www.wadsworth.com

wadsworth.com is the World Wide Web site for Wadsworth and is your direct source to dozens of online resources.

At *wadsworth.com* you can find out about supplements, demonstration software, and student resources. You can also send email to many of our authors and preview new publications and exciting new technologies.

www.wadsworth.com
Changing the way the world learns®

CALIFORNIA
The Politics of Diversity

BRIEF EDITION

David G. Lawrence
Westmont College

THOMSON
™
WADSWORTH

Australia • Canada • Mexico • Singapore • Spain • United Kingdom • United States

THOMSON

★

™

WADSWORTH

Publisher: Clark Baxter
Executive Editor: David Tatom
Assistant Editor: Julie Yardley
Editorial Assistant: Reena Thomas
Technology Project Manager: Melinda Newfarmer
Marketing Manager: Janise Fry
Marketing Assistant: Mary Ho
Advertising Project Manager: Nathaniel Bergson-Michelson
Project Manager, Editorial Production: Ray Crawford
Print/Media Buyer: Jessica Reed
Permissions Editor: Kiely Sexton

Production Service: Matrix Productions
Photo Researcher: Sarah Evertson, ImageQuest
Copy Editor: Kay Mikel
Illustrator: Thompson Type & Lois Stanfield,
  Light Source Images
Cover Designer: Jeanette Barber
Cover Image: © Roberto Soncin Gerometta/PictureQuest
Cover Printer: Webcom Limited
Compositor: Thompson Type
Printer: Webcom Limited

Printed in Canada
3 4 5 6 7 07 06 05

For more information about our products, contact us at:
Thomson Learning Academic Resource Center
1-800-423-0563
For permission to use material from this text, contact us by:
Phone: 1-800-730-2214   **Fax:** 1-800-730-2215
Web: http://www.thomsonrights.com

Library of Congress Control Number: 2003105247

Student Edition with InfoTrac College Edition:
  ISBN 0-534-54382-0

Wadsworth/Thomson Learning
10 Davis Drive
Belmont, CA 94002-3098
USA

Asia
Thomson Learning
5 Shenton Way #01-01
UIC Building
Singapore 068808

Australia/New Zealand
Thomson Learning
102 Dodds Street
Southbank, Victoria 3006
Australia

Canada
Nelson
1120 Birchmount Road
Toronto, Ontario M1K 5G4
Canada

Europe/Middle East/Africa
Thomson Learning
High Holborn House
50/51 Bedford Row
London WC1R 4LR
United Kingdom

Latin America
Thomson Learning
Seneca, 53
Colonia Polanco
11560 Mexico D.F.
Mexico

Spain/Portugal
Paraninfo
Calle/Magallanes, 25
280115 Madrid, Spain

Brief Contents

1 Explaining California Politics 1

2 California's Political Development 13

3 Constitutionalism and Federalism 26

4 Direct Democracy in a
Hyperpluralistic Age 38

5 The Political Behavior of Californians 49

6 Linking People and Policymakers 60

7 Legislative Politics 76

8 Executive Politics 94

9 California's Judiciary 108

10 Community Politics 123

11 Public Policy in California 138

Index 163

Contents

1 Explaining California Politics   1

Introduction   1
How Diversity Explains
   California Politics   2
Land   3
Regions   3
Resources   4
People   4
Economy   6
How Political Theory
   Explains California Politics   7
Democratic Theory   7
Elite Theory   8
Pluralist Theory   8
Hyperpluralism   9
How Hyperpluralism
   Explains California Politics   9
The Constancy of Individualism   9
A Diversity of Interests   9
A Diversity of Cultures   10
Fading Majoritarianism   10
Structural Conflict   10
California: The Ironies of Diversity   11
Conclusion   11
Key Terms   11
Review Questions   12
Web Site Activities   12
InfoTrac College Edition Articles   12
Notes   12

2 California's Political Development   13

Introduction   13
The Idea of Political Culture   14
The Idea of Political Development   14
The Politics of Unification   15
Spanish "Rule"   15
Mexican "Control"   15
Statehood   16
The 1849 Constitution   16
The Politics of Modernization   17
The Gold Rush   17
The Big Four   17
Water   18
Other Modernizing Factors   20
The Politics of Welfare   20
The Progressive Movement   20
The Great Depression   20
Earl Warren and Edmund G.
   (Pat) Brown   21
The Politics of Abundance
   and Beyond   22
Conclusion   24
Key Terms   24
Review Questions   24
Web Site Activities   24
InfoTrac College Edition Articles   25
Notes   25

3 Constitutionalism and Federalism 26

Introduction: Rules and Boundaries 26
California's Constitution 27
What It Contains 28
What Makes It Distinctive 29
California and the Nation:
   The Boundaries of Federalism 31
Dual Federalism 31
Cooperative Federalism 31
Centralized Federalism 31
On-Your-Own and Pragmatic Federalism 32
California in Washington 32
"Saturation Bombing" 33
Coalition Politics 33
"Bury" the California Connection 34
California and the World:
   The Politics of Fences 34
Immigration 34
Trade 35
Conclusion 36
Key Terms 36
Review Questions 36
Web Site Activities 36
InfoTrac College Edition Articles 37
Notes 37

**4 Direct Democracy in a
Hyperpluralistic Age** 38

Introduction: The Impact
   of Progressivism 38
Selected Initiative Battles in
   California 39
Proposition 13: Give the Money Back 39
Proposition 22: Gay Marriage 40
The Initiative Mess 41
Prospects for Reform 45
Progressive Cousins: Referendum
   and Recall 45
Conclusion: The Legacy and
   the Paradox 47
Key Terms 47
Review Questions 47
Web Site Activities 48
InfoTrac College Edition Articles 48
Notes 48

**5 The Political Behavior
of Californians** 49

Introduction 49
Forms of Participation in
   a Democracy 50
Conventional Participation 50
The Exit Option 50
The Protest Option 50
Voters and Nonvoters in California 51
Who Votes in California? 51
Those Who Cannot Vote 51
Those Who Will Not Vote 53
Partisanship in California 54
Party Affiliation 55
The Partisan Geography of California 55
California's Electoral Gaps 57
Conclusion: Divided by Diversity 58
Key Terms 58
Review Questions 58
Web Site Activities 58
InfoTrac College Edition Articles 59
Notes 59

6 Linking People and Policymakers 60

Introduction 60
Mass Media 61
Newspapers 61
Television 62
The Internet 64
Political Parties 64
Political Parties: California Style 65
How the Parties Are Organized 65
Surrogate "Parties" 66
Endorsement Politics 66
Elections 66
Campaign Professionals 67
The Role of Money 68
*California Elections and
   National Politics* 69
Interest Groups 70
California Groups: Who Are They? 70
How Interest Groups Organize 71
What Interest Groups Do 72
Conclusion:
   Competing for Influence 73

Key Terms	73
Review Questions	73
Web Site Activities	74
InfoTrac College Edition Articles	74
Notes	74

7   Legislative Politics   76

Introduction:	
The Road to Proposition 140	76
California's Legislative History	77
The Early Years	77
The Progressive Era	77
Stagnation Amid Change	77
Reform	77
The Golden Years	77
Inching Toward 140	78
The Post-140 Legislature	78
What the Legislature Does	78
Policymaking	78
Representation	79
Executive Oversight	81
Civic Education	81
Getting There and Staying There	81
Recruitment	82
Why They Stay: Rewards of Office	82
How They Stay: Reapportionment Politics	83
The 2001 Reapportionment	83
Organizing to Legislate	84
The Role of Leadership	84
The Committee System	85
The Staff	88
The Legislative Process	88
The Third House	90
Conclusion	91
Key Terms	92
Review Questions	92
Web Site Activities	92
InfoTrac College Edition Articles	93
Notes	93

8   Executive Politics   94

Introduction	94
How Governors Lead	95
The Governor's Duties and Powers	97
Executive Powers	97
Budget Leadership	98
Legislative Power	98
Judicial Powers	100
Other Powers	101
The Plural Executive:	
Competing for Power	101
Lieutenant Governor	101
Attorney General	102
Secretary of State	102
Superintendent of Public Instruction	102
Insurance Commissioner	103
Fiscal Officers	103
California's Bureaucracy and	
the Politics of Diversity	104
Functions of Bureaucracy	104
Power Sharing and Clout	105
Conclusion	106
Key Terms	106
Review Questions	106
Web Site Activities	107
InfoTrac College Edition Articles	107
Notes	107

9   California's Judiciary   108

Introduction	108
State Courts in Our Legal "System"	109
How California Courts	
Are Organized	109
Trial Courts	110
Appellate Courts	110
Supreme Court	111
So You Want to Be a Judge	111
Entering the Profession	111
The Right Experience	112
Selection Mechanics	112
Judicial Discipline	113
How Courts Make Decisions	114
The Criminal Process	114
The Civil Process	116
Juries and Popular Justice	116
How Courts Make Policy	116
Trial Court Policymaking	117
Appellate Court Policymaking	117
Criminal Justice and Punishment	118
Conclusion	120

Key Terms 121
Review Questions 121
Web Site Activities 122
InfoTrac College Edition Articles 122
Notes 122

10 Community Politics 123

Introduction 123
The Role of Community 125
The Limits of Community Government 125
Counties 126
The Shape of California Counties 126
How Counties Are Governed 126
County Troubles 129
Cities 130
How Communities Become Municipalities 130
"Cities" Without "Government" 131
How California Cities Are Run 131
Special Districts 132
What Makes Them Special? 132
The Stealth Governments of California 133
The Future of Special Districts 133
School Districts 134
Regional Governments 135
Regional Coordination 135
Regional Regulation 135
Conclusion: Diverse Communities,
    Diverse Governments 136
Key Terms 136
Review Questions 137
Web Site Activities 137
InfoTrac College Edition Articles 137
Notes 137

11 Public Policy in California 138

Introduction 138
Budget Policy: The Cost of Diversity 138
California's Economy 139
State and Local Budget Processes 139
State and Local Revenues 141
State and Local Expenditures 144
Policies Stemming from Growth 146
Water Policy 147
Housing Policy 147
Transportation Policy 149
Energy and Environmental Policy 150
Larger Growth Strategies 152
Policies Stemming from Diversity 152
Social Issues: Abortion and Gay Rights 152
Education Policy 153
Higher Education Policy 155
Social Programs 156
Health Policy 157
California's Immigration "Policy" 158
Conclusion 159
Key Terms 159
Review Questions 160
Web Site Activities 160
InfoTrac College Edition Articles 160
Notes 160

Index 163

Preface

As California's budget crisis deepened during 2003, an effort to recall Governor Gray Davis was launched. If a recall election went forward, potential Davis replacements would appear on the same ballot alongside the recall itself. What would be the prize? As Daniel Weintraub of the *Sacramento Bee* put it, "Nominal leadership of a troubled state of 35 million, with a struggling economy, a crumbling health care system, an electricity industry in disarray, schools unsure of their future, and ethnic and racial diversity that could make it a model for the world or an American Yugoslavia." Fellow columnist Dan Walters called recent crises in California "really a crisis of governance."

If ever there was a time to study California politics, the time is now. The state's remarkable diversity is a major factor in its politics. Euro-Americans are less than 50 percent of California's population but remain a sizable majority of the electorate. Racial and ethnic minorities now constitute most of the state's school-age population. Recent elections suggest that California's Latino population is beginning to flex its political muscles and choose political sides. In fact, the twenty-first century has been dubbed the Latino Century. But diversity in California is much more than a colorful rainbow of faces. From a political perspective, diversity includes the rich variety of individuals, groups, regions, locales, traditions, and institutions that constitute California's political culture.

The remarkable diversity that is California drove my writing of the first edition of *California: The Politics of Diversity* and its two revisions. Since its initial release in 1995, virtually all the trends originally chronicled and examined—for better or worse—are now more pronounced. Simply put, today's California is like yesterday's California, only more so. This streamlined edition of *California* continues to underscore the growing diversity of California and its impact on how the state and its communities are governed. In doing so, I draw on a wide array of valuable resources including think tanks, Web sites, media, and academic scholarship.

Text Features

As with its longer companions, this brief edition covers the basics of California politics in light of two broad themes—*diversity* and *hyperpluralism*. I have tried to show two things: (1) how demographic, cultural, economic, geographic, and political diversity affect how politics actually works in California; and (2) how that diversity expresses itself in political hyperpluralism—the view that California politics is exceedingly pluralistic.

The exercise of political power in California is a highly competitive tug-of-war between ideologies, institutions, policymakers, political parties, interest groups, and voters. So many groups now compete and the political system is so complex that governing of any sort is most challenging. Much of the time, power is thinly scattered, not just unevenly scattered.

As with many California political scientists, my own teaching assignments have included both California politics and American government. The brief edition continues to apply important political science and American government concepts to the California experience, and it does so in a lean, lucid, student-friendly manner.

Helping Students Learn

The streamlined version of *California* offers numerous pedagogical features to help students learn. Each chapter includes the following features:

• A consistent perspective that really makes sense to today's students

• An attractive and functional two-column design that aids in reading

• Introductory outlines that organize student thinking

• A conclusion that revisits key points and ties them to book themes

• Key terms italicized in the text and referenced by page number at the end of each chapter

• Study questions that help students review and apply chapter content

• Endnotes that invite further reading and research

• InfoTrac College Edition articles that create, in effect, a California politics reader

• Illustrations that underscore key points and ask probing questions

• End-of-chapter Internet Web sites that encourage further exploration

• "Did You Know?" boxes that feature interesting facts related to chapter topics

What's New?

The brief edition of *California: The Politics of Diversity* retains an organizational format familiar to many political scientists who teach American government courses. Important ideas should be intelligible ones, especially in an undergraduate textbook, and the material is presented in a lively writing style that many students have found accessible. In terms of substance, the brief edition reflects the latest developments in California politics, including:

• Updated discussion of the state's recent budget crisis

• Frequent use of new 2000 Census data

• Results and impacts of the 2001 reapportionment

• Coverage of women's issues, Latino political power, gay rights, and the 2001 energy crisis

• Recent California-originated U.S. Supreme Court cases

• Results and analysis of the 2002 gubernatorial election

• New public opinion data from the state's top polling organizations

• Cutting-edge research on demographic, economic, voting, and immigration trends

• Helpful comparisons with other states highlighting state spending, taxes, and population growth

All in all, the brief edition is especially suitable for those teaching and studying California politics in the context of American government and for others who need a streamlined version of the full text.

Supplements

As a Wadsworth text, *California* offers a number of attractive supplements that aid both professors and students; they consist of the following resources:

• An instructor's manual with test questions and other helpful instructional tips

• Transparency masters of charts and graphs to augment lectures and discussions

• InfoTrac College Edition, an online university library that lets students explore full-length articles from hundreds of periodicals. When students log on with their personal ID, they will see immediately how easy it is to search, read, and print out articles from the last four years. Periodicals include *State Legislatures, U.S. News & World Report, The Economist,* and *Campaigns & Elections.*

• The Wadsworth Political Science Resource Center (http://politicalscience.wadsworth. com/), which includes information on all Wadsworth political science texts including those on California politics. The Resource Center contains information on surfing the Net, links to general political sites, a career center, election updates, monthly news online, and a discussion forum.

Acknowledgments

Textbook writing is a team effort. It involves many more people than a title page would suggest. I am indebted to several teams. The first is uniquely mine. From my own years in and around state and local politics, I must credit the many practitioners who have shared their political insights with me—former city council colleagues, internship supervisors, classroom speakers, journalists, and countless Sacramento Legislative Seminar panelists, including policymakers, lobbyists, and journalists. Fellow board members of the California Center for Education in Public Affairs provide constant stimulation. I am also grateful to colleague Richard Burnweit, whose own expertise and keen eye aided recent revisions, and student researcher and indexer Brooke Early. As always, my wife and best friend Carolyn has been a source of insight and encouragement. I am grateful.

A second team consists of the good people at Wadsworth who provide helpful direction, assistance, and encouragement. They are publisher Clark Baxter, executive editor David Tatom, assistant editor Julie Yardley, production manager Ray Crawford, permissions editor Kiely Sexton, marketing manager Janise Fry, and technology project manager Mindy Newfarmer. Merrill Peterson of Matrix Productions and copyeditor Kay Mikel of Word-Works ably assisted the production process. Professor Dianne Long (California Polytechnic State University, San Luis Obispo) authored the instructor's manual and test bank.

A third team consists of the political scientists who reviewed all or some of *California* along the way. They include Theodore J. Anagnoson, California State University, Los Angeles; John H. Culver, California Polytechnic State University, San Luis Obispo; Robert L. Delorme, California State University, Long Beach; Lawrence L. Giventer, California State University, Stanislaus; Drake C. Hawkins, Glendale Community College; Peter H. Howse, American River College; Donald J. Matthewson, California State University, Fullerton; Stanley W. Moore, Pepperdine University; William W. Lammers, University of Southern California; Marilyn J. Loufek, Long Beach City College; Edward S. Malecki, California State University, Los Angeles; Charles H. McCall,

California State University, Bakersfield; Steve Monsma, Pepperdine University; Eugene Price, California State University, Northridge; Donald Ranish, Antelope Valley College; Alvin D. Sokolow, University of California, Davis; Richard S. Unruh, Fresno Pacific University; and Alan J. Wyner, University of California, Santa Barbara.

As helpful as these veteran colleagues were, I take full responsibility for the end product.

David Lawrence

CALIFORNIA
The Politics of Diversity

CHAPTER 1

Explaining California Politics

OUTLINE

Introduction

**How Diversity Explains
California Politics**
Land
Regions
Resources
People
Economy

**How Political Theory
Explains California Politics**
Democratic Theory
Elite Theory
Pluralist Theory
Hyperpluralism

**How Hyperpluralism
Explains California Politics**
The Constancy of
   Individualism
A Diversity of Interests
A Diversity of Cultures

Fading Majoritarianism
Structural Conflict

**California:
The Ironies of Diversity**

Conclusion
Key Terms
Review Questions
Web Site Activities
InfoTrac College Edition
   Articles
Notes

Introduction

If you think about it, the state of California and theme park roller coasters have much in common. People flock to both—enduring congestion in the process and experiencing the exhilaration of both ups and downs. In the Golden State, the highs include better jobs, economic opportunities, and living conditions that people could only have imagined back home, whether they are from Missouri or Mexico. People envision California as a place where these dreams can come true. The lows include periodic recessions, occasional droughts, smog, crime, crowded freeways, and unaffordable housing.

Some Californians endure the lows to appreciate the highs, but others find California, like the roller coaster, a bit too much. They flee the state for Washington, Oregon, Nevada, Colorado, and so forth. Or they move within the state, seeking a calmer ride. As a whole, Californians' confidence in the future of the state can vary remarkably from year to year (see Figure 1.1).

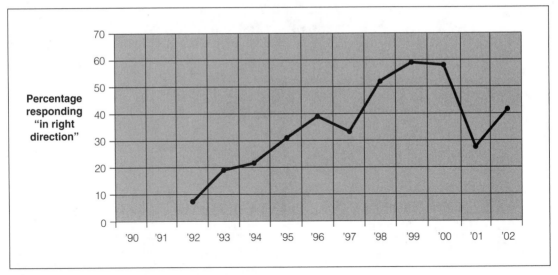

FIGURE 1.1   How Californians view California

When pollsters ask, "Do you think things in California are generally going in the right direction, or do you feel things are seriously off track?" Californians' responses can vary significantly within a 10-year period. *Question:* In your opinion, to what extent do these data affect perceptions of government institutions and policymakers?

Source: The Field Poll (May 6, 2002), 6. Note: Results are based on representative statewide samples of up to 1,021 California adults. The sampling error ranges from ±3.2 to 4.5 percentage points.

Many observers speak of the Golden State as a unique, one-of-a-kind place. Others put it differently. Political analyst William Schneider put it, "California is just like the rest of the country, only more so."[1] Author Kevin Phillips thinks that California is "almost a mirror—or perhaps a simulcast—of the most important things starting to happen to America."[2] To be sure, California has a larger-than-life quality about it. Whatever your view, California will continue to represent people's search for the "good life" however they define it. As you will see, coloring this search is the state's growing diversity of peoples and cultures.

As far as California is concerned, this search began centuries ago. In the 1500s, Spaniards desired to find and explore a mythical island of *California*. Writer Garci Ordonez de Montalvo described this place as rich in "gold and precious stones"; its people were "robust of body, with strong and passionate

hearts and great virtues." As for government, the queen "had ambitions to execute nobler actions than had been performed by any other ruler."[3] Wealth and good intentions—what a combination! No wonder California has been called not only a state, but a state of mind.

Chapter 1 introduces two approaches to understanding California politics. The first is the state's remarkable diversity. The second is a set of theories political scientists use to explain aspects of American politics generally. These two broad approaches (diversity and theory) are revisited throughout the book.

How Diversity Explains California Politics

To understand California, one must understand how its public sector works. Political scientist David Easton defined *politics* as "the authoritative allocation of values for a society as a whole."[4] Politics occurs within the context of a *political system.* In our federal arrangement, there are 50 state systems and one national political system. These systems reflect ongoing patterns of human behavior involving control, influence, power, and authority. The process of making public policy—that is, deciding "who gets what, when and how"[5]—exists within the context of a larger environment. The *political environment* is a set of social, cultural, economic, and physical attributes that inform and limit how politics is done. To begin this study of California politics, we must examine California's diverse environment: the land and regions of the state as well as its resources, people, and economy.

LAND

Diverse is truly the only word to describe the physical geography of California. The state's diversity is made possible in part by its sheer size. California's length covers the distance between New York City and Jacksonville, Florida. The nation's third largest state in square miles (behind Alaska and Texas), California supports a rich variety of terrain.

Coastal communities enjoy moderate, semi-arid Mediterranean weather in the south and wetter, cooler weather in the far north. Thick forests including the Giant Redwoods occur in the north. In fact, 40 percent of the entire state is forested. The naturally barren south has been made less so over the years by farmers and gardeners alike. Numerous mountain ranges criss-cross the state. The defining north/south range is the Sierra Nevada. Less imposing coastal ranges help define the attractive but expensive environments around such places as Santa Barbara, Carmel, and Santa Cruz.

The transverse ranges, those mountains that lie in an east/west direction, once defined the limits of urbanization and, to some people's minds, the boundary between Northern and Southern California. The Los Angeles Basin (surrounded by the Sierra Madre, Tehachapi, Santa Ana, San Gabriel, and San Jacinto ranges) once kept its poor air quality to itself. But urban growth and automobile proliferation have spread smog over the mountains to communities on the other side (Palm Springs and Lancaster, for example) and locales as far away as the Grand Canyon in Arizona. The increasingly smoggy Central Valley supports some of the most productive agriculture in the world.

REGIONS

The configuration of the land influences how people settle on and use it—leading to regional differences. These differences are partly a matter of perception. Consider the idea of Northern and Southern California, the most familiar division of the state. People know Northern California for San Francisco (called simply "The City"), wineries, the redwoods, heavy water-consuming crops such as rice, and mountain resorts such as Lake Tahoe. They identify Southern California with its warm days, wide beaches, automobile culture, show business, Latino roots, and, of course, smog. Some suggest that these two regions are actually two states divided by water. The north has it, the south wants it, and the north knows it. Some pundits have divided California from north to south into Logland, Fogland, and Smogland.

Perceptions aside, observers have divided the state into anywhere from 4 to 14 distinct regions based on geography, economy, populations, political behavior, and public attitudes.[6] Public opinion surveys of 4 regions—Los Angeles County, the San Francisco Bay Area, the Central Valley, and the Orange County/Inland Empire region—document a number of differences. For example, Central Valley residents are more opposed to affirmative action, illegal immigration, and environmental regulations than their counterparts elsewhere. Based on these surveys, analyst and pollster Mark Baldassare believes "the major

TABLE 1.1 Californians at a Glance

Group	Percentage of State Population		
	1990	2000	2025*
Non–Hispanic White	57	46	33
Hispanic	26	31	42
Asian and Pacific Islander	9	11	18
Black/African American	7	7	7
Other/Multiple[a]	—	1	<1
Native American	<1	1	<1

Source: California Department of Finance, Demographic Research Unit, 2000.

Notes: California's population was 29,760,021 in 1990 and grew to 33,871,648 according to the 2000 Census. Projections (*) suggest the state's share of Hispanics will continue to grow; its share of whites will continue to shrink. [a]The 2000 Census allowed individuals to self-report other races/ethnicities including mixed or multiple races.

Question: To what extent are these changes already evident where you live?

regions are drifting further apart at a time when there is a need to reach a statewide consensus on social, environmental, land use, and infrastructure issues."[7]

RESOURCES

In addition to regional perceptions, a state's natural resources affect its politics. Ironically, California's most important resource is its most precious—water. The availability and redistribution of water has had a profound effect on growth in the Golden State. Water has transformed parched land into the nation's salad bowl and fruit basket. Water has enabled imaginative people in a semiarid climate to turn their front, back, and side yards into tropical and subtropical gardens. And most important, dams, canals, and aqueducts have channeled water from the north to the south, allowing millions of people to live where nature alone could support very few.

California's overall climate is itself a resource and has directly and indirectly caused the state's phenomenal growth. Americans have always been lured to California because of its weather. Years ago, winter exports of citrus and newspaper ads in the Midwest created a "Garden of Eden" image, which served as a magnet. Doctors would recommend California's milder climate to patients suffering from respiratory and arthritic ailments.

All this has resulted in a subtle attitude found in the Golden State. Just as people thought they could change their destiny by moving to California in the first place, many believe they can engineer their destiny once they arrive. Californians seek what they call the "good life" despite hindrances of all sorts. They expect their state and local governments to deliver policies fostering and protecting their chosen lifestyles. They become disillusioned and angry when policymakers fail to meet those expectations.

PEOPLE

California's resources have encouraged waves of human settlement. In short, diversity and growth characterize the demographics of California. As in the past, the state attracts immigrants from all over the world. Furthermore, they are settling throughout the state. The ethnic and geographic diversity of today's Californians is astounding. California's population currently is growing at a rate of 1,400 per day. By 2000, no racial or ethnic group constituted a majority of Californians. This trend can be seen in Table 1.1.

California's first dwellers were widely dispersed Indians living off the land in small communities. As peaceful peoples, they were no match for the succession of more aggressive Spanish, Mexican, and Anglo American settlers. Due primarily to disease imported from these settlers, they and their cultures were driven to near extinction. The Spanish, as elsewhere, treated Mexican California as a colony to be conquered, civilized, and exploited, not necessarily to be populated with Spaniards.

By the time of Mexican independence from Spain in 1822, the province of *del norte* was populated by the remaining Indians, a few Spaniards, Mexicans, and the offspring of mixed marriages between various groups. Like their predecessors, contemporary Mexicans come to California seeking prosperity. Be they citizens, resident aliens, or undocumented workers, Latinos staff the growing service economy in California. Due to continuing in-migration and relatively high birthrates, they have become a sizable cultural and socioeconomic force in the state. The state's largest minority group, Latinos now number 11 million. Their numbers are not limited to Southern California as old images would suggest. For instance, the 2000 Census revealed that the Latino population of Monterey and Tulare Counties was 47 and 51 percent, respectively. Latinos have been known for low voter turnout, in part because many of them are not yet citizens or are too young to vote. Yet a growing number of Latinos have been elected to public office. In 2003, there were seven California Latinos in Congress, including two Latina sisters, Loretta and Linda Sanchez. Both Cruz Bustemante and Antonio Villaraigosa attained the state Assembly speakership, and Bustemante won the lieutenant governorship in 1998, the first Latino elected to statewide office since 1871. There are now 28 Latinos in the state legislature. Both population data and electoral returns suggest that Latino political clout will grow in the future but that the Latino community is itself rather diverse and will not likely be a monolithic force.[8]

The Gold Rush of 1849 began what is known as the "American era." This provincial-sounding term refers to the successive waves of American citizens who moved to California from other parts of the United States. Population figures tell the story. In 1840, Californians numbered about 116,000, including 110,000 to 112,000 Indians. Two decades later, they numbered 380,000, including only 30,000 Indians.

A second population rush followed completion of the Transcontinental Railroad in 1869. That last spike linked California both physically and symbolically with the rest of the nation. For urban Americans, the lure of open space "out West" actually made possible a newly emerging dream in the late 1800s—a single-family house on a single-family lot. Later, the mass production of automobiles allowed others to bypass trains altogether on their way to sunny California.

In the 1900s, additional waves of Americans moved westward to seek various employment opportunities. Beginning with Summerland near Santa Barbara in 1920, the discovery and

Did You Know...?

In response to the 2000 Census, 1.6 million Californians indicated that they were of two or more races. Of that number, more than 94,000 indicated that they were of three or more races.

Question: *In the future, will racial categories be more difficult to keep distinct in California?*

SOURCE: U.S. Census Bureau; 2000 Census Redistricting Data.

drilling of oil led to new jobs and still more land speculation. The Depression-era jobless and Dust Bowl refugees (many were called Okies and Arkies for their home states of Oklahoma and Arkansas) came to California in search of any opportunity they could find. John Steinbeck's *Grapes of Wrath* fictionalized the real misery of these migrants and what they hoped for in California. World War II brought numerous Americans to California for training and war production efforts. Many of them vowed to return to California—for keeps—and they did.

Many African Americans migrated to California during World War II. Today, most of California's 2.4 million African Americans live in the state's large metropolitan areas. As elsewhere, they have suffered racial discrimination, and many lag behind other groups in education and income. Current African American officeholders include San Francisco mayor (and former Assembly speaker) Willie Brown, Assembly Speaker Herb Wesson, California Supreme Court Associate Justice Janice Rogers Brown, and various state legislators, members of Congress, judges, and city officials.

A succession of other minorities entered California over the years. Notable have been California's 3.6 million Asian Americans. Many Chinese were brought to the state during the Gold Rush or to work on railroad construction gangs. Many of them were subject to economic exploitation and discrimination. Today, the Chinese population of California numbers more than 981,000.

Japanese Americans in California number about 229,000 according to the most recent Census. In a stunning example of racial discrimination, many were moved to relocation camps after Japan attacked Pearl Harbor in 1941. Branded temporarily as "enemy aliens," Japanese Americans rose above this wholesale discrimination and economic dislocation to become successful both educationally and economically.

Filipinos are the largest Asian group, slightly outnumbering Chinese Americans with about 919,000 people. Yet they do not command the economic influence of either the Chinese or the Japanese in California. The Vietnam War resulted in an influx of Southeast Asians to California. Few Vietnamese were in California in 1970. The 2000 Census counted more than 447,000. Some have achieved material success in the Golden State, but others work at poverty wages in Southern California sweatshops.

Ethnic diversity in California also translates into language diversity. The 2000 Census revealed that an impressive 40 percent of Californians speak a language other than English in the home, the highest percentage of any state. In general, children speak English more fluently than the adults in these homes.

What does all this racial and ethnic data tell us? Other parts of America are largely thought of in biracial (black and white) terms, but describing the people of California is much more complex. In fact, according to journalist Steve Scott, "California is on the leading edge of a national redefinition of racial diversity, one which acknowledges that race is no longer merely a 'black and white' issue."[9]

ECONOMY

A state's economy helps explain its politics and so it is with California. California's modern economy has four characteristics: postindustrialism, change, diversity, and a two-tier structure.

1. *Postindustrialism.* California's economy is *postindustrial,* meaning it is characterized by a large service sector, economic interdependence, rapid change, innovation, and advanced technology. Today's postindustrial service economy includes education, research, finance, insurance, and real estate. The sleek buildings, professional office "parks," and shopping malls dotting suburban California epitomize this sector. It also includes both wholesale and retail sales of groceries, clothing, and other consumer items. To many Californians, fast food franchises and technology firms symbolize postindustrialism.

2. *Change.* California's economic history has been one of constant change. The Gold Rush encouraged a "rush" of workers. The expansion of railroads (including the invention of refrigerated rolling stock), plus government financed water projects, secured agriculture as an economic mainstay. The discovery of oil attracted still more workers and fueled the state's emerging automobile-oriented transportation system. World War II spawned a military-industrial complex, which anchored the state's manufacturing sector, and the technological revolution laid the groundwork for the service-based economy. Change has also meant increased international competition from Asia and Mexico.

3. *Diversity.* California's economy is richly *diverse.* The sheer size of California's economy (the sixth largest in the world) would suggest diversity. Although less than 2 percent of California's workers are in agriculture, the state is the nation's top producer of more than 50 crops and livestock commodities. (This does not include what some speculate to be the state's most lucrative cash crop—marijuana!) The state ranks first among the 50 in international trade. Governors and mayors alike travel abroad to promote trade with California. Geographically, the state is a Pacific Rim "nation" dependent on international investment and trade opportunities. In recent years, economic diversity has been tinged with economic uncertainty. In the early 1990s, factory closings reduced the number of well-paying, blue-collar jobs. Cuts in defense and aerospace spending hurt large numbers of the state's military contractors. California's economy surged in the late 1990s but reversed course in the early 2000s. Despite Asian economic troubles, a nationwide economic slowdown, and the state's recent energy crisis, long-term prospects seemed bright.

4. *Two-Tier Structure.* Lastly, California's economy has a roughly *two-tiered structure.* In terms of the workforce, the top tier or layer consists of highly educated, well-paid employees in high technology, knowledge-intensive busi-nesses. Included are the fields of education, medicine, communications, law, finance, real estate, transportation, and government. The bottom tier consists of those working in low-paying, low-status service jobs found in retail outlets, the tourism industry, agriculture, and marginal manufacturing concerns. Research suggests that there is a growing income disparity between these two tiers, especially among male workers and low-skill immigrants.[10]

How Political Theory Explains California Politics

As important as it is, a state's political environment alone (land, regions, resources, people, and economy) does not explain its politics. Politics deals with very complex sets of human relationships involving influence and power. To understand the complexity of politics, theories help explain who governs and why. But not all political scientists can agree on a single theory. As a result, alternative theories have emerged, which we will briefly explore and apply to California politics.

DEMOCRATIC THEORY

According to traditional democratic theory, the answer to "Who governs?" is "All of us," in a sense. Two forms of democracy exist. *Participatory democracy* envisions rule by the many as described by the ancient philosopher Aristotle. *Representative democracy* suggests rule by the few on behalf of the many. In a representative democracy, policymakers may negotiate and compromise with each other but are influenced and ultimately controlled by the electorate. When we refer to *democratic theory* in the U.S. context, we mean representative democracy.

American democratic theory also includes the states. In part it explains California politics, especially its political ideals. The preamble to the state's Constitution reads: "*We, the People* of the State of California, grateful to Almighty God for our freedom, in order to secure and perpetuate its blessings, do establish this Constitution" (emphasis added). It contains the state's own "bill of rights" and establishes various institutions of government that, on paper, are responsible to the electorate. Furthermore, voters have the power to adopt their own legislation (initiatives), approve or disapprove various laws passed by the state legislature (referenda), and fire elected officials between elections (recall). They can do all this on a statewide basis and in their respective communities.

Traditional democratic theory advances political ideals better than it explains political reality. A representative democracy assumes greater citizen interest than often is the case. In California, the politically disinterested and the economically weak are at a clear disadvantage. Democratic theory, then, needs to account for the relationship between government and wealth, the persistence of unequal subgroups in the polity, and what, if any, common ground exists between the haves and the have-nots.

ELITE THEORY

Other theories also attempt to explain the origins and exercise of power. According to *elite theorists,* all societies naturally divide into two classes: the few who rule and the many who do not. As political scientist Harold Lasswell once put it, "Government is always government by the few, whether in the name of the few, the one, or the many."[11] Some elites consist of corporate owners and other wealthy persons who exercise political power directly or control those who do on their behalf.

As with democratic theory, elements of elite and class politics can be seen in California. Historically, significant power was wielded by one corporation, the Southern Pacific Railroad, and the "Big Four" (Leland Stanford, Collis Huntington, Charles Crocker, and Mark Hopkins). Considered a virtual political machine, they shaped the state's early commerce, land development, and overall growth. Elites abound in modern California. The state's media exercise considerable influence through major television stations and a small handful of newspaper chains. Among the most influential groups in Sacramento are large corporations or clusters of them, such as the California Manufacturers Association.

Californians themselves sense the power of elites and distrust the results. According to one recent survey, 64 percent of respondents thought that the state government was "pretty much run by a few big interests looking out for themselves" instead of for the benefit of all Californians.[12]

As compelling as elite theory sounds, it, too, cannot fully explain California politics. The influence of the Big Four was ultimately broken in the Progressive era. Today, many California businesses of all sizes compete for power—reducing the influence of any single one. In short, because elites exist does not necessarily mean that they win on, or even care about, all issues. California's elites tend to husband their resources for issues they regard as most important.

PLURALIST THEORY

Pluralist theory tries to correct aspects of both democratic and elite theory. Electoral majorities, a cornerstone of democratic theory, are something of a myth, given voter apathy. No single group dominates all the time. In many ways, American politics *is* group politics—a fluid process of competing interests winning or losing, rising or falling, as they seek to influence transitory issues.

Pluralism is an attractive option for students of California politics. If you look up "Associations" in the Sacramento Yellow Pages, you will be amazed at the breadth of interest groups in the state's capital. Group-inspired lunch hour rallies are a common sight on the Capitol steps. Proposition "wars" now feature dueling initiatives sponsored by opposing groups. Increasingly, ethnic groups are creating *multicultural pluralism* in California politics.

But not all politics in California can be labeled group politics. First, structural features of California's political system (its constitution and institutions) to some extent limit group power. Second, group competition alone does not explain the occasional rise of policy entrepreneurs—individuals who make a substantial difference, such as anti-tax crusader Howard Jarvis, three-strikes proponent Mike Reynolds, bilingual education opponent Ron Unz, and tobacco tax advocate and Hollywood director Rob Reiner. Third, pluralism seems to suggest a satisfactory equilibrium among competing groups. But how does one explain policy indecision, delay, or paralysis—what is often called gridlock?

HYPERPLURALISM

Elements of truth in these three theories may suggest what Dahl calls an "American hybrid,"[13] but a nagging problem remains. All three presume governing does in fact occur. Yet some observers claim that no one "rules" effectively anymore. State governments, California included, lurch from fiscal year to fiscal year. In a sense, recent budget crises serve to magnify the ongoing challenge of governing in the Golden State. Even in economic good times perennial problems seem to defy permanent solutions, and many policy proposals are little more than leftovers from the past. In addition, initiatives sponsored by some organized interests, once passed, are challenged in court by other groups. Some political scientists call this state of affairs *hyperpluralism*. In this view, power is thinly scattered, not just widely or unevenly scattered as previous theories would suggest. The exercise of political power has become a highly competitive tug-of-war between institutions, policymakers, political parties, numerous interest groups, and voters.

Hyperpluralism seems increasingly helpful in explaining how aspects of American politics work. In explaining California politics, it is

downright compelling. Let us consider it in more depth.

How Hyperpluralism Explains California Politics

There is ample evidence of hyperpluralism in American politics, and in California politics in particular: individualism in political life, a growing diversity of group interests and cultures, the changing nature of majoritarian politics, and "built-in" or structural conflict. These components of California hyperpluralism are somewhat intertwined and dependent on each other.

THE CONSTANCY OF INDIVIDUALISM

Individualism is a hallmark of American life, and it is nothing new. The proliferation of interest groups, the pursuit of leisure, gated communities, private security systems, solitary rush hour commutes, and growing gun ownership—a do-it-yourself law enforcement of sorts—all suggest dependence on self rather than on society to fulfill both needs and wants. In a sense, even low voter turnout in California elections reflects individualism in a culture where political participation is considered optional and even unimportant.

A DIVERSITY OF INTERESTS

California has experienced a number of changes in how groups of people behave politically. As these groups proliferate, each tends to represent a narrower spectrum of views or interests. Some even define themselves and behave politically in terms of one, single issue—giving rise to what has been called *single-issue politics*. When public problems are viewed in such narrow terms, policy solutions seem obvious and clear cut, but only to the group espousing them. Absent a broader consensus, policymakers find that supporting certain groups has a price—the wrath of other groups.

A DIVERSITY OF CULTURES

At a deeper level than group politics, California has experienced a growing number of ethnically and other-based cultures. The most rapidly growing group is the Latino population, but Asian groups are growing as well. The dominant white or Euro-American culture in California will soon be a minority itself. One survey detected nearly 100 distinct ethnic groups in California. But multiculturalism is broader than ethnicity. "Gay pride" parades and "life chain" marches by abortion foes reflect cultural differences based on sexual orientation, religious belief, and other nonethnic value systems. As we saw earlier, California's various regions to some extent reflect different cultural values. When the diversity of California cultures is coupled with the group behavior just described, the result is a diversification of California's *social structure,* not just its politics. Some use terms like "tribalization" and "Balkanization" to describe this state of affairs. Again, the political system mirrors these trends. Public officials are torn between the demands of California's newer, immigrant-dominated groups and those of older, white, largely middle-class voters.

FADING MAJORITARIANISM

Another evidence of hyperpluralism is the changing nature of *majority rule*—a major principle of American politics. The nation's Founders thought that, in a representative democracy,

elected officials would seek the common good agreeable to a functioning majority. In California politics, a single public interest and a single majority seem to be endangered political species. In a sense, "minorities" already rule in the Golden State. On a statewide basis, a relatively small number of individuals and groups set legislative agendas and determine which issues make it to the ballot. A relatively small percentage of Californians who qualify to vote actually register to vote; an even smaller percentage turn out on election day; and only a *simple majority of those* determine election outcomes. "Minority rule" is commonplace in numerous California cities.

STRUCTURAL CONFLICT

California's political structure itself invites political conflict. First, the state's Constitution in effect predestines a horizontal power struggle between the executive, legislative, and judicial branches. Second, by dictating certain roles for local government, it guarantees a vertical power struggle between the "locals" (cities, counties, and special districts) and the state itself. Third, allowing voters to directly make policy and even restructure government further complicates matters. According to journalist Peter Schrag, the result has been "an increasingly unmanageable and incomprehensible structure of state and local government that exacerbates the same public disaffection and alienation that brought it on."[14]

Did You Know ... ?

Based on 43 factors ranging from median household income, crime rates, infant mortality rates, and education success to the annual number of sunny days, Morgan Quitno Press ranks the "livability" of all 50 states.

In 2003, California ranked only thirty-eighth. Minnesota was first and Mississippi last.

Question: *In your opinion, why do so many Californians rank their own state higher than this publisher does?*

SOURCE: *State Rankings, 2003* (Lawrence, KS: Morgan Quitno Press, 2003). Available online at www.morganquitno.com/.

California: The Ironies of Diversity

In this introductory chapter, we have surveyed California's rich diversity, the theories that help explain its politics, and the hyperpluralism that is increasingly evident. As California becomes increasingly diverse and hyperpluralistic, several ironies have emerged. First, compared to other states, California has become both policy innovator and laggard. Over the years, it has "led the way" with such measures as Proposition 13 (which reduced property taxes) and "Three Strikes, You're Out" legislation (which imposed lengthy sentences for three-time felons). Years ago, its investment in freeways was the envy of other states. Yet by the mid-1990s, California ranked forty-ninth in per capita state spending on highways. Recent spending on education has not kept pace with the state's growth. In 1961, California ranked twelfth in average per-pupil spending; in 2001, it ranked thirty-second, having been nearly fortieth a few years earlier. While enrolling more higher education students than 24 other states *combined,* in 2000–2001 California ranked only thirty-eighth in per-student support of higher education.

Second, as diverse as California's economy is, the state's dependence on inherently volatile sources of revenue such as the income tax can significantly alter budget priorities. For example, in 1971, California ranked eighth among the states in state and local revenue as a percentage of personal income. By 1977, it had dropped to twenty-third; by 2000, it rose again to eighth, and has likely dropped since that time due to stock market and technology sector declines. Spending commitments rise and fall accordingly.[15]

Third, while policy paralysis often grips Sacramento, policy progress can be found closer to home. The state's 478 cities have developed entrepreneurial ways to raise needed revenue. Numerous counties have increased sales taxes to pay for transportation projects once thought to be the state's responsibility. Those Californians who can afford to (the upper tier) are buying services their state or local government cannot afford or will not provide. Examples include private recreation clubs, security systems, housing associations, and private schools. What does the bottom tier do? They rely on government programs despite the cuts, live by their wits, or simply do without.

Conclusion

The California portrayed in this chapter is of immense proportions. The challenges facing the most populous state in the Union are abundant to be sure, as they always have been. The capacity and potential for California governments to address these challenges is and always has been great. Its political system reflects a state that "is ever Californianizing: searching for what it is and for what it wants to be."[16]

Political scientists search for theories to explain why California functions the way it does. Although no single theory or approach will suffice, both the state's diversity and its hyperpluralistic political system seem useful in explaining California's current state of affairs.

As a subject of study, California politics is both fascinating and challenging. Due to term limits and demographic shifts, it is also ever changing. As you read this book, you will discover why.

KEY TERMS

politics (p. 2)

political system (p. 3)

political environment (p. 3)

diversity (p. 3)

postindustrial economy (p. 6)

two-tier economy (p. 7)

democratic theory (p. 7)

elite theory (p. 8)

pluralist theory (p. 8)

hyperpluralism (p. 9)

components of California hyperpluralism (p. 9)

REVIEW QUESTIONS

1. Identify the ways in which diversity explains California politics.

2. How have water and climate affected the state's growth?

4. What demographic groups have come to California and why?

5. Describe the four keys to understanding the state's economy. What makes it two-tiered in nature?

6. Survey the four theories political scientists use to describe power and influence in American politics. Illustrate each theory with California examples.

7. Discuss and illustrate California's ironies of diversity.

WEB SITE ACTIVITIES

California Home Page
(www.ca.gov/)
A good starting point, this site will take you in many different directions regarding life and politics in the Golden State.

California Department of Finance, Demographic Research Unit
(www.dof.ca.gov/HTML/DEMOGRAP/Druhpar.htm/)
This "single official source of demographic data for state planning and budgeting" provides helpful information on population growth, change, and diversity in California.

INFOTRAC COLLEGE EDITION ARTICLES

For additional reading, go to InfoTrac College Edition, your online research library, at http://infotrac-college.com/wadsworth

Tragic California?

Where America Is Heading

California's Language Wars, Part II

NOTES

1. William Schneider, "Roads Not Taken," *Los Angeles Times,* May 31, 1992.

2. Kevin Phillips, "California," *Los Angeles Times,* November 19, 1989.

3. Quoted in Andrew F. Rolle, *California: A History* (New York: Crowell, 1969), 34.

4. Harold D. Lasswell, *Politics: Who Gets What, When and How* (New York: McGraw-Hill, 1938).

5. David Easton, *The Political System* (New York: Alfred A. Knopf), chap. 5.

6. Hans P. Johnson, "A State of Diversity in California Regions: Demographic Trends," *California Counts* (San Francisco: Public Policy Institute of California, May 2002).

7. Mark Baldesarre, *PPIC Statewide Survey: Californians and Their Government* (San Francisco: Public Policy Institute of California, July 2001), 13.

8. See Anthony York, "Latino Politics," *California Journal* 30 (April 1999): 26–34; Gregory Rodriguez, "The Latino Century," *California Journal* 31 (January 2000): 8–14.

9. Steve Scott, "Reality Votes," *California Journal* 29 (January 1998): 25–26.

10. Legislative Analyst's Office, *California's Changing Income Distribution* (Sacramento: Legislative Analyst's Office, August 2000); Marla Dickerson, "State's Workers Making Progress," *Los Angeles Times,* June 10, 2002.

11. Harold Lasswell and Daniel Lerner, *The Comparative Study of Elites* (Stanford, CA: Stanford University Press, 1952), 7.

12. Mark Baldassare, *California in the New Millennium: The Changing Social and Political Landscape* (Berkeley: University of California Press, 2000), 47.

13. Robert A. Dahl, *Preface to Democratic Theory* (Chicago: University of Chicago Press, 1956), chap. 5.

14. Peter Schrag, *Paradise Lost: California's Experience, America's Future* (New York: New Press, 1998), 12.

15. Data derived from the *California Statistical Abstract* and Kendra A. Hovey and Harold A. Hovey, *CQ's State Fact Finder, 2003: Rankings Across America* (Washington, DC: CQ Press, 2003).

CHAPTER 2

California's Political Development

OUTLINE

Introduction
The Idea of Political Culture
The Idea of Political
Development

The Politics of Unification
Spanish "Rule"
Mexican "Control"
Statehood
The 1849 Constitution

**The Politics of
Modernization**
The Gold Rush
The Big Four
Water
Other Modernizing Factors

The Politics of Welfare
The Progressive Movement
The Great Depression
Earl Warren and Edmund G.
(Pat) Brown

**The Politics of Abundance
and Beyond**

Conclusion
Key Terms
Review Questions
Web Site Activities
InfoTrac College Edition Articles
Notes

Introduction

Why is California different from New York? Both states have large, diverse populations, complex economies, megacities, huge state budgets, and geographic variety (seashore, mountains, farms, forests, and so forth). Although Californians struggle to obtain water and New Yorkers do not, there are many similarities. Yet Californians and New Yorkers know their states are different—and in profound ways. Political scientist Daniel Elazar calls these variations the "geology of political culture."[1] A primary difference stems from how the states grew and changed as political and cultural identities. Chapter 2 surveys aspects of California's past that help explain its current political system. This process of growth and change is called "political development." The focus will be on the development of California's political system and its impact on both political culture and modern policymaking.

THE IDEA OF POLITICAL CULTURE

To understand the stages of political development found in California, we need to briefly examine the concept of political culture. *Political culture* is the product of historical events, migration and settlement patterns, and the presence of various social groups. It refers to *the shared beliefs, values, customs, and symbols of a society that affect how the society governs itself.* Political culture helps explain the policy choices made within political systems and why those choices vary between political systems.

In many respects the United States reflects one broad political culture, but Elazar has identified three distinct political subcultures: traditional, moralistic, and individualistic.[2] Although the descriptions of each are largely impressionistic, they do help explain why some states are so different from others. The *traditionalistic* political subculture is characterized by the dominance of a small, self-perpetuating, paternalistic ruling elite and a large, compliant non-elite.

The *moralistic* political subculture emphasizes a public-spirited citizenry dedicated to the common betterment of all its members. Widespread participation is both valued and expected. Dedicated, selfless, incorruptible public officials strive toward an assumed "general welfare."

The *individualistic* political subculture emphasizes the goals, aspirations, and initiative of private individuals or groups. Government exists to serve and facilitate these interests. Policymaking is transactional, a process of bargaining between self-interested individuals and groups.

As more people immigrated to the United States and Americans already here migrated west, the features of these three subcultures moved and mingled as well. Historically, each of these three subcultures has played an important role in California's political development; elements of all three still persist. Although Elazar once thought the Golden State was primarily moralistic, a persistent individualistic subculture helps account for the state's hyperpluralistic politics.

THE IDEA OF POLITICAL DEVELOPMENT

Political development refers to the growth and change that occurs within political systems. Political scientists view this term differently. Some think it simply refers to government's increasing capacity to manage its affairs and respond to demands placed upon it. Others suggest it means the extension of democratic practices including increased citizen participation and greater sensitivity to the ideals of equality. That view is understandable given the world in which we now live. Still others view political development as what happens when societies become more complex, their labor more specialized, their groups more divided, and their social structures more differentiated.[3] Many political systems in the Western world have proceeded through distinct stages of political development: (1) unification, (2) modernization, (3) welfare, and (4) abundance.[4] These stages do not have neat beginnings and endings; they merge into each other.

Do states have their own stages of political development? Yes, to some extent. To be sure, the states together form a national political culture. Also, the nation's founding documents such as the U.S. Constitution have steered each state's political development in similar directions. Yet the subsystems we call states entered the union at different times and are distinctly different in terms of the people they attracted, the economies they established, and the political practices they developed.

To view California's political history as its political development allows the student of California politics not only to understand the state's history but to interpret it as well. Author Theodore White once observed, "California politics squirm with a complexity and intrigue that defies reasonable analysis."[5] Not really. Larger than most nations, California has passed through all four stages of political development. To be sure, today's abundance does not affect all parts of the state and its people in equal measure. To analyze the present and anticipate the future, we must first make sense of the past—the goal of this chapter.

The Politics of Unification

During an early *unification* stage of political development, the primary function of government is making a society into a state. Government needs to establish its own central role, guard against early disunion, and develop a network of viable local economies. Early California from Native American times through the Gold Rush and statehood embodies this stage.

The West Coast has been a population magnet since prehistoric times. Archaeological evidence suggests nomadic peoples from Asia once crossed a land bridge (now the Bering Strait) through Alaska and down the coast some 25,000 years ago. Native Californians were the eventual products of these early migration patterns. These first Californians were gatherers and coastal fishermen who spoke 135 different languages. They were peaceable, nomadic, agrarian, and needed little or no government. They resisted change, as well-meaning missionaries discovered, but were not resistant to European diseases and violence, which decimated their numbers.

The first non-native visitors to California were European explorers who sailed California's coastal waters in the 1500s. They included Juan Rodriguez Cabrillo, Bartolome Ferrelo, and Sir Francis Drake. In 1579, Drake claimed the area north of modern-day San Francisco as Nova Albion (New England) 41 years *before* the Pilgrims touched shore at Plymouth.

SPANISH "RULE"

Spain colonized Mexico in 1519 but did not extend its reach into Alta California until 1769. Governor Gaspar de Portola and Father Junipero Serra established a European settlement and Franciscan mission at San Diego. The missions (eventually numbering 21 and stretching from San Diego to Sonoma) were religious and evangelistic outposts intended to convert the Native Californians both to Christianity and to more "progressive" (European) lifestyles. As a colonial power, Spain promptly built military bases (*presidios*). Nearby civilian towns (*pueblos*) accommodated modest population growth. At the height of their influence, the Spanish numbered no more than 3,000 people spread thinly along the California coast from San Diego to Sonoma.

Preoccupied with the balance of the crumbling empire, Spain saw no need to "unify" Alta California. To the responsible viceroy in Mexico City, California was "out of sight, out of mind."

MEXICAN "CONTROL"

After years of Mexican frustration and Spanish inattention, Mexico obtained its independence from Spain in 1821. Ironically, the gold-hungry Spanish government abandoned Mexican California, unaware of the rich gold deposits to be discovered only a few decades later. California was now Mexico's colony—a distant and not too important province in Mexico's federal system. Concerned with solidifying its power base and unifying the rest of Mexico, the central government in Mexico City paid even less attention to California than did Spain. Feuds between the presidios and the missions and between the fledgling regions of California continued unabated during this Mexican era.

One act of unification during this time was to reduce the role of the church, which in California meant the vast mission enterprises developed under Spain. The Mexican government secularized the missions and distributed their massive landholdings to government loyalists.[5] Individuals could obtain 48,000-acre grants, and some influential families were able to accumulate *ranchos* as large as 250,000 acres. Many places familiar to Californians today derive their names from these ranchos. The myth of an idyllic, rural California persisted from the rancho period on.

Another development during this period had nothing to do with Mexican policy. A gradual but steady trickle of rugged Euro-Americans found their way to California. These intrepid individuals included whalers, trappers, mountaineers, and adventurers. Some remained on the "wild side," but others turned to farming and married into landholding Mexican families. Most of these travelers were peaceful. Not so with Lieutenant John C. Fremont, who led several military expeditions into California. A "Bear Flag Revolt" ensued between the *Californios* (native-born, Spanish-speaking Californians) and the American settlers, aided and abetted by Fremont and his associates. The symbol was a flag portraying a grizzly bear with the inscription "California Republic." It remains the state flag today.

Mexico's lax control ended with its defeat by the United States in the Mexican American War of 1848. Physical remnants of California's Spanish and Mexican past are everywhere from red tile roofs to local fiesta celebrations. Mexico did not appear to exercise a unifying influence, but during its interim control, Mexico introduced several governing patterns that would become part of California's constitution. Also, both Spain and Mexico left behind a traditionalistic political subculture, elements of which we see today among newly arrived immigrants.

STATEHOOD

The unification stage of political development was completed with California's admission to the Union. To the Americans, California came to represent a logical stepping-stone in meeting the nation's "manifest destiny." By the end of the war, Mexico had "sold" not only California but also Nevada, Utah, and portions of Wyoming, Colorado, New Mexico, and Arizona. This $15 million bargain was known as the Mexican Cession. The 1848 Treaty of Guadalupe Hidalgo concluded the war, ceded California to the United States, and granted U.S. citizenship and all its rights to the conquered peoples. Private property rights, important to the wealthy *rancheros*, were maintained. California was now a U.S. territory under temporary military control.

The United States, despite its euphoric westward expansion and sense of mission, did not bring unification to California instantly. Its fragmented governance structure was based on a now-collapsed Spanish system of *presidios*. Furthermore, the bits of gold found by James Marshall on the American River only nine days before the treaty was signed would bring anything but peace to America's newest possession.

THE 1849 CONSTITUTION

A very important instrument in unifying a civil society is a constitution. This basic law provides general vision, establishes rights, creates political structures, and places limits on power and those who claim it. Theoretically it is a contract between the government and the governed as well as a covenant among society's members.

California's first constitution was the result of a constitutional convention held in the fall of 1849. The process was a curious mixture of elitism and pluralism. All 48 delegates were relatively young men. Thirteen had lived in California for less than one year. The non-native Californians came from 13 other states and five other nations.[6] Closer to their Mexican roots, Southern Californians preferred territorial status, thinking that would give them the best of both cultures. Northern Californians generally favored statehood, sent a majority of the delegates, and eventually controlled the convention.

The new constitution blended several theories of governing. The Constitution began with a lofty, unifying preamble and a strong "bill of rights" reflecting democratic ideals. The idea of checks and balances (and the potential for structural gridlock) was found in a plural executive (a governor and several statewide officers) and a bicameral (two-house) legislature. Reflecting Mexican practice, it established a four-tier judicial system of elected judges. As elsewhere, suffrage (the right to vote) was limited to white males. Due to the *Californios*, the document was to be printed in both English and Spanish; so were all future official documents. The Constitution won overwhelming voter approval in November 1849, and on September 9, 1850, Congress admitted California as the thirty-first state. California was to remain slave free, a condition not applied to other ceded Mexican territories. At that moment, unification, to the extent California would ever experience it, was complete. The Mexican era ended; the North American era began.

The Politics of Modernization

This sense of opportunity led to *modernization*, the next stage in the process of political development. This is a time when new political leaders emerge, a statewide economy is forged, and the political masses become fully incorporated—becoming the polity of the state. Government's purpose is to encourage economic modernization or industrialization. During this stage, California became a magnet of opportunity and a destination for those seeking jobs or simply a better way of life. Historic benchmarks during this stage were the Gold Rush, the rise of the Big Four, the industrialization of agriculture, and the consequences of World War II.

THE GOLD RUSH

Discovery of gold created the mining frenzy noted earlier. In retrospect, gold did not change California; the rush for it did. For a time, the population doubled every six months: from 9,000 in 1846 to 264,000 six years later. Seemingly overnight, a heavily Latino California become 80 percent Euro-American. The newcomers were primarily young, single men from every state in the Union and from as far away as Europe and China. A spirit of entrepreneurialism merged with hard labor and racism. Chinese immigrants were allowed to mine the gold but not own rights to it. Policing the mining towns was rough business. Committees of vigilance—*vigilantes*—often used violence to quell violence. A few found the gold they sought, but many more found unprecedented opportunities of other types. One luckless miner found he could make more money selling pants to other miners; his name was Levi Strauss.

Those who stayed created a new base for California's emerging economy. In effect, the Gold Rush jump-started the state's second stage of development by adding instant diversity to California's population. It created numerous spillover effects (planned or unplanned consequences), such as heightened demand for goods and services. In turn, new demands for transportation improvements created still more opportunities for future entrepreneurs. Lastly, it created a worker base consisting of individuals with steely nerve to take a risk, not just on gold, but on California itself.

THE BIG FOUR

Four Sacramento merchants dared to believe that "the fabulous could be realized." As already noted, some Americans brought an individualistic political subculture to California; these men personified it. Eventually, they controlled 85 percent of the state's rails. This elite became a monopoly and behaved accordingly.

By varying freight rates, they rewarded their friends and punished their enemies. For every mile of track, the owners of the Southern Pacific Railroad would receive up to 12,800 acres from the public domain. Frank Norris's 1901 novel, *The Octopus*, was a chilling and transparent description of how the SPR operated in the state.

Fearing that popular resentment might lead to state regulation, the Southern Pacific established a Political Bureau, a forerunner of the modern political action committee (PAC). Unlike today's PACs, which operate primarily in Sacramento, the Political Bureau was active at all levels of government. Due to its influence, the California legislature was regarded as the most corrupt in the state's brief history.

As politically successful as the Big Four were, they could not cope with a national depression in the late 1800s that left many out of work. The unemployed blamed the railroads for importing poorly paid Chinese laborers who competed with whites for nonrailroad jobs. One such worker, the fiery Denis Kearney of San Francisco, helped found the radical Workingmen's Party. His incendiary rhetoric was both anti-Chinese and anti-Big Four.

Ironically, the same voters that elected a railroad-controlled State Senate also authorized the calling of a constitutional convention— one noted for its antirailroad temperament. Original state constitutions seem to need revision within several decades, and California was no exception. In California's case, the 1878–1879 convention coincided with economic troubles, antirailroad fervor, and worker radicalism. The revised constitution literally banned the employment of the Chinese and instituted regulations aimed at the railroads. In retrospect, a constitutionally authorized railroad "proved as clay in the hands of the great corporations."[7] Furthermore, occasional regulatory victories were often voided by economically conservative courts. A popular political cartoon of the day entitled "The Curse of California" symbolized not only the power of the Big Four but also the elite theory of politics described in Chapter 1 (see Cartoon 2.1).

Eventually, the power of the Big Four waned. The Sante Fe, a competing southern transcontinental railroad initiated a rate war, thereby ruining the Southern Pacific monopoly. Further industrialization of California would depend less on parochial, intrastate concerns and more on national and international forces.

WATER

A third factor in the modernization of California was water. This commodity affected both agriculture and urbanization in the state. A growing interstate network of railroad routes plus the advent of refrigerated rolling stock enabled the nation to enjoy an increasing variety of fruit and vegetables. The early padres, and later farmers, found California's geography could accommodate at least some crops, anytime, anywhere in the state. This led not only to highly specialized farming but also to a demand for adequate water. Specialty crops increased a farmer's return per acre but only if there was a sufficient, continual supply of water. The state's endless cycles of wet and dry years produced a yo-yo economy from a grower's perspective.

The late 1800s and early 1900s witnessed numerous efforts to increase the volume and dependability of water. The Wright Act of 1887 authorized the formation of local water conservation districts. From that point on, the agricultural sector, in partnership with the state and federal governments, pursued the construction of dams, well, canals, reservoirs, catchment basins, and aqueducts to move water ever farther from its source. Examples include the L.A. Aqueduct (that diverted water from the Owens Valley to Los Angeles), Hoover Dam (that diverted water from the Colorado River to Southern California), the Central Valley Project (that stabilized agricultural water supplies), and the State Water Project

THE CURSE OF CALIFORNIA.

CARTOON 2.1 Edward Keller's "The Curse of California" was published in *The Wasp* on August 19, 1882, and is regarded as the most influential political cartoon in California history. Keller employed the often-used octopus symbol to caricature the political and economic reach of the Big Four.

(that moved still more water from North to South). As a result of all this activity, during this industrialization period, California would become one of the world's great "hydraulic societies," as Donald Worster put it.[8]

OTHER MODERNIZING FACTORS

The impact of the Gold Rush and visionary water planning were only two features of California's modernization. Several others also deserve mention.

Oil

"Black gold" was discovered in various parts of Southern California between 1900 and 1940, creating new economic opportunities. Unlike California's farmers and their crops, the oil companies faced tremendous obstacles shipping crude to distant out-of-state markets. Despite logistical challenges of drilling and shipping oil, this activity helped to diversify California's mushrooming economy. Like yellow gold, early discoveries of black gold produced ripple effects—land speculation and further population growth. It became still another magnet drawing both job seekers and environmentalists concerned about oil-generated pollution.

World War II

A second event that propelled California's industrialization was World War II. Nearly 2 million people came to or through California to work in defense plants, neighboring communities, or on military bases.

Although military spending predated the war, the war itself helped the state to both grow and urbanize. When people moved to California, they moved to its cities. By the 1990s, remnants of wartime California remained visible, including numerous military bases that had never closed after the war. The closure of some of these bases has been met with anguish by public officials and neighboring communities alike.

The Politics of Welfare

The third stage of political development is the *politics of welfare*. In this stage, government's task is to shield the citizenry from hardship, manage a smooth running economy, improve standards of living, and assist the less fortunate. It takes an industrial base to afford these activities.[9] In California, several factors influenced this stage of development: the Progressive Movement, the Depression, and the leadership of two governors, Earl Warren and Edmund G. (Pat) Brown. Combined, they represented the state's moralistic political subculture on a grand scale.

THE PROGRESSIVE MOVEMENT

Although California's role as a modern welfare state came after World War II, the foundation for welfare politics was built earlier. California's version of the nationwide Progressive Movement, led by Governor Hiram Johnson (1911–1917), eliminated the overbearing political influence of the railroads and stressed political individualism and nonpartisanship (see Chapter 4). Progressive reforms weakened political parties by requiring many officeholders to run as nonpartisans.

Furthermore, the Progressives in effect created a leadership vacuum by allowing voters to make decisions previously reserved for elected representatives.

THE GREAT DEPRESSION

The Depression itself accelerated demands for public assistance to those crushed by economic hardship. In 1934, novelist and socialist Upton Sinclair became the Democratic nominee for governor. His platform, End Poverty in California (EPIC), combined the goals of tax reform and public employment. Some voters, especially senior citizens, became Sinclair enthusiasts; big business labeled him a radical, a crackpot, and even a communist. Republican Frank Merriam won. Four years later, the same year *Grapes of Wrath* was published, Democrat Culbert L. Olson won the governorship. Although he served only one term, he too developed ambitious policies to aid those untouched by progress in California.[10] What really helped California was the New Deal, which converted good intentions into actual assistance. The Works Progress Administration (WPA) funded projects from Shasta Dam and the Golden Gate Bridge to lesser-scale schools, libraries, and hospitals.

EARL WARREN AND
EDMUND G. (PAT) BROWN

World War II expedited the welfare era by pumping even more federal dollars into the state's economy. Politically, it helped produce a coalition of business and labor dedicated to one common goal: a healthy economic future for California. Elected in 1942, Governor Earl Warren was just the leader this coalition needed. He was so bipartisan he took advantage of a Progressive era reform called crossfiling to run on both party tickets in 1946. He won a third term in 1952, the only California governor ever to do so, but resigned in 1953 when President Eisenhower appointed him Chief Justice of the U.S. Supreme Court.

During Warren's tenure as governor, California made great strides in education and various social programs. In some respects, Warren continued a moralistic political subculture advanced by the Progressives. His social reforms included improvements to old-age pensions, unemployment benefits, medical care, labor law, prisons, and mental hospitals. A massive freeway-building program was launched in 1947, financed through increased gasoline taxes. No wonder President Harry Truman

once said of Warren, "He's a Democrat—and doesn't know it."[10]

Growing state services in the Warren years meant a growing bureaucracy. State employees swelled from 24,000 in 1943 to 56,000 in 1953. An expanding economy made this growth affordable. A 50 percent population increase during this period made it necessary. Historian Robert Glass Cleland credited the state's economy for all this policy vigor: "The war and postwar booms gave Warren only problems of prosperity to solve."[11]

In 1958 Democratic votes finally caught up with Democratic registration trends, and Pat Brown succeeded Knight as governor. Like Warren, Brown had been state attorney general and had avoided overly partisan election campaigns. He too avoided close ties with his own party. Under Brown's leadership, the state's Water Project was funded, providing the infrastructure to move vast amounts of water from the mountains to the growing Bay Area and Southern California cities. School and university enrollments mushroomed, reflecting the state's continued growth.

In 1959 Brown called for a master plan for higher education. This plan allocated different tasks to the University of California, the state colleges, and the junior colleges (as they were called then). Access to higher education by all Californians became part of the state's implicit social contract. Brown continued Warren's progressive welfare policies—an agenda he called "responsible liberalism." Brown oversaw massive public construction projects including new college campuses, public schools, and freeways. Actor and conservative spokesperson Ronald Reagan succeeded Brown in 1966, but his election did not slow the momentum of activist government. Although the bureaucracy did not increase appreciably, state budgets continued to climb. Neither legislative Democrats nor Reagan's own pragmatism allowed his "Squeeze, cut, and trim" rhetoric to become reality. Furthermore, by the 1960s, many of California's social programs were federally required. In a sense,

California mirrored the nation at this stage in its political development.

The Politics of Abundance and Beyond

Ironically, responsible liberalism can produce negative reactions, even by those it helps. True, the standard of living had increased in California through both public and private spending. The state had moved into the *politics of abundance*. A growing economy provided the taxes to fund a social welfare state and a plethora of services Californians had come to expect. These policies were *majoritarian* in nature: the majority both paid for them and received their benefits. For instance, low-cost public higher education was available to every resident regardless of need. These policies were not only widely supported but attracted still more people to the Golden State.

When does growth become too much of a good thing? By the 1960s, many Californians were asking that question. Growth had funded their favorite programs but had also replaced orange groves with endless housing tracts and fueled freeway congestion, air pollution, and overcrowded parks and schools. Although many effects of growth are privately generated, Californians sensed that "politics as usual" was somehow to blame. Responsible liberalism apparently had become irresponsible. A succession of governors including Reagan would try to reverse the politics of growth, especially governmental growth, which had characterized the state's history. California entered an era of lowered expectations. Reagan's successor and Pat Brown's son, Jerry Brown (1975–1983), declared "small is beautiful" and claimed that Californians were living in an *era of limits*, hardly the language his father would have used. Jerry Brown had rejected the bipartisan growth consensus of the Warren–Brown era. George Deukmejian (1983–1991) suc-

ceeded Brown. As Reagan did, Deukmejian championed free enterprise, claimed government was the problem, not the solution, and rejected most tax and spending increases. When the Democratic legislature allowed him to, he pared back the state's regulatory activity, especially that opposed by business.[12]

Political leaders in the 1970s and 1980s heeded Californians' pleas to preserve the "abundant state." If government was the problem, cut off its lifeblood—in a word taxes. Some of these tax limits were self-imposed by elected officials in the annual budget process. Others, like Proposition 13 (which drastically cut property taxes), were imposed by voters led by policy entrepreneurs Howard Jarvis, Paul Gann, and others. The state's middle-class voters have always been a powerful, albeit fickle, influence on the political process. Buffeted by raging inflation and tax increases in the 1970s, they sincerely believed government revenue could be cut without reducing the services they enjoyed.

While governmental growth slowed down, the state's population growth did not. By the early 2000s, observers were conflicted over the future of Abundant California. Given the constant drumbeat of population growth (1,000 plus per day!), would there continue to be enough abundance to go around? This was a fundamental policy dilemma for Deukmejian's successor Pete Wilson (1991–1998) and continues to be for Wilson's successor, Gray Davis (1999–). The 2001 electricity shortage and massive budget shortfalls in the years following underscore this point. Nancy Vogel's observations in 1991 seem equally instructive today: "[G]one is [Earl] Warren's cornucopian sense of California. Where Warren dreamed of a garden cottage for every new 'settler,' as he called them, his successors in Sacramento see smog-choked suburbs. Where Warren welcomed migrant muscle power to develop 'latent resources,' today's leaders fear depletion of those resources."[13] Those who fear a "post-abundant" future see a shrinking number of "tax payers" supporting the service demands

CARTOON 2.2 In 1975 cartoonist Dennis Renault captured the "era of limits" rhetoric of Governor Jerry Brown. To Californians used to the leadership of Governors Earl Warren and Pat Brown, the politics of the 1970s and 1980s did seem to be characterized by lowered expectations.

Source: Dennis Renault, *Sacramento Bee.*

of a soaring number of "tax spenders." Furthermore, they see clashes, not only of competing political interests but of diverse political and ethnic cultures. They question whether there is any longer a single public interest acceptable to most Californians. Others speculate that even a hyperdiverse, constantly growing California will continue to offer hope and prosperity to succeeding generations regardless of wealth or ethnic background.

Conclusion

When British ambassador Lord Bryce visited California in 1906, 2 million people inhabited the state. He asked: "What will happen when California is filled by 50 millions of people and its valuation is five times what it is now? There will be more people—as many as the country can support—and the real question will be not about making more wealth or having more people, but whether the people will then be happier or better than they have been hitherto or are at this moment."[14]

Thirty-two million people later, his question remains compelling. As noted in Chapter 1, the gap between the state's haves and have-nots is growing larger. The moralistic and individualistic political subcultures, which have historically lived side by side in California, seem at war with each other. Individualism may be winning. The state's upper tier, wanting to maintain the abundant state as they see it, readily participate in California's political system. Meanwhile, the lower tier, which participates to a lesser extent, in effect seems to be asking: "Where is the moralistic political subculture when *we* need it?"

Caught in the middle, the political leadership of California has exercised the "politics of caution." They face certain wrath from some constituents regardless of the policy choices they make. Consequently, they hesitate to do anything bold or significant, especially if it means more or higher taxes. Earlier, I attributed this policy paralysis to an increasingly diverse and hyperpluralistic political system. Chapter 2 adds to this equation a pattern of political development characterized by individualism and a move toward abundance experienced by many, but apparently not all, Californians.

KEY TERMS

political culture (p. 14)

traditional, moralistic, and individualistic subcultures (p. 14)

political development (p. 14)

politics of unification, industrialization, welfare, abundance (pp. 15–23)

presidios and pueblos (p. 15)

1849 and 1879 Constitutions (pp. 16–18)

Gold Rush (p. 17)

Big Four (p. 17)

Southern Pacific Railroad (p. 18)

Progressive movement (p. 20)

majoritarian policies (p. 22)

era of limits (p. 22)

REVIEW QUESTIONS

1. Describe Elazar's three political subcultures. How do they apply to California?

2. Describe political history as a process of political development. Describe and illustrate the four stages of political development used in this chapter.

3. Who were the most influential Californians during these stages and what made them so?

4. Describe the politics of abundance and why some Californians worry that it will not continue.

5. What do you think will be the next stage of California's political development and why?

WEB SITE ACTIVITIES

California Historical Society
(www.calhist.org/)
The Golden State's official historical society provides historical data and numerous links to statewide and local resources.

INFOTRAC COLLEGE EDITION ARTICLES

For additional reading, go to InfoTrac College Edition, your online research library at http://infotrac-college.com/wadsworth

California Becomes a State of the Union

Gold Rush Legacy

Reagan's Rise

NOTES

1. Daniel Elazar, *American Federalism: A View from the States*, 3rd. ed. (New York: Harper and Row, 1984), 122–123.
2. Ibid., chap. 4.
3. Various theories of political development are summarized in David E. Apter, *Introduction to Political Analysis* (Cambridge, MA: Winthrop, 1977), chap. 15.
4. A. F. K. Organski, *The Stages of Political Development* (New York: Alfred A. Knopf, 1965).
5. Quoted in Gladwin Hill, *Dancing Bear: An Inside Look at California Politics* (Cleveland, OH: World Publishing Co., 1968), 4.
6. Paul Mason, "Constitutional History of California," *Constitution of the State of California (1879) and Related Documents* (Sacramento: California State Senate, 1973), 75–105.
7. Ibid., 112.
8. Donald Worster, *Rivers of Empire* (New York, Pantheon Books, 1985).
9. Organski, *The Stages of Political Development*, 12.
10. See Robert E. Burke, *Olson's New Deal for California* (Berkeley: University of California Press, 1953).
11. Robert Glass Cleland, *From Wilderness to Empire: A History of California* (New York: Alfred A. Knopf, 1959), 419.
12. David Kutzman, Teresa Watanabe, and Arnold J. Hamilton, "The Terminator: Deukmejian Dismantles the State's Regulatory System," *California Journal* 19 (February 1988): 85–88.
13. Nancy Vogel, "Is California Bursting at the Seams?" *California Journal* 22 (July 1991): 295–299.
14. Quoted in Dan Walters, *The New California: Facing the 21st Century*, 2nd ed. (Sacramento: California Journal Press, 1992), 7.

CHAPTER 3

Constitutionalism and Federalism

OUTLINE

Introduction:
Rules and Boundaries

California's Constitution
What It Contains
What Makes It Distinctive

California and the Nation: The
Boundaries of Federalism
Dual Federalism

Cooperative Federalism
Centralized Federalism
On-Your-Own and Pragmatic
Federalism

California in Washington
"Saturation Bombing"
Coalition Politics
"Bury" the California
Connection

California and the World:
The Politics of Fences
Immigration
Trade

Conclusion
Key Terms
Review Questions
Web Site Activities
InfoTrac College Edition
   Articles
Notes

Introduction:
Rules and Boundaries

Western democracies place certain limits on governments. Some of these limitations may be rules that dictate how and under what circumstances power can be exercised and policy made, and by whom. State constitutions and local governing charters contain such rules. Other limitations take the form of boundaries that demarcate territorial jurisdiction. These are legal borders beyond which influence

wanes and power means little. National and state borders as well as city, county, and special district lines mark off the legal reach of most public policy efforts. From a state perspective, constitutions and federalism are the *perimeters of politics*—the outer limits that in effect contain the scope of political power.

Political scientists call the idea of limited government—government operating within certain rules—*constitutionalism.* According to English political theorist John Locke (1632–1704), constitutions were essentially contracts between "the People" and those who governed them. Such documents, approved by the people, would specify the powers public officials would have and the limits on those powers.

Locke deeply influenced America's Founders as they drafted the U.S. Constitution. They were largely successful in limiting the document to basic fundamental law and to only 8,700 words. It would be the "Supreme Law of the Land," superseding the Articles of Confederation. With revisions, the colonial constitutions became state constitutions in 1789. Despite Locke's preferences, ordinary citizens never voted on the original document and have never directly ratified its amendments.

America's constitutional history actually predates the U.S. Constitution. Those 13 original colonies possessed extensive governing charters reflecting their respective political cultures. Later states brought with them comparable experiences and traditions. Although state constitutions were destined to look alike in many respects, they were never intended to be clones of the federal government. For better or for worse, they would reflect not only those beliefs shared by American society as a whole but also the culture, traditions, and unique attributes of each state.

As you explore California's constitution, consider what constitutions are and should be. Some reformers think that a state constitution should contain only basic, fundamental law. As several California political scientists once put it, a constitution should be "brief, clean and unambiguous . . . [expressing] a philosophy of government that has been thoroughly discussed and represents the consensus of thought." Still others believe constitutions are political documents; living, breathing expressions of policy conflict, not policy consensus. Constitution writing is "a struggle between competing groups of people who try to get as many of their ideas and interests as possible expressed in law, so the resulting document represents compromises between numerous groups."[1] State constitutions reflect policy victories and defeats, not just com-

promise. Even the rules of the game reward one group over another.

California's Constitution

California's current constitution contains more than 54,000 words and has been amended nearly 500 times, second only to Alabama. Some of the document's most interesting provisions are certain amendments, which will be discussed shortly. Yet the basic framework for California's government was established in the 1800s by two separate conventions producing two distinct constitutions.

The 1849 Constitution provided the basic structure of state government and a 16-section Declaration of Rights. Slavery was banned. Married women were granted separate property rights, the first such guarantee found in any state (see Figure 3.1). Certain policy directions were also set in this constitution. Provisions for public education were specified in some detail, and public debt of any magnitude was disallowed. This constitution lasted 30 years, longer than many observers thought it would. The voters repeatedly rejected legislative calls for a second constitutional convention. Finally, a second one was held in 1878 amid population growth pressures (a 17-fold increase in only 30 years), farmer–railroad feuds, and the rise of the militant Workingman's Party. Many Californians thought constitutional reform would solve these problems.

The new constitution, ratified by voters in 1879, was three times longer and more detailed than the old one. Over the years, it has grown still further just as the state has. In the modern paperback version published by the California State Senate, the U.S. Constitution is included. The California Constitution's index alone is twice the length of the entire U.S. Constitution! Over the years, many original provisions have survived intact. Others

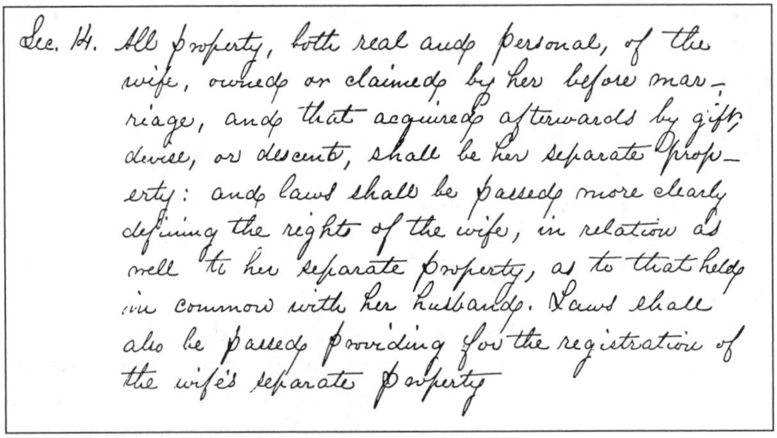

> Sec. 14. All property, both real and personal, of the wife, owned or claimed by her before marriage, and that acquired afterwards by gift, devise, or descent, shall be her separate property: and laws shall be passed more clearly defining the rights of the wife, in relation as well to her separate property, as to that held in common with her husband. Laws shall also be passed providing for the registration of the wife's separate property

FIGURE 3.1   Women and the Constitution of 1849

At a time in American history when women were considered legally subservient to their husbands, California's first constitution suggested otherwise. Consider Section 14 of Article 11 (Miscellaneous Provisions) as it appeared in the original.

Source: The Original Constitution of the State of California, 1849: The Engrossed Copy with the Official Spanish Translation (Sacramento: Telefact Foundation, 1965), p. 94.

have been slightly revised. Entire new sections have been added, and other sections have been reorganized.

WHAT IT CONTAINS

California's constitution illustrates features common to all state constitutions.

Duties of Government

It reflects the particular obligations of state government overall and necessary institutions such as the governor, legislature, and judiciary. Since local governments are really subdivisions of the state, the constitution must spell out their duties and powers. Therefore, extensive sections of California's constitution deal with cities, counties, special districts, and school districts.

Mistrust of Politicians

California's constitution, like those of other states, has reflected historic mistrust of elected officials. Regarded as corrupt, the legislature's powers were sharply delineated. For instance, the 1879 document enumerated 33 instances in which the legislature was *prohibited* from passing laws. Governors have not been spared either. California's constitution requires the governor to share power with separately elected executive officers—the lieutenant governor, attorney general, secretary of state, treasurer, controller, insurance commissioner, and school superintendent plus numerous boards and commissions.

Group Benefits

Typical of other state constitutions, California's has conferred particular advantages or imposed various regulations on interest groups. Numerous provisions address corporations generally and a host of specific groups including financial institutions, the legal profession, the alcoholic beverage industry, churches, contractors, utility companies, the fishing industry, farmers, realtors, and transportation providers. Although the constitution does not exactly mirror hyperpluralism as we use the term, any and all groups with requisite political power can use it to garner benefits for themselves or deny them to others.

Money

California's constitution addresses taxation and finance in detail. Tax policies embedded in this document are used to promote a plethora of interests: charitable groups, orchards and vineyards, historical preservation, nonprofit hospitals, the elderly, renters, home owners, museums, and veterans. Also, public indebtedness in California is severely restricted.

Clutter and Trivia

Like other states, California's constitution is filled with clutter and trivia. For instance, today's public school teachers can be grateful the state's constitution prevents their annual salaries from dipping below $2,400![2] In the early 1900s, the length of boxing matches and rounds was specified (12 rounds and three minutes, respectively). Occasionally the voters eliminate such provisions, but others remain simply because they are politically irrelevant. More important, some constitutional trivia remains because trivia is relative in a pluralistic society; what is undue clutter to one group may be economic survival to another. In a sense, it is pluralism at work.

Change

California, like other states, allows its basic document to change. Three methods are available. First is a *constitutional convention*. The legislature, by a two-thirds vote, may call for a constitutional convention. The last such convention was in 1878. In the 1960s, the legislature modified this method by appointing a "blue ribbon" constitutional revision commission to study the document and recommend changes for legisla-

tive approval and voter ratification. In the mid-1990s, a 23-member Constitutional Revision Commission studied the constitution and how government operates under it. It's recommendations died in the legislature.

A second method is change by *legislative proposal*, a method common to all states. Here the legislature proposes amendments and with a two-thirds vote forwards them to the voters for approval. "Housekeeping" changes and more significant policy proposals have resulted from this method. For instance, in 2000 voters approved Proposition 17, a legislatively drawn proposal to allow private nonprofit groups to conduct raffles; previously, the Constitution sanctioned only the official California Lottery. A third method is the *initiative*, a product of the Progressive era. The initiative allows individuals and groups to bypass the legislature entirely by placing proposed statutes or constitutional amendments on the ballot. In 2003–2006, it takes 598,105 valid signatures (8 percent of the 7,476,311 votes cast in the 2002 gubernatorial election) to qualify an initiative constitutional amendment. Eighteen states allow this method, but no state uses it more than California. Chapter 4 discusses the initiative process in depth.

WHAT MAKES IT DISTINCTIVE

Structurally, all state constitutions resemble the U.S. Constitution. Yet state constitutions invariably reflect their regional context, dominant political subcultures, historical experience, and subsequent political trends. At this point, I will briefly spotlight several provisions in California's Constitution that are quintessentially "Californian."

Power to the People

As noted earlier, one significant result of California's Progressive movement was the addition of initiatives, referenda, and recall. None of these is provided for in the U.S. Constitution. The *initiative*, allowing voters to directly place constitutional amendments and statutory proposals on the ballot, was approved in 1911. The *referendum* allows voters to approve or reject statutes already passed by the legislature. In 2003–2006, initiative statutes and referenda required 373,816 valid signatures to be placed on a California ballot (5 percent of the votes cast in the 2002 election). The *recall* allows the electorate to remove elective officials between elections. This provision applies to all elective officials at both the state and local levels, including judges.

The Right of Privacy

Only eight state constitutions contain a right of privacy, and California is one of them. Even though it is not specifically mentioned in the U.S. Constitution, the U.S. Supreme Court in *Roe v. Wade* (1973) established a right of privacy relative to reproductive choice.[3] California's original "Declaration of Rights" in 1849 did not include privacy. It read: "All men are by nature free and independent, and have certain inalienable rights, among which are those of enjoying and defending life and liberty; acquiring, possessing, and protecting property; and pursuing and obtaining safety and happiness." In 1974, the year after *Roe v. Wade*, California voters replaced "men" with "people," and added "privacy" after "happiness." Although the emerging abortion controversy was not a key issue in its passage, this rewording has been used to support a pro-choice policy in California.

Water

Many states take water for granted, but not those in the West. California's history of drought, coupled with its agricultural potential, virtually required government's attention from the start. Over the years, much water policy has made its way into the Constitution itself. A separate article is simply titled "Water" (Article 10).

English Only

The original 1849 Constitution was clear: "All laws, decrees, regulations, and provisions, which, from their nature, require publication, shall be published in English and Spanish." The constitution itself was handwritten in both languages, reflecting California's two dominant cultures. Possibly due to the influx of Euro-Americans during the Gold Rush, that bilingual requirement was eliminated in the 1879 Constitution. Californians have struggled with this issue ever since. In 1986, voters overwhelmingly approved Proposition 63, which declared English as the official language of the state. Its purpose was to "preserve, protect and strengthen the English language." In 1998, voters also rejected bilingual education in the public schools by approving Proposition 227.

Proposition 13

In June 1978, California voters approved Proposition 13, a property-tax-cutting measure that fundamentally altered the relationship between the state and its local governments. The media widely portrayed its passage as the opening volley of a national tax revolt. Although other states have adopted their own tax cuts in the intervening years, Proposition 13 captured the nation's attention like no other.

From a governing perspective, California's constitution has fostered fragmentation and gridlock in state politics and policymaking. The state's governors must share their power with other elected executives. Legislative prerogatives are curtailed or limited. Protections for powerful interest groups are sprinkled throughout the document. The initiative process allows well-funded interest groups and individuals, via the electorate, to share legislative power. California's constitutional clutter actually encourages litigation, as groups seek to determine what a particular provision really means. This increases the policy role of the courts with which the executive and legislative branches must share power.

California and the Nation: The Boundaries of Federalism

California's relationship to the national government, as with other states, has depended on both constitutional language and political practice. As times have changed, so has this relationship. The Tenth Amendment to the U.S. Constitution defines the general relationship that was supposed to exist between all the states and the national government: "The powers not delegated to the United States by the constitution, nor prohibited by it to the states, are reserved to the states respectively, or to the people."

The Founders never thought the national government would dominate the states in domestic policy. On the contrary, James Madison believed that, in most respects, the national government would be subservient to the states: "The State governments may be regarded as constituent and essential parts of the federal government; whilst the latter is nowise essential to the operation or organization of the former" (The Federalist, #45). Alexander Hamilton considered citizens' loyalties to be primarily local. If national representatives were tempted to encroach on the states, "the people of the several States would control the indulgence of so extravagant an appetite" (The Federalist, #17).

To modern-day Americans and Californians, these arguments seem both idealistic and unrealistic. The Founders simply could not have anticipated the profound changes that would take place in the federal system. Political scientists have grouped these changes into four historic periods.

DUAL FEDERALISM

This is the original pattern of which Madison and Hamilton wrote. From the founding to about 1913, the national government largely limited itself to activities specifically mentioned in the U.S. Constitution (such as national defense, foreign affairs, coining money, issuing tariffs, and maintaining a post office). The states were expected to make policy on domestic matters such as education, welfare, health, and law enforcement. With few exceptions, such as aid for the transcontinental railroad, the federal presence in California politics was minimal and indirect.

COOPERATIVE FEDERALISM

As American society became more complex and the Industrial Revolution produced a national economy, a "cooperative federalism" pattern emerged. A national income tax, two world wars, and the Great Depression combined to make both levels active policy partners concerned with health, welfare, transportation, education, crime, and other issues. During this period, California benefited greatly from federal spending on water projects, New Deal programs, highway construction, and defense contracts.

CENTRALIZED FEDERALISM

"He who pays the piper calls the tune," claims the old adage. As the federal government's capacity to tax and spend grew, it also became more than simply a cooperative partner in policymaking. The "feds" (as state and local officials call national level policymakers) gradually established their own goals. President Lyndon Johnson's Great Society legislation in the 1960s epitomized the next stage, centralized federalism.

The rationale was simple: If policy problems are national in *scope*, they must be national in *nature*—requiring a centralized response. People assumed that states could not or would not provide policy leadership or needed funding. From 1964 to 1980, the Tenth Amendment lost much of its original meaning. California followed the national pattern—depending on federal grants for everything from highways to health care. Along with these categorical grants came federal conditions and expectations. Control shifted from Sacramento to Washington, D.C. California public officials at all levels developed both an appetite for federal funds and a distaste for the federal conditions or "strings" that were attached. Increasingly, they had to lobby Washington, not just Sacramento, to get more funds and to avoid more strings.

ON-YOUR-OWN AND PRAGMATIC FEDERALISM

The 1980s and the "Reagan revolution" partially shifted this centralization pattern. Building on his experience as California's governor, President Ronald Reagan sought to decrease the national government's role vis-à-vis state and local government. He hoped to return many responsibilities to the states and, short of that, to simply reduce spending on programs he disliked. California officials, like their colleagues across the nation, felt that they would need to carry out a number of important programs on their own, without generous federal subsidies.

Today, the relationship between the federal government and subnational governments, including California, has been called *pragmatic federalism*—"a constantly evolving, problem solving attempt to work out solutions to major problems on an issue by issue basis."[4] Intergovernmental relations still exhibit some on-your-own, do-it-yourself characteristics. At each level of our federal system, public officials seek to maximize services to the people, take credit for providing such services, and where feasible, transfer the costs to some other level of government. Federal officials prefer unfunded mandates—telling California officials to do something without helping to pay for it. Many environmental regulations and anti-terrorism expenditures exemplify

this. Within California, state officials try to do much the same with local governments. For example, state officials require local governments to develop transportation plans or tell school districts to teach this or that. Are ordinary Californians pragmatic? Apparently so. They want favored services such as adequate transportation or education programs provided; which level of government does it or pays for it is of no concern. They simply want the job done.

California in Washington

The mixed signals from Washington in recent decades—less grant money, more preemptions—left California policymakers in a quandary. Do they solve pressing public problems on their own or continue to play the "Washington federalism game"? They have had to do both. In fact, California has developed its own approaches to policy issues apart from the national government. But given the federal structure of American politics, California's interests invariably reach to the nation's capital.

Compared to less diverse states, representing California in Washington is more challenging than size alone would suggest. According to many observers, California does not even receive in federal funds what it is presumably entitled to receive. In fiscal year 2000, the state sent a record $30 billion *more* to Washington in taxes than it received back in federal spending. This balance of payments problem is largely due to reduced defense procurement and insufficient spending on highway projects.[5]

The reasons for California's relative lack of influence in Washington are numerous and complex. First, the rules of the federalism game have shifted in the last two decades. Earlier, lobbyists in Washington worked routinely with executive branch bureaucrats who controlled the distribution of grant monies. As both funding and federal programs were reduced in the 1980s, some power over grants shifted from anonymous bureaucrats to Congress. As a result, California lobbyists found they had to influence the very content of legislation, not just "touch base" with grant administrators. This trend put a diverse and conflict-prone state at the mercy of a more diverse and conflict-ridden Congress.

Second, California lacks clout because it is so "distant" from the rest of the nation. Members of Congress from other states resent the state's sheer size and potential influence. According to a California Institute Report, "opportunistic legislators from other states continue to view California as a drain on the federal treasury and as a competitor for the federal dollars they covet."[6] Washington veterans call this attitude the *ABC syndrome*—Anybody or Anywhere But California.

Third, California's congressional delegation (two senators and 53 House members) is by far the nation's largest and most diverse. One problem is structural. High-growth states like California are outnumbered in the U.S. Senate, where each state, regardless of size, gets two senators and, accordingly, two votes. Another is ideological. The California delegation includes some of the most liberal and most conservative members in the entire House. Sharp ideological divisions exist not only between Republicans and Democrats but also within both parties. According to former Superintendent of Public Instruction Delaine Eastin, keeping the delegation unified on important issues such as education is like "herding cats."[7] In addition, California's diverse political geography (north/south, coastal/inland, urban/rural) creates diverse agendas within the

delegation. In the 1990s, the California Institute was founded to advise the state's congressional delegation on federal issues.

Given California's diversity of interests in Washington, several strategies have been employed to maximize the state's political effectiveness.

"SATURATION BOMBING"

A testimony to diverse, hyperpluralistic California, growing numbers of the state's public and private interest groups now saturate the federal government with lobbying activity. Dozens of California counties, cities, special districts, and state agencies (including the legislature) are represented in Washington. All three public higher education systems (the community colleges, the California State University, and the University of California) have registered lobbyists.

COALITION POLITICS

To make any issue a "California" issue is politically risky, especially on Capitol Hill. As a result, California's congressional delegation and California-based organizations have been most successful when they have framed their needs in broader terms and looked outside California for support. A few examples include the Committee for Education Funding, NOISE (the airport noise coalition), and the State and Local Clean Air Coalition. Because many issues come and go, California lobbyists must constantly build new coalitions to deal with new policy challenges. For instance, when Congress failed to appropriate needed funds

Did You Know . . . ?

Did you know that it takes the population of 23 other states to equal the population of California? Those states have a total of 46 U.S. senators to California's two.

under the 1986 Immigration Reform and Control Act, Californians from numerous state agencies and affected local governments worked together with officials from Texas and Florida to pressure Congress.

"BURY" THE CALIFORNIA CONNECTION

Ironically, another strategy for coping with the ABC syndrome is to downplay California interests. State agencies have been known to quietly support or oppose a bill in Congress without actually acknowledging its impact on California. Private businesses from California, such as defense contractors and Silicon Valley computer companies, maintain the usual ties with home-district members but rarely coordinate their lobbying efforts, fearing a so-called anti-California bias.

California and the World: The Politics of Fences

In an article entitled "California's Foreign Policy," James O. Goldsborough argues that "California is in many ways not a state, but a nation."[8] As such, it needs and deserves its own foreign policy. International pressures on the Golden State are primarily twofold. First, California is by far the most popular destination for both legal and illegal immigrants. What made the state attractive to early immigrants makes it attractive today. Second, California's colossal economy—the seventh largest in the world—is increasingly dependent on international trade. As the nation's largest exporter, the state relies on the ability to trade freely with Canada, Mexico, Europe, and its largest trading source— Asia. Much of California's "foreign policy" is related to immigration and trade.

IMMIGRATION

One gets the impression that there are few fences between California and the world. According to Immigration and Naturalization Service (INS) estimates, immigrants now account for one in four California residents, the highest proportion in the nation. In 2001, the United States became home to more than one million legal immigrants; 27 percent of those called California home. Furthermore, about 40 percent of all undocumented or illegal immigrants (totaling about 2 million) locate in California. Although about 40 percent of immigrants to California come from Asian nations, by far the most frequent country of birth for these newcomers is Mexico. All in all, people cross the California–Mexico border more than 60 million times each year.

Movement across California's border with Mexico is nothing new. Historically, the nation's approach toward Mexican workers, one shared in California, has been called the "flower petal policy": "I need you, I need you not, I need you. . . ." That is, immigrants are welcome depending upon whether the American workforce needs them. For instance, California welcomed Mexican immigrants after the Mexican Revolution of 1910 when Japanese and Chinese workers were unwelcome. During the Depression, people thought Mexicans were taking "American" jobs. But World War II resulted in another labor shortage, and Mexican laborers were welcomed once again. Renewed deportation efforts occurred in the 1950s and early in the 1980s. Although the "I need you not" rhetoric has been common in recent years, in reality Mexican labor has been essential to numerous California industries including garment makers, electronics, furniture manufacturing, food processing, and tourism.

The attraction of *El Norte* to Mexicans is understandable. California's minimum wage workers earn more per hour than comparably skilled Mexicans earn per day. This disparity has made the United States, and California in particular, economic magnets. Once they arrive and obtain jobs, Mexican American workers often use excess income to support family members left behind.

Recent immigration policy has been to shore up the fence. Facing the reality of illegal immigrants already here, Congress passed the Immigration Reform and Control Act of 1986 (IRCA). This law created an amnesty program leading to legal residency for more than 3 million foreigners, over half of whom lived in California. About 75 percent of those were from Mexico. One purpose was to unite family members divided only by national boundaries. The children of these newly legalized aliens became fully eligible for any and all government services and benefits. Critics of current policy complain that some immigrants, mindful of the benefits, cross the border in order to give birth in the United States. California has received only a portion of the federal aid intended to cushion the fiscal impact of the IRCA.

In 1994 the INS launched "Operation Gatekeeper" to stem the tide of illegal immigrants pouring into California along the San Diego–Tijuana border—the busiest land-border crossing in the world. In 1996, Congress followed up with the Illegal Immigration Reform and Immigrant Responsibility Act. This law increased criminal penalties for immigration-related offenses and authorized the INS to more aggressively police the border. Has the law worked? Evidence is mixed. Illegals still come but enter through less patrolled regions. Many depend on border-wise smugglers and guides to make this dangerous journey. While growing in numbers, immigrants from Asia and other nations do not seem to engender the negative reactions among some Californians that immigrants from Mexico do. In fact, many of California's technology firms have sought out highly skilled immigrants to fill labor shortages.

TRADE

In contrast to immigration, the approach of California and the federal government to world trade is to lower economic fences. In 1993, Congress passed the North American Free Trade Act (NAFTA) to encourage trade between Canada, the United States, and Mexico. Over time, it will eliminate tariffs completely and remove many nontariff barriers to trade such as import licenses. On the whole, the agreement has fostered trade and increased California exports to NAFTA's partners, especially in the high technology sector. In the first six years of NAFTA, California's exports to Mexico alone increased nearly 129 percent, or $8.4 billion.

In addition, California has taken action on its own. In the 1980s, it established the California World Trade Commission with offices in numerous foreign capitals. Recognizing the need to do more, state lawmakers created a Technology Trade and Commerce Agency. This agency assists California businesses wishing to expand markets domestically and abroad. In recent years, California has experienced a surge in exports to its most significant markets: Canada, Asia, and Europe. In sum, California's approach to its own borders has

---

Did You Know . . . ?

Did you know that 25.9 percent of all Californians are foreign born? That 33.1 percent of all foreign-born residents in the United States live in the metropolitan areas of Los Angeles and New York City? That, of the largest metropolitan areas, Los Angeles and San Francisco have the highest proportion of foreign-born at 30 percent each?

SOURCE: *Profile of the Foreign Born Population in the United States: 2000* (Washington, DC: Census Bureau, 2001), 2–3.

been to heighten the immigration fence and lower the economic fence.

Conclusion

California's position relative to the nation as a whole is most interesting. Its political development has resulted in constitutional provisions both similar and dissimilar to constitutions in other states. California's diversity is mirrored both in its constitution and in the variety of representatives it sends to Congress. Its sheer size makes it the focal point of media attention when voters dramatically alter their constitution. As a result, California can give birth to national political movements through such changes (for example, Proposition 13 and the "taxpayers' revolt").

California's size and diversity have affected its relationship to the national government of which it is a part. The state is both the automatic recipient of large amounts of federal spending and the source of resentment at the money being spent. But California's interests are so diffuse and its congressional delegation so diverse that the state rarely speaks with one voice, even when doing so would be in its own best interest. Finally, California's relationships with the rest of the world present an ongoing challenge and reflect the politics of diversity. A solid black line on maps, California's border is in reality a porous screen door through which flow workers, families, jobs, and dollars. Efforts have been made to raise the fence in terms of immigration but at the same time lower the fence in terms of international trade.

KEY TERMS

perimeters of politics (p. 26)

constitutionalism (p. 26)

Constitutions of 1849 and 1879 (pp. 27–29)

constitutional convention, legislative proposal, initiative (p. 29)

referendum and recall (p. 30)

stages of federalism (pp. 31–32)

ABC syndrome (p. 33)

Immigration Reform and Control Act (1986) (p. 35)

Illegal Immigration Reform and Immigrant Responsibility Act (1996) (p. 35)

NAFTA (p. 35)

REVIEW QUESTIONS

1. Describe the concept of constitutionalism and illustrate from California's two constitutions.
2. In what ways is California's constitution much like those of other states? In what ways is it different or unique?
3. California's constitution both planted the seeds of hyperpluralism and over time mirrored the varied political subcultures of the state. Illustrate this statement.
4. What developments were occurring in California during each stage of American federalism? How does the state relate to the federal government today?
5. How is California politics impacted by its proximity to Mexico and the Pacific Rim?

WEB SITE ACTIVITIES

The California Constitution
(www.leginfo/ca.gov/const.html/)
The Legislative Counsel of California maintains this Web site, which contains a fully searchable copy of the state constitution. Contrast it to the U.S. Constitution.

The California Institute
(www.calinst.org/)
This nonprofit Washington, D.C.–based organization analyzes federal policy as it relates to California and advises the California delega-

tion in Congress accordingly. The site helps you to assess the impact of a particular federal policy on California.

INFOTRAC COLLEGE EDITION ARTICLES

For additional reading, go to InfoTrac College Edition, your online research library, at http://infotrac-college.com/wadsworth

English Only for California Children

Little Federal Aid for California Terrorism and Public Safety Efforts

The California Cauldron

NOTES

1. Winston W. Crouch, John C. Bollens, and Stanley Scott, *California Government and Politics,* 6th ed. (Englewood Cliffs, NJ: Prentice-Hall, 1977), 29, 30.

2. See Article IX, Section 6 adopted November 4, 1952.

3. *Roe v. Wade,* 410 U.S. 113 (1973).

4. Parris N. Glendening and Mavis Mann Reeves, *Pragmatic Federalism: An Intergovernmental View of American Government,* 2nd ed. (Pacific Palisades, CA: Palisades Publishers, 1984), 27–28.

5. California Institute, *California's Balance of Payments with the Federal Treasury FY 1981–2000* (April 2002).

6. California Institute, p. 7.

7. Quoted in Ralph Frammolino, "California Lags in Slice of U.S. Funds for Schools," *Los Angeles Times,* October 28, 1998.

8. James O. Goldsborough, "California's Foreign Policy," *Foreign Affairs* 72 (Spring 1993): 88–96.

C H A P T E R   4

Direct Democracy in a Hyperpluralistic Age

OUTLINE

Introduction:
The Impact of Progressivism

Selected Initiative Battles in California
Proposition 13: Give the Money Back

Proposition 22: Gay Marriage

The Initiative Mess

Prospects for Reform

Progressive Cousins:
Referendum and Recall

Conclusion: The Legacy and the Paradox

Key Terms
Review Questions
Web Site Activities
InfoTrac College Edition Articles
Notes

Introduction: The Impact of Progressivism

It seems Californians are perennially voting, thinking about the next election, or recovering from the last one. They are inundated with more candidate and policy choices than most Americans could imagine. In some respects, Progressive reforms predestined this state of affairs. *Progressivism* was a turn-of-the-century political movement that sought to rid politics of corrupting influences, return power to "the people," and make government more businesslike.

The era from about 1900 to 1920 was one of social upheaval and intense political competition among social classes in the United States. The Progressive reformers were in the middle of this upheaval. Across the nation, these reformers were appalled by the political dark side of the Industrial Revolution. From coast to coast, new immigrant voters were routinely bribed by members of urban political machines. Unelected bosses of both parties easily controlled many city halls and statehouses. Rather than being above the dirt, political parties were rolling around in it.

Californians easily equate the Progressive era with the introduction of the initiative, referendum, and recall. Yet across the nation as well as in California, an entire set of other reforms were enacted to inhibit the influence of political machines. They included:

1. Direct primaries (allowing voters to nominate candidates)

2. At-large elections (where local government candidates run city-wide rather than by district)

3. Nonpartisan elections (where party designations do not appear on the ballot)

4. Merit systems and short ballots (government employees hired based on qualifications, not connections; fewer directly elected offices)

5. Professional management (such as presumably apolitical city managers)[1]

Selected Initiative Battles in California

Progressive era reforms are so familiar that modern Californians take them for granted. One reform that is both defended and criticized is the *initiative*. Those dissatisfied with the way initiatives have been manipulated by interest groups seem to think this is a recent phenomenon. Not so. In 1924, Artie Samish, then employed by the Motor Carriers Association, used the initiative to stabilize taxes on bus companies. Samish later became an infamous lobbyist.

In theory, the initiative would empower ordinary people to fight entrenched special interests. In reality, it was a weapon quite readily available to any group willing and able to use it. Since the individualist political subculture runs deeply in California's political development, it did not take long for individuals and groups to discover how valuable the initiative process could be. By 1939, well-financed interest groups were initiating measures more often

than ad hoc reform groups. The trend has continued to the present. Instead of using it as the safety valve it was intended to be, interest groups *and* politicians use the initiative to bypass the legislature. A closer look at two representative initiatives will demonstrate the role they have played in California's electoral politics.

**PROPOSITION 13:
GIVE THE MONEY BACK**

The first of these initiatives, 1978s Proposition 13, was rooted in California's real estate market. In the 1970s, California home prices skyrocketed and so did property taxes. Legislators and Governor Jerry Brown could not agree on how to best provide tax relief. Homeowner frustration mounted. A Los Angeles real estate developer and apartment owner Howard Jarvis proposed cutting property taxes by half and curbing their subsequent growth. He formed the populist-sounding United Organization of Taxpayers. They gathered a record 1.2 million signatures to qualify this historic tax reduction measure for the June 1978 ballot. Despite the dire predictions about its potential consequences, Proposition 13 passed with 64 percent of the vote. Nearly every electoral group as measured by political scientists supported it.

The consequences *were* dire. With property taxes cut by 57 percent, local services were slashed severely. Local governments, especially counties and school districts, became increasingly dependent on state "bailouts" to fill in revenue shortfalls. The bailouts became an annual feature of the state budget, and, in the process, local government lost a measure of its autonomy. The crowning blow to this autonomy was the passage of the 1993–94 state budget, which not only eliminated the bailout but transferred $2.6 billion in local property taxes to the state for education spending.

Another consequence was the so-called Proposition 13 effect. The measure limited property tax growth to only 2 percent per year, much less than real estate inflation. Only when a property was sold would the tax jump dramatically (to 1 percent of the new price). Over time the property tax paid by two neighbors living in identical houses could vary substantially depending on when the homes were purchased. In 1992, the U.S. Supreme Court, in *Nordlinger v. Hahn,* upheld Proposition 13, including this unequal treatment of property owners. Proposition 13 also made it exceedingly difficult to raise most taxes (a two-thirds vote of the people is usually required). It encouraged local officials to approve land use projects that generated sales taxes not controlled by Proposition 13, and it spawned a generation of political leaders loathe to reform the measure or even to question its wisdom, at least in public.

PROPOSITION 22: GAY MARRIAGE

PROPOSED LAW

SECTION 1. This act may be cited as the "California Defense of Marriage Act."
SECTION 2. Section 308.5 is added to the Family Code, to read:
308.5. Only marriage between a man and a woman is valid or recognized in California.

The above language was the actual text of Proposition 22, a controversial measure on the March 7, 2000, ballot. Those 14 words galvanized both supporters and opponents of gay rights and gay marriage in California. Although the proposition seemed simple enough, the issue it addressed was quite complex.

In an effort to seek societal recognition and fight discrimination, gay rights activists had demanded that gay marriages be given the same legal footing as heterosexual marriages. If they could achieve that in one state, presumably such marriages would need to be recognized in other states. The United States Constitution provides that "Full Faith and Credit shall be given in each State to the public acts, Records, and judicial Proceedings of every other State" (Article IV, Section 1). Concerned about that possibility, Congress passed and President Bill Clinton signed the Defense of Marriage Act in 1996. This law permitted states to not recognize gay marriages performed in other states. By early 2000, 30 states had passed similar laws.

The concerns of the gay community extend beyond the legal recognition of same-gender marriages. They feared that nonrecognition would result in the denial of various rights, including hospital visitations, inheritance, and dependent health insurance.

California does not allow same-sex couples to marry; Proposition 22 did not change that. But before Proposition 22, California recognized as legally valid all marriages occurring outside the state. Proposition 22 proponents had become alarmed because Hawaii had come close to recognizing gay marriages and Vermont was on the verge of doing so (it legalized gay marriages in May 2000).

The impetus for Proposition 22 came from California State Senator William "Pete" Knight (R–Palmdale) who had unsuccessfully sought similar limits in the state legislature. Knight's

Did You Know . . . ?

All nine pages of Article XIII Section A in the California State Constitution are devoted to Proposition 13 and voter-approved revisions of it. This is about the same length as Article I in the United States Constitution detailing the powers of Congress.

involvement was intriguing to say the least. Knight's son was gay and his gay brother had died of AIDS. Lining up to support the measure were various religious groups, the Mormon Church, the California Catholic Conference of Bishops, the state Republican Party, and the Hispanic Business Roundtable. Opposed were various gay rights organizations, the American Civil Liberties Union, a number of labor unions, the California Democratic Party, and still other religious leaders. By the end of the campaign, Proposition 22's supporters outspent their opponents by a wide margin—$9.5 million versus $5 million. As usual, much of this money was spent on television advertising.

In the end, Proposition 22 passed with 61 percent of the vote. The only region to oppose it was the Bay Area; they rejected it by a 69 to 31 percent margin. The statewide margin of support for Proposition 22 was even higher than pre-election polling would have predicted. Analysts speculated that large numbers of conservatives turned out because of a competitive Republican presidential primary campaign and effective get-out-the-vote efforts by groups like the Traditional Values Coalition.

Gay rights advocates were both disheartened and energized. Some thought they should seek to qualify their own pro-gay marriage initiative. Others thought that they should press their agenda in the state legislature. Most observers predicted that the struggle over gay marriage was hardly over. Polls suggest that fully 81 percent of Californians oppose discrimination based on sexual orientation; 54 percent think that homophobia is morally wrong. In addition, it appears that younger voters are more concerned about discrimination against gays than are older voters.[2]

The Initiative Mess

The stories behind Propositions 13 and 22 are typical of many others, and they point to some disturbing trends. Article titles give you some

clues: "Initiatives: Too Much of a Good Thing," "Hiram's Folly?" "California Initiatives: Out of Control," "California: The State That Tied Its Own Hands," and "Is This Any Way to Run a State?" Former assembly speaker and San Francisco Mayor Willie Brown goes so far as to call the initiative process "the single greatest threat to democracy in California."[3] Veteran journalist Peter Schrag believes that today's initiative process has caused a "seismic shift in the state's political center of gravity."[4]

What has happened to this ultimate tool of the sovereign voter? In terms of democratic theory, there were two faulty assumptions. Before the initiative was instituted, there was *misplaced confidence in legislators as competent representatives.* This assumes that elected representatives will choose decision over indecision; that they will consult public opinion rather than the preferences of special interests, especially when the two conflict. Consider this question: Are legislators primarily trustees using their own best judgment to represent the broad interests of their constituents or delegates following each and every constituent preference? The classic debate between trustee and delegate functions of legislators usually assumes constituents are the voters back home, not the lobbyists with whom contemporary legislators have much more contact.[5]

After the initiative process was established, there was *misplaced confidence in the voters as competent legislators.* Admittedly, political scientists do not always agree on this point. Years ago, Lester Milbrath observed, "we should not expect [the average voter] to give a lot of attention to, and be active in resolving issues of public policy."[6] Recent critics have called the initiative process "laws without government" and "simulated democracy." Political scientist Thomas Cronin is more sanguine: "Voters who do vote on ballot measures do so more responsibly and intelligently than we have any right to expect."[7]

Many observers blame the state's initiative mess largely on how the process has evolved. In

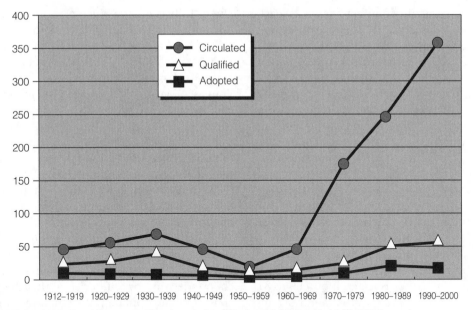

FIGURE 4.1 Initiative Measures Circulated, Qualified, and Adopted, 1912–2000

A growing number of groups and individuals have attempted to use the initiative process to make and influence public policy. But voters are rather selective in what they are willing to adopt.

Question: Why do California voters refuse to adopt most ballot initiatives? Which initiatives have you voted for, against, and why?

Source: Public Policy Institute of California.

many respects, it epitomizes *hyperpluralistic politics in a technological age.* Remember, California is a large, diverse, industrial state with a complex economy and a large, relatively intrusive state government. The initiative was intended to be a profound but infrequently used tool against singular interests. But California has long since passed the stage of one monopolistic interest like the Southern Pacific Railroad. Writer Carey McWilliams once called the state capital the "market place of California" where competing groups "bid for allotments of state power."[8] As Figure 4.1 indicates, the initiative process itself has become California's new marketplace where all manner of groups seek, if not receive, public favor. Political scientist Elizabeth R. Gerber has observed that citizen groups use direct legislation to bring about policy change whereas economic groups use it to block policy change.[9]

Widespread access to and use of the initiative process has had numerous consequences:

1. *Many ballot measures represent big money, not just good ideas.* A significant feature of the process today is the amount of money spent to affect the outcome. In 1998, more money was spent on ballot initiatives than on all state legislative races combined. In 2000, opponents and proponents of Proposition 38, the school voucher initiative, spent more than $60 million. To be sure, not all initiative campaigns require heavy spending, and big money does not always ensure victory. Proposition 38 was soundly defeated by a 71 to 29 percent vote.

2. *New policy and process entrepreneurs can emerge,* rivaling the importance and influence of legislative leaders and even the governor. Some Cali-

fornians are synonymous with measures they have supported or opposed: Howard Jarvis and Paul Gann (property tax cuts), Howard Rosenfield (auto insurance reform), Mike Reynolds (three-strikes sentencing reform), Ron Unz (bilingual education), and Tim Draper (school vouchers).[10] The initiative process itself has spawned its own business entrepreneurs, a so-called initiative industrial complex. Although it takes only $250 to file an initiative with the Secretary of State, gathering a million-plus signatures to qualify it for the ballot is no job for amateurs. Major firms such as Kimball Petition Management, National Petition Management, American Petition Consultants, and Progressive Campaigns hire independent subcontractors who in turn employ solicitors who receive $1.50 or more per signature. Some solicitors handle up to 10 petitions at a time, often pushing the ones that pay the most. Using these firms, it is possible to garner more than 1 million signatures in one month. In fact, 90 percent of all initiatives require professional assistance.[11]

3. *Initiative campaigns increasingly rely on television.* California's television stations do a remarkably poor job covering the policy process in a representative democracy. Complicated issues do not lend themselves to short, visually entertaining stories. Lobbyists need not buy commercial time to woo a legislative subcommittee majority. But a "plebiscitarian" democracy is different. Lacking cues (endorsements or preferences) from candidates and political parties on ballot measures, information overload— including thick voter information guides— gives way to simplistic but graphic emotional appeals. As a result, two-thirds of respondents in one California survey believe media are the most influential sources of information on initiatives.[12] Lacking cues (endorsements or preferences) from candidates and political parties on ballot measures, information overload gives way to simplistic but graphic emotional appeals.

4. *The initiative process itself is constantly changing.* The process engenders different and evolving techniques. One technique is for groups to simply outspend their opponents. In March 2000, California's Indian tribes spent more than $25 million to lock Indian gaming into the state constitution. Opponents spent a paltry $45,000. A second technique has been for opponents of a particular measure to offer their own less objectionable measure, hoping voters will be attracted to it. Recent examples of *dueling initiatives* include term limits, insurance reform, and campaign finance reform. These competing measures may represent valid approaches or efforts to blur issues and confuse voters. Confused voters are often "no" voters.[13] The newest technique has been to "campaign against the campaign," in other words, to head off a new initiative effort before it gets to the ballot. This has been done with health insurance reform.

5. *Elected officials themselves employ the initiative.* Criticized as damaging representative government, the initiative has actually become another tool *of* representative government. Statewide officeholders and legislators alike see it as a new route to public policy and electoral popularity. Policy gridlock in Sacramento has driven some policymakers to bypass their own process. The initiative serves a variety of motives. Depending on the situation, it can be an opportunity for minority party members to go around majority party leaders, a policy vehicle for legislative mavericks or outsiders, a platform for higher office, or one more bargaining chip on pending legislation.[14] Then Governor Pete Wilson built at least part of his policy agenda around initiatives dealing with illegal immigration, three strikes, and affirmative action.

6. *Government's workload actually increases when initiatives pass.* To work at all, many measures require the legislature to fill in the missing details or to establish implementing measures. For instance, Proposition 20, the 1972 coastal protection initiative, required the appointment, staffing, and funding of a State Coastal Commission and several regional coastal commissions. Proposition 10, a 1998 initiative that raised the

Did You Know ... ?

Did you know that in a two-year period in California, on average,

   70 initiatives will be filed,
   12 will qualify for the ballot,

4 will win voter approval, and
3 of those will be challenged in court?

SOURCE: Charles M. Price, "Shadow Government," *California Journal* 28 (October 1997): 33.

---

cigarette tax 50 cents per pack (to a total of 87 cents), established a new state commission to provide information and formulate guidelines for newly funded early childhood development and smoking prevention programs. Initiative-driven governing becomes an ongoing process.

7. *Many initiatives end up in court.* Initiatives are often poorly drafted or patently unconstitutional. A lawsuit is so likely that initiative drafters usually insert severability clauses; if the courts find one section unconstitutional, the balance of the measure survives. In our dual judicial system, initiatives can be challenged in state or federal courts. The results are mixed. Sometimes the courts may remove an offending provision while affirming the balance of the initiative. For example, the California Supreme Court upheld Proposition 140, which established term limits for state officeholders, but removed the retroactive elimination of legislative pensions. At times courts take more drastic action. In 1999, the Court struck down all of Proposition 5, the 1998 Indian gaming initiative, because it violated a 1984 constitutional amendment that created the state lottery. As noted earlier, Proposition 1A in 2000 inoculated Indian gaming from further interference by placing it in the state constitution. Law professor Gerald F. Uelman believes that the "validity of initiative measures will occupy a steadily growing segment of the California Supreme Court docket."[15]

Federal judges and justices are less generous, possibly because they do not face periodic election. For instance, Proposition 187, the illegal immigration measure, stalled in a Los Angeles federal district court as soon as it passed in 1994. The enforcement of Proposition 209 that banned affirmative action programs eventually became law but only after the Ninth Circuit Court of Appeals (which handles cases from California) upheld it. The U.S. Supreme Court ruled unconstitutional California's Three-Strikes Law after someone was sentenced to 25 years to life in prison for stealing some videotapes.

Clearly state and federal courts play important roles in the initiative process. Although they tend to infuriate initiative zealots, the courts can modify, rewrite, overturn, or uphold challenged initiatives. In effect, they repair faulty provisions or put the brakes on what they consider unconstitutional ones.[16]

Prospects for Reform

If the initiative process in California is such a mess, what are the odds of reforming it? Not very good. In the mid-1990s, the California Constitution Revision Commission made three modest recommendations: (1) allow the legislature to rewrite an initiative before it is submitted to the voters; (2) limit initiative constitutional amendments to November elections, when voter turnout is higher; and (3) permit the legislature, with the governor's approval, to amend statutory initiatives after they have been in effect for six years. The legislature has not acted on any of these recommendations.

Ordinary Californians appear to be ambivalent regarding the initiative process. Polls suggest they are relatively aware of its shortcomings as described in this chapter. They admit that many initiatives are confusingly worded, unnecessarily complicated, and often represent the concerns of special interests, not the state as a whole. Yet fully 71 percent of Californians prefer initiatives over decisions by the legislature and governor as the best way to address issues facing the state.[17] Given these views, significant reform is unlikely.

Progressive Cousins: Referendum and Recall

In contrast to the initiative process, two other Progressive era reforms—referendum and recall—are less important and less utilized. For example, the *referendum* allows voters to prevent a legislative statute from taking effect. There are two kinds of referenda: *petition* and *compulsory*. The petition version is relatively rare. For instance, in 1982, a petition referendum was placed on the statewide ballot to block a legislative decision to build the Peripheral Canal through the Sacramento Delta. Northern Californians opposed to diverting more water to the south were behind this effort. The compulsory referendum is more common. All constitutional amendments initiated by the legislature and all bond issues over $300,000 require voter approval. In recent years, bond issues have appeared on nearly every ballot as legislators seek additional revenue for schools, prisons, and highways without raising taxes.

The mechanics of the referendum are simple enough. Within three months of a state law's passage, opponents may gather a requisite number of signatures to place the matter on the next regularly scheduled statewide ballot. Certain categories of legislation are ex-

empt: calls for special elections, tax levies, urgency measures, and spending bills. To be successful, referendum supporters must gather 373,816 valid signatures within 90 days (the figure needed during 2003–2006). In contrast, initiative backers have 150 days to gather the necessary signatures.

The *recall* allows voters to remove from office state or local elected officials between elections. California is one of 15 states allowing statewide recall, but in 59 attempts it has never been successful here. The hurdles to statewide recall are substantial. To place a recall on the ballot, people must gather signatures equal to 12 percent of the votes cast in the previous election for that office. In 2003, opponents of Governor Gray Davis, led by U.S. Representative Darrell Issa, launched a campaign to recall him from office; by July, the imposing requirements of 897,157 signatures seemed well within reach. A few state legislators have been ousted in this manner. In the aftermath of a bitter struggle over the Assembly speakership in the 1990s, Southern California voters recalled Republicans Paul Horcher and Doris Allen for cooperating too closely with the Democrats.

Recall is much more common at the local level (as is defeating incumbents at regular elections). A relatively small number of qualifying signatures makes it quite feasible indeed. Such recall efforts are often characterized by bitter conflict. What angers local voters enough to recall an official? Most controversies involve unpopular policy decisions, personnel controversies, "cronyism," outrageous behavior, or other local issues. Consider these examples. Latino voters in Bell Gardens ousted four white, "out-of-touch" city council members. In predominantly Latino South Gate, voters rejected their mayor, two council members, and the city treasurer, calling them thieves and crooks. Glendora voters removed the mayor and two council members after they fired the city manager and replaced several planning commission members with "cronies." A Santa

AP Photo/Nick Ut

PHOTO 4.1 How Voters Vent

South Gate, Calif., Treasurer Albert Robles receives his ballot as he arrives to vote in a recall election in the Los Angeles suburb Tuesday, Jan. 29, 2003. The Secretary of State monitored a bid Tuesday to recall four top city officials amid allegations that they squandered nearly $8 million in city reserves, while handing out contracts and kickbacks to friends. At the top of the recall list is Robles, who is facing assault weapons possession charges. South Gate gained notoriety last year after city officials were accused of interfering with an earlier effort against them, prompting Gov. Gray Davis to sign a bill giving Los Angeles County control over the city's special elections.

Barbara county supervisor survived a recall rooted in redistricting, a flag salute dispute, and chronic intradistrict feuding.

Conclusion:
The Legacy and the Paradox

The legacy of the Progressive era cannot be overemphasized. In fact, it has fostered hyperpluralism. By kicking one group—the Southern Pacific Railroad—out of politics, Californians invited many other groups into politics. Numerous reforms at both the state and local levels were implemented in those early years. We take many of them for granted, such as nonpartisan local elections and city managers. Some reforms, like the referendum, have proved to be rather unworkable. Others, like the local recall, have truly become the safety valve they were meant to be. The initiative gets the most attention and with good reason. Savvy individuals with enough money can qualify most any pet policy or project for the ballot. But historically, most California initiatives have resulted from interest group activity and, more recently, major policymakers. Progressives defeated one powerful interest group and limited what they considered the negative influence of political parties, as Chapter 6 will attest. But inadvertently they also strengthened the long-term role of California's interest groups for generations to come.

The process now appears to be a function of hyperpluralism in a technological age. Interest groups participate via initiatives, not just statehouse bills. Truly revolutionary policy can result from this process. But so can policy paralysis. An initiative victory can be whittled away or substantially revised in its implementation. A stunning initiative victory or defeat can actually inhibit further discussion on the policy involved as with Proposition 13. The process has produced more choices and information about them than typical voters can handle. At the same time, it has produced media-centered campaigns that insult voter intelligence. Yet, for all its faults and abuses, contemporary Californians resist efforts to tamper with the system they have inherited. Voters may well realize that if they do not understand an issue, in spite of or due to an information blizzard on it, they can simply vote "No."

The initiative process is analogous to true-or-false tests. At the polls voters are faced with highly technical issues with uncertain and far-reaching ramifications. Wise policy alternatives come in shades of gray, not black or white. Yet the voters are examined on these complex subjects with up or down decisions. No multiple-choice, fill-ins, or essay questions are allowed. The requirements of direct democracy are such that only the well-educated and homework-inclined can vote wisely. But a growing number of Californians do not fit that description. As we will see in Chapter 5, all Californians are affected by the state's policies, but a much smaller number actually participate in the system that produces those policies.

KEY TERMS

Progressivism (p. 38)

Progressive reforms (p. 39)

Propositions 13, 22 (pp. 39–41)

policy and process entrepreneurs (p. 43)

dueling initiatives (p. 43)

petition referendum (p. 45)

compulsory referendum (p. 45)

statewide and local recall (pp. 45–46)

REVIEW QUESTIONS

1. What factors explain the rise of Progressivism nationwide? In California?

2. How do the initiative cases described here

illustrate the pros and cons of the initiative process?

3. Is the initiative process as much a mess as some believe?

4. Based on this chapter, are recalls a good idea? Why or why not?

5. What larger issues of California politics does the modern initiative process illustrate?

WEB SITE ACTIVITIES

Initiative and Referendum Institute
(http://www.dnet.org/initiatives/)
As you will see from this site, California is not alone or unique in allowing voters to legislate.

California Secretary of State
(http://www.ss.ca.gov/)
Go to the elections area for progress reports on initiatives currently in circulation. If you want to circulate your own, complete how-to instructions are available.

California Voter Foundation
(www.calvoter.org/)
This watchdog and educational group tracks contributions to recent proposition campaigns. Click on "Follow the Money."

INFOTRAC COLLEGE EDITION ARTICLES

For additional reading, go to InfoTrac College Edition, your online research library, at http://infotrac-college.com/wadsworth

Initiative Reform

Laws for Sale

Proposition 22: Unintended Consequences

NOTES

1. For a historical treatment of direct democracy in California, see John M. Allswang, *The Initiative and Referendum in California, 1898–1998* (Stanford: Stanford University Press, 2000).

2. Jennifer Warren, "Gays Gaining Acceptance, Poll Finds," *Los Angeles Times*, June 14, 2000.

3. John Balzar, "Brown Labels Anti-Proposition 39 Ads 'Con Jobs,'" *Los Angeles Times*, November 22, 1984.

4. Peter Schrag, *Paradise Lost: California's Experience, America's Future* (New York: New Press, 1998), 189.

5. Political scientists regard legislators as *trustees* if they are primarily guided by personal conscience and as *delegates* if they are primarily guided by the wishes of the constituents who elect them.

6. Lester Milbrath, *Political Participation* (Chicago: Rand McNally, 1965), 144–145.

7. Thomas E. Cronin, *Direct Democracy: The Politics of Initiative, Referendum and Recall* (Cambridge, MA: Harvard University Press, 1989), 84–88, 89, 210.

8. Carey McWilliams, *California: The Great Exception* (New York: Current Books, 1949), 213.

10. Elizabeth R. Gerber, *The Populist Paradox: Interest Group Influence and the Promise of Direct Legislation* (Princeton, NJ: Princeton University Press, 1999).

10. For a profile of Unz, see Steve Scott, "Gadfly Extraordinaire," *California Journal* 30 (August 1999): 18–22.

11. David Broder, "Collecting Signatures for a Price," *Washington Post*, April 12, 1998.

12. *The California Initiative Process—How Democratic Is It?* [An Occasional Paper] (San Francisco: Public Policy Institute of California, 2002). Available online at http://www.ppic.org/.

13. Bill Ainsworth, "Initiative Wars: If You Can't Beat 'Em, Swamp 'Em," *California Journal* 21 (March 1990): 147–149.

14. Charles Bell and Charles Price, "Lawmakers and Initiatives: Are Ballot Measures the Magic Ride to Success?" *California Journal* 19 (September 1988): 380–384.

15. Gerald F. Uelman, "Taming the Initiative," *California Lawyer* 20 (August 2000): 50.

16. For more on the courts' role in the initiative process, see Charles M. Price, "Shadow Government," *California Journal* 28 (October 1997): 32–38.

17. Mark Baldassare, *California in the New Millennium: The Changing Social and Political Landscape* (Berkeley: University of California Press, 2000), 84–88.

CHAPTER 5

The Political Behavior of Californians

OUTLINE

Introduction

**Forms of Participation
in a Democracy**
Conventional Participation
The Exit Option
The Protest Option

**Voters and Nonvoters
in California**
Who Votes in California?
Those Who Cannot Vote
Those Who Will Not Vote

Partisanship in California
Party Affiliation
The Partisan Geography of
California

California's Electoral Gaps

**Conclusion:
Divided by Diversity**
Key Terms
Review Questions
Web Site Activities
*InfoTrac College Edition
Articles*
Notes

Introduction

California's fondness for initiatives creates the impression that all Californians are reasonably knowledgeable, politically active, and ready to vote on any issue or candidate placed before them. A seemingly constant parade of candidates and policy issues fills their political "space." Yet despite the political demands placed on them, Californians are much like other Americans in their political activity. Only a few are very involved, a larger number vote, and still others choose not to participate in any meaningful way. Yet specific groups of Cal-

ifornians differ from each other in their political behavior. To understand how Californians behave politically, we need to review what political scientists know about generic political behavior. Researchers have collected huge amounts of data, but iron laws of voting behavior are nonexistent. Voting is an individual, private act, and it is also a continuous activity. Electoral attitudes and behavior can and do change. Researchers find voters and nonvoters hard to pin down. Also, voting is only one political behavior among many to measure and analyze. First, we consider the larger idea of political participation.

Forms of Participation in a Democracy

How ordinary citizens participate in a representative democracy has always intrigued political scientists. In recent years, political scientists have identified and categorized the political activities of Americans. *Political participation* consists of individual or group activity intended to exercise influence in the political system. Methods used to exercise such influence are either conventional or unconventional in nature: that is, inside or outside the norms considered acceptable by the larger society. We will explore briefly these channels of influence.

CONVENTIONAL PARTICIPATION

Political scientists have identified a wide range of civic activities engaged in by Americans. Voting is the most widely shared political activity (71 percent reporting doing it regularly), followed by joining a political organization (48 percent), contacting political officials (34 percent), attending political meetings (29 percent), and making political contributions (24 percent).[1] Also, many people participate in voluntary associations that political scientists call "civil societies." These include service organizations (Rotary, Lions, Soroptimists), youth clubs (Boys and Girls Clubs, Girls, Inc.), and churches, mosques, or synagogues. Many parents are deeply involved in their children's schooling and sports activities. Yet there is growing evidence that many Americans are becoming more disengaged from civic life. That is, although they may do charity work, many do not volunteer or work on national, state, local, or neighborhood issues.[2]

THE EXIT OPTION

These types of political and social behavior do not tell the whole story below the national level. Some people become so dissatisfied with conditions or public policies in their communities that they leave for other communities and even other states. In the wake of California's energy crisis in 2001, some electricity-dependent technology firms threatened to leave the state or take their expansion plans elsewhere than California. This is the *exit option*—an unconventional but not unusual form of political participation.

This exit option also applies to individual Californians who may be fed up with crime, smog, and congestion. Given the chance, many move from crowded metropolitan areas to rural, inland locations (urban refugees); they sell expensive homes and move to Oregon, Washington, Nevada, or anywhere that is cheaper (equity refugees); or they pull their children out of ethnically diverse public schools and send them to less diverse, private ones (ethnic refugees). Some may even home school their children—the ultimate educational exit program. Demographers monitor this exiting trend in California by analyzing automobile registration data (each driver represents about 1.5 persons). For instance, in the early 1990s, many urban Californians were moving to suburbia, rural areas, or beyond—anywhere that was smaller or less dense. By the early 2000s, some of these trends were reversed. Large numbers of people were migrating to California's job-generating urban counties.

THE PROTEST OPTION

A less conventional form of political participation is the *protest option*. Sporadic political protest, both violent and nonviolent, has always been a part of America's political heritage. Historically, California has had its fair share. Most of the well-publicized incidents of protest and violence in California have been ethnic in nature. Consider the anti-Chinese demonstrations in San Francisco inspired by the Workingman's Party (1877); union strikes and the union-inspired bombing of the *Los Angeles Times* building (early 1900s); the "zoot suit" riots in Los Angeles (1943); free speech and Vietnam War protests on university campuses (1960s); the Watts riot in Los Angeles following a controversial police arrest (1965); and the 1992 Los Angeles riot (following the acquittal of four Los Angeles police officers accused of beating motorist Rodney King). In 2002, facing the prospect of significant budget cuts, numerous groups traveled to Sacramento to "demonstrate" and to communicate their views to lawmakers.

As forms of political behavior, political protest and violence are difficult to study. Developing a direct cause-and-effect relationship between arson or looting and some conscious political message can be rather speculative. To be sure, protest is a form of political behavior used by groups who lack more conventional resources. These groups may not be able to articulate clearly why they do what they do. While some rioters may be acting out pent up rage over lack of jobs, others are simply looting or caught up in the emotions of the moment. All in all, the connection between protest and violence is tenuous, albeit related. In short, *not all protest is violent, and not all violence is protest.*

Voters and Nonvoters in California

To better understand conventional participation and voting in particular, political scientists examine voters (those who show up at the polls on election day or vote absentee) and nonvoters (those who cannot or will not vote). Some Californians are not qualified to vote. Those who are eligible are considered to be the *voting age population* (VAP). For instance, in the 2000 presidential election, California's voting age population numbered about 21.5 million, and only 51.9 percent of that group voted. Another measure of voting is *voter turnout*—those registered voters who turn out to vote in any particular election. In that 2000

election, almost 71 percent of those Californians registered to vote actually did so.

WHO VOTES IN CALIFORNIA?

Political scientists want to know not only how many people vote but who votes and what those voters are like. One way to do this is through *exit polls*—questioning voters as they leave polling places on election day. What do California voters look like? Closely examine Table 5.1, an exit poll conducted on November 5, 2002. Here are some of the highlights. There were somewhat more female than male voters. The largest age group was 45- to 64-year-olds. White voters constituted 76 percent of the turnout, a much larger percentage than their share of the population. A majority had at least a college degree. There were more Democrats than Republicans, but many of them appeared to consider themselves moderates, not liberals. Well over half of all voters had household incomes over $60,000. Religiously, the largest group was Protestant. Lastly, an impressive 56 percent resided in Southern California, including Los Angeles County.

THOSE WHO CANNOT VOTE

The health of representative democracy depends on voting. Yet California and other states have experienced rather high levels of nonparticipation, especially at the ballot box. Nonparticipation takes two forms: *structural nonvoting* (those disenfranchised by the rules) and *preferential nonvoting* (those disenfranchised by their own behavior and attitudes). We will explore both forms.

In our federal system, states administer all elections. "Universal suffrage" does not mean all people get to vote. In fact, states can and do make it difficult and, for some, impossible to vote. California is no exception. Of 34 million Californians in 2002, only 21.5 million were legally qualified to vote. The other 12.5 million included people in the following categories:

TABLE 5.1 California Voters: A Snapshot (November 2002 Exit Poll)

% of all voters	Gender		Political Ideology
49%	Male	35%	Liberal
51%	Female	30%	Moderate
		35%	Conservative
	Age		**Party and Ideology**
11%	18 to 29	27%	Liberal Democrat
25%	30 to 44	19%	Moderate Democrat
40%	45 to 64	7%	Moderate Independent
24%	65 or older	13%	Moderate Republican
		27%	Conservative Republican
	Race/Ethnicity		**Annual Family Income**
76%	White	24%	Less than $40,000
4%	Black	19%	$40,000 to $59,000
10%	Latino	32%	$60,000 to $100,000
6%	Asian	25%	More than $100,000
	Education		**Religion**
18%	High school graduate or less	46%	Non-Catholic Christian
24%	Some college	25%	Roman Catholic
58%	College degree or more	4%	Jewish
	Party Registration		**Union Membership**
46%	Democrats	17%	Union member
10%	Independents	11%	Union member in household
40%	Republicans	72%	Non-union household
	Gender/Race/Ethnicity		**Region**
37%	White men	23%	Los Angeles County
39%	White women	33%	Rest of Southern California
12%	Minority men	14%	Bay Area
12%	Minority women	30%	Rest of Northern California (including Central Valley)

Source: The *Los Angeles Times* Poll.

Note: The *Times* Poll interviewed 3,444 voters as they left 60 polling places across California during the November 2002 election. Percentages were adjusted slightly to account for absentee ballots and those who declined to participate. The margin of error for the entire sample is ± 2 percent.

- Those under 18 years of age

- Nearly 5 million noncitizens (legal and illegal immigrants)

- Those who moved into a precinct within 15 days of an election

- Prisoners and parolees (ex-convicts regain their voting rights; those serving jail time for misdemeanor convictions may vote, by absentee ballot, of course!)

- The legally insane (but only if a judge formally disqualifies such persons)

Qualifying is not enough. Individuals must also declare their desire to vote by filing a brief registration form with the appropriate county office (usually a registrar of voters or the county clerk's office). During spurts of activity before big elections, these forms are available at shopping centers, public buildings, and on street corners. Originally designed to inhibit voter fraud, registration requirements effectively inhibit many Californians from voting. Because one must reregister after every move, highly mobile groups (such as agricultural employees, some construction workers, and college students) find they are unregistered on election day. Recent surveys suggest that many unregistered Californians are relatively young Latino males with modest levels of income and education. They pay little or no attention to politics or political news. According to pollster and analyst Mark Baldassare, they are "quite oblivious to the election process."[3]

Today, registering to vote is less difficult than in the past. A 1993 federal "motor voter" law requires states to lower registration hurdles, for instance, by allowing people to register at motor vehicle or welfare offices. By the November 2000 election, millions of Californians had registered or reregistered under the law's provisions. To vote in that election, another 40,000 used a first-ever online voter registration process from the comfort of their own homes or workplaces. Under these various methods, a record 15.7 million Californians registered to vote, about 73 percent of those eligible to vote.

THOSE WHO WILL NOT VOTE

When political scientists, media pundits, and election officials bemoan low voter turnout, they refer to the eligible voters who choose not to vote—preferential nonvoters. As previously noted, only 51.9 percent of California's voting age population (those qualified to vote) bothered to vote in November 2000. Why do those eligible to vote choose not to? The reasons can be divided into personal factors and structural factors.

Personal Factors

Many Californians consider themselves disengaged from government and politics. In a 1998 poll, habitual nonvoting Californians were asked why they do not always vote.[4] Thirty-six percent said they lack enough knowledge to vote. This is understandable. To these people, voting is a daunting task. Primary elections, general elections, special elections, off-year elections, advisory elections—if it is Tuesday, it must be election day, or so it seems. Consolidated elections (combining various municipal, special district, and state ballots) have lengthened considerably. Some voters experience information overload, including official voter pamphlets, incessant television commercials, political "junk-mail," door hangers, and precinct walkers. This is especially true when propositions are on the ballot. For some, the cost of voting (including the homework involved) is not worth the trouble, especially if the benefit is not clear. Also, some observers believe that negative campaigning by candidates demotivates some voters.

Another 24 percent in that survey claimed to be too busy to vote. The better-off of these pursue a full routine of activities and feel no need to vote. The less well-off are preoccupied with getting or staying employed, holding families together, and simply living from day to day. Still another 16 percent viewed voting as useless. To these political alienated Californians, voting produces no change, so why not boycott elections entirely? Finally, 9 percent say they are "just not interested in politics."[5]

The personal factor of age may also affect voter turnout. Turnout is relatively high among older Californians, but the oldest of them may be too infirm to vote. "The youngest voters—members of Generation X—are less attuned to politics and voting. They have been raised on MTV, view public officials as corrupt, and do not look to government as a problem solver."[6]

Structural Factors

Many Californians (as do other Americans) pick and choose elections in which to vote. They seem to ask: Is this election important? Does it stir my interest? They tend to think that higher-level elections are more important than lower-level ones. Voter turnout drops successively from presidential to state to local elections. In the 2002 gubernatorial election, turnout of those eligible to vote was a dismal 36 percent, the lowest turnout *ever* in a statewide gubernatorial election. Turnout in separate local elections normally hovers around 30 percent but can go lower. When incumbents run unopposed, as often happens in state legislative primaries, voters lose interest. Understandably, special elections garner fewer voters than regularly scheduled ones.

Partisan Factors

Political scientists also know that voter turnout varies by political party. The conventional wisdom suggests that Republicans have higher turnouts than Democrats, and the 2002 general election confirmed this. While Democratic turnout mirrored their registration numbers, Republicans experienced a higher turnout. Their turnout was 40 percent despite the fact that they were only 35 percent of registered voters. Republicans occasionally can benefit from this gap, especially in low-turnout elections. The gap widens a bit in primary elections, then narrows somewhat in general elections. Nonetheless, this phenomenon forces both Republican and Democratic candidates to appeal to California's independent voters. And appeal they must, because independents and minor party members comprise 17 percent of the state's likely voters.

Regional Factors

All these general explanations apply to California as a whole but not to all parts of the state. Dramatic differences exist between the state's 58 counties. For the 2002 gubernatorial election, over 70 percent of registered voters in sparsely populated Amador County turned out to vote. Only 48 percent of registered voters in San Bernardino turned out. Of those simply eligible to vote, Alpine County had the highest turnout at 64 percent, and San Bernardino had the lowest at 27 percent. Why the differences? One explanation is that counties with high numbers of Latinos, immigrants, and other low-propensity voters tend to experience lower turnouts than those with lower concentrations of such groups.

What are the long-term trends in California? Even though absolute numbers of voters continue to increase, a gradually smaller percentage of Californians are bothering to register and, once registered, to vote. Take a moment to study Table 5.2, which shows voting in presidential election years when voter turnout is highest. Particularly striking is the declining turnout of those Californians eligible to vote.

Partisanship in California

How citizens participate in the electoral process and why many do not is only part of the picture. Another part includes the various

TABLE 5.2 Voter Turnout in California, 1976–2000: Presidential Election Years

Year	Eligible to register (%)	Turnout of registered (%)	Turnout of those eligible (%)
1976	70.3	81.5	57.3
1980	73.8	77.2	57.0
1984	78.8	74.9	59.1
1988	73.5	72.8	55.5
1992	72.4	75.3	54.5
1996	80.5	65.5	52.6
2000	73.2	70.9	51.9

Source: California Secretary of State.

frames of reference citizens use to contextualize their participation. A *frame of reference* is a set of beliefs or observations that gives meaning to ideas and actions. They are "hooks" on which to hang numerous political messages. One of the most important hooks for Americans is political party identification.

PARTY AFFILIATION

A *political party* is a relatively permanent coalition that exists to win public offices for its candidates, promote policy positions, and serve as a primary frame of reference for voters. *Party identification* is the extent to which citizens affiliate with, relate to, or support a specific political party. Identifiers believe support for a party makes their vote more meaningful. In November 2002, 44.5 percent of California's registered voters identified themselves as Democrats; only 35.2 percent registered as Republicans.

More than 15 percent of registered voters checked "Decline to State"—they consider themselves to be independents. Understandably, Democratic and Republican voters hold at least some of the views of their respective parties, but what motivates independent voters? One poll suggests that independents are more concerned with issues than with partisan ideology. While they are relatively moderate in

their overall views, they tend to be liberal on social issues and conservative on fiscal issues. Furthermore, compared to party loyalists, independents are more distrustful of government. These factors combine to make independents a powerful, but unpredictable, electoral force in California.[7]

The biggest news in recent elections has been the alignment of Latinos with the Democratic Party. Given their status as a minority group and their relatively conservative views on family and social issues, Latinos were once considered "up for grabs" by both major parties. Many observers credit Latinos' recent voting behavior to Republican Party support for Proposition 187 (a 1994 anti-immigration measure) and Proposition 209 (a 1996 anti-affirmative action measure). In recent years, large numbers of Latinos have registered, many for the first time, and many of those votes have gone Democratic. In 1992, just under 800,000 California Latinos voted, and 63 percent of them voted for Bill Clinton. In 2000, 1.45 million Latinos voted, and 75 percent voted for Al Gore. Whether Latino influence increases in the future depends on whether their citizenship and participation rates match their population growth.[8]

THE PARTISAN GEOGRAPHY OF CALIFORNIA

Generalizations about party affiliation in California can only be understood in the context of the state's diverse geographical regions. Those regions have different voting habits and partisan loyalties. Pollsters often identify five distinct voting regions of California—Los Angeles County, the rest of Southern California, the San Francisco Bay Area, the rest of Northern California, and the Central Valley.

FIGURE 5.1 California's preference pluralities by county (November 2000)

Source: California Secretary of State.

Within Southern California, Los Angeles County remains a Democratic island amid a large and more conservative region. Inner city African Americans remain loyally Democratic, and they are joined by lower income Latinos and some urban whites. In 2000, Al Gore garnered 67 percent of the vote there. The rest of Southern California is more conservative, in some places much more so. Although it is more white and middle class in Los Angeles, the surrounding Southland counties have a growing number of Asians and Latinos. In 2000, Southern

Californians voted for George W. Bush by a 53 to 44 margin.

In general, Northern California, and especially the San Francisco Bay Area, is more liberal and Democratic than the rest of the state. According to the *Almanac of American Politics,* the Bay Area is overwhelmingly the most Democratic of any metropolitan area.[9] In 2000, Bay Area voters preferred Gore to Bush by a 67 to 27 percent margin.

A more recent and telling regional contrast has been between coastal and inland California. Note the contrasts portrayed in Figure 5.1. This map shows which 2000 potential candidates won pluralities in each county. Most coastal Californians—and that means most Californians—preferred Gore over Bush. Even where Bush won a plurality in coastal counties, his margins of victory were relatively slim. Voters in portions of the Central Valley and the Sierras preferred Bush. Gore received 53.5 percent of the vote statewide, thereby amassing all 54 of the state's electoral votes. An east-west contrast is also evident in political ideologies. In one 1999 poll, Central Valley respondents were more conservative and less liberal than the Bay Area or greater Los Angeles residents.[10]

California's Electoral Gaps

In addition to partisan and geographic differences between Californians, other differences also emerge. For example, one such gap is a *voter-nonvoter gap*. That is, the people who vote appear to be unrepresentative of the entire population of the state. Comparing demographic date and election day exit polls reveals this dichotomy. In 2000, 73 percent of California voters were white, but they constituted only 53 percent of the population. Those who voted had higher levels of education and family income than the overall population. Only 13 percent of voters were Latino although they constituted 26 percent of the population. That said, Latino voters have become the fastest growing segment of the California electorate. From 1990 to 2000, they increased in numbers from 1.35 million to 2.35 million.

Gaps also emerge between different groups of voters. Consider the state's *racial-ethnic gap.* For example, only 47 percent of California whites voted for Al Gore. That figure jumps to 75 percent among Latino voters and 85 percent among African American voters. In 2002, whites split their votes for governor—43 percent for Gray Davis and 46 percent for Bill Simon. But minorities voted for Davis by much

larger margins—54 percent of Asian voters, 65 percent of Latinos, and 79 percent of blacks. This gap is evident on some policy issues as well as candidates. For instance, in November 1996, Californian voters as a whole rejected affirmative action by passing Proposition 209. A substantial majority of whites supported the measure (63 percent) compared to Latinos (24 percent), African Americans (26 percent), and Asians (39 percent). Differences are also evident on less transparently racial issues. In 2002, voters rejected Proposition 52, which would have allowed election day voter registration. Only 35 percent of whites supported the measure, but other racial and ethnic groups did support it (51 percent of Asians, 53 percent of blacks, and 65 percent of Latinos).

Another gap among Californians is a *gender gap*—the margin of difference between the opinions and votes of men and women. In general, more women side with Democrats than with Republicans; the opposite is true with men. This gap is clear in California elections. For instance, in 2000, 57 percent of women voted for Al Gore, but only 49 percent of men did. In 2002, larger percentages of white and minority women voted for Davis (47 and 67 percent) than white and minority men (39 and 53 percent). In other words, even controlling for race and ethnicity, gender makes a difference. In 1996, only 48 percent of women voted to ban affirmative action (Proposition 209), but fully 62 percent of men did.

Should these gaps concern us? Less than one might think. To attract voters and win elections, parties and candidates will need to stress voter commonalities, not differences. As more ethnic and racial minorities enter the middle class, they will to some extent vote as breadwinners and taxpayers, not just as Latinos, African Americans, or Asians. This will have an impact on party politics, not just on election outcomes. For example, to the extent Latinos align with the Democrats, according to observer Gregory Rodriguez, "Latinos will keep the party focused less on, say, environmentalism and more on old-fashioned, bread-and-butter issues such as jobs, education and crime."[11] For Republicans to attract those voters, they will need to emphasize similar issues as well.

Conclusion:
Divided by Diversity

This survey of California's political behavior underscores its diversity. In a sense, California's electorate was destined to be diverse from the beginning. After all, Mexican and American cultures merged to produce early California. As noted in Chapter 2, a broad electorate consensus in the post-World War II years, based on a less diverse electorate, resulted in bipartisan policies such as new highways and university campuses. These Progressive policies accommodated and encouraged growth. But recent demographic growth patterns have created diverse subelectorates, each with different interests. Californians possess viewpoints and cast votes differently based on partisanship and regional, racial and ethnic, gender, and other factors. These factors contribute to the state's hyperpluralistic political system. While policy division may often result, this is not an inevitable fate. Consider Proposition 38, a November 2000 initiative that would have provided state-funded vouchers for private schools. Virtually every major group of California voters rejected the measure.

KEY TERMS

political participation (p. 50)

exit option (p. 50)

protest option (p. 50)

voting age population, voter turnout (p. 51)

exit polls (p. 51)

structural and preferential nonvoting (p. 51)

frame of reference (p. 55)

political party (p. 55)

party identification (p. 55)

electoral gaps; voter-nonvoter, racial-ethnic, and gender (pp. 57–58)

REVIEW QUESTIONS

1. Survey the various forms of political participation identified by political scientists. Which forms most aptly describe your own participation in the political system?
2. Why are the exit and protest options exercised by some Californians? Give some examples. Under what conditions might you consider these options?
3. Why do people not register to vote or, once registered, not turn out on election day?
4. Why do sizable numbers of Californians consider themselves independents?
5. How do recent election results underscore trends in voter demographics, turnout, and behavior?
6. Describe the various electoral gaps in California. To what extent are they troublesome for the nation's largest and most diverse state?

WEB SITE ACTIVITIES

Los Angeles Times Poll
(www.latimes.com/HOME/NEWS/POLLS/)
This site has excellent national and statewide polling data including periodic election day exit polls.

California Voter Foundation
(www.calvoter.org/)
Use this site to "follow the money" and to check on recent state and local election results.

California Secretary of State
(www.ss.ca.gov)
Click on "Elections" to locate online registration forms, voter registration statistics, turnout data, and past election results.

INFOTRAC COLLEGE EDITION ARTICLES

For additional reading, go to InfoTrac College Edition, your online research library, at http://infotrac-college.com/wadsworth

The Disempowerment of the Gender Gap

The GOP's California Blues

The Absentees Are Also Present

NOTES

1. Sidney Verba, Kay Lehman Scholzman, and Henry E. Brady, *Voice and Equality: Civic Volunteerism in American Politics* (Cambridge, MA: Harvard University Press, 1995), 51.

2. Mark Baldassare, *California in the New Millennium: The Changing Social and Political Landscape* (Berkeley: University of California Press, 2000), 34–36; see also Robert Putnam, *Bowling Alone: The Collapse and Revival of American Community* (New York: Simon and Schuster, 2000).

3. Baldassare, *Caifornia in the New Millennium,* 31.

4. Mark Baldassare, *The Changing Political Landscape of California: Statewide Survey* (San Fran-cisco: Public Policy Institute of California, September, 1998), 22.

5. Ibid.

6. See Noel Brinkerhoff, "Gen X: The Unknown Quantity," *California Journal* 30 (December 1999): 16–22.

7. For an extended discussion of California independents, see Baldassare, *California in the New Millennium,* 61–80; and David Lesher, "A Decline to State," *California Journal* 33 (February 2002): 8–12.

8. See Jack Citron and Benjamin Highton, "When the Sleeping Giant Is Awake," *California Journal* 33 (December 2002): 42–46.

9. Michael Barone and Richard E. Cohen, *The Almanac of American Politics 2002* (Washington, DC: National Journal, 2001), 146.

10. Mark Baldassare, *The Changing Political Landscape of California: Statewide Survey* (San Francisco: Public Policy Institute of California, 1999) (www.ppic.org/publications/calsurvey5/survey5.ch4.html/).

11. Gregory Rodriguez, "Latino Clout Depends on GOP Remake," *Los Angeles Times,* November 15, 1998.

CHAPTER 6

Linking People and Policymakers

OUTLINE

Introduction

Mass Media
Newspapers
Television
The Internet

Political Parties
Political Parties: California
Style
How the Parties Are Organized

Surrogate "Parties"
Endorsement Politics

Elections
Campaign Professionals
The Role of Money
California Elections and
National Politics

Interest Groups
California Groups: Who Are
They?

How Interest Groups Organize
What Interest Groups Do

Conclusion:
Competing for Influence
Key Terms
Review Questions
Web Site Activities
InfoTrac College Edition
  Articles
Notes

Introduction

Chapter 6 concerns those activities, processes, and political experts that link individual Californians to those officials and institutions that make policy—what people think of as "the government." In a representative democracy, such linkage institutions build necessary bridges between the governed and those who govern.[1] They help to organize the political attitudes of ordinary citizens (the activity of opinion leaders), frame their political choices (elections and political parties), and both structure and

communicate their policy preferences to the government (through interest groups). Linkage institutions help place the policy concerns of citizens on the government's policy agenda. In a representative democracy (where the people are sovereign but delegate decision making to a relative few), linkage institutions are essential. In California's evolving, complex, and pluralistic society, linkage institutions are the only practical way ordinary citizens can speak or relate to those making policy on their behalf. Even with initiatives, Californians depend on these institutions to structure policy choices.

Political scientist Kay Lawson has identified three types of linkages shared by democratic governments:[2] (1) *Participatory linkage* allows direct citizen participation in government decision making. In California, the initiative, referendum, and recall provide that kind of link. (2) *Policy-responsive linkage* encourages political leaders to be responsive to the policy views of ordinary citizens. This is done through elections, political parties, and interest groups. (3) *Clientele linkage* often involves political leaders offering specific rewards in exchange for public support. Citizens act as "clients" who "buy" favored services by supporting particular leaders. Interest groups are the dominant clients in California politics.

Scholars of American politics commonly focus on the media, political parties, elections, and interest groups. Chapter 6 describes and evaluates each of these links and the role they play in connecting California's diverse citizenry and its government.

Mass Media

A primary linkage institution in national and California state politics is the mass media. The *mass media* funnel information to large numbers of people without direct, face-to-face contact. They include print media (newspapers and magazines), electronic media (radio and television), and new media (the Internet). Citizens and public officials alike depend on the media to send and receive messages. Their resulting power is enormous.

In addition to mass media, various *elite media* (those catering to select groups) thrive in California. For instance, the *California Journal,* which covers state politics, personalities, and issues, claims a relatively small but highly influential readership. Numerous political newsletters (*Political Pulse, California Political Week,* and *The Political Animal*) provide timely inside news and gossip considered essential to their subscribers. But their readership is small.

So, on which of these news sources do Californians most rely? In one statewide survey, television was the most cited source of political news, followed by newspapers and radio. Only 3 percent cite the Internet as their primary news source, although this number is expected to rise (see Figure 6.1). Combined, these media warrant particular attention.

NEWSPAPERS

The rise of California's newspapers parallels the state's political development. Wealthy individuals and families managed the earliest newspapers. One example was the crusading James McClatchy of the *Sacramento Bee,* who fought for land reform and the transcontinental railroad while opposing business monopolies and environmentally disastrous hydrologic mining. Today, the McClatchy Corporation owns communications properties in six states. The *Los Angeles Times* was decidedly more conservative than McClatchy's *Bee.* Harrison Gray Otis of the *Los Angeles Times* preached pro-business, antiunion sermons in editorials. He shared with the Big Four a desire for economic growth, personal power, and enormous income. On the other hand, William Randolph Hearst's *San Francisco Examiner* was decidedly antirailroad and friendly to Progressive reforms.

Today, California has more newspapers and newspaper readers than any other state. Yet newspapers across the state have gradually shrunk in number. Many have merged to create "one-newspaper" towns or have been acquired by media chains such as McClatchy, Copley, Gannett, and Knight Ridder. Some smaller newspapers are now owned by larger newspapers. While corporations dominate the newspaper scene, other newspapers reflect California's ethnic diversity. For example, *La Opinion* is the largest Spanish language newspaper in the nation. In Los Angeles, only the *Los Angeles Times* has higher circulation. The Web site New California Media lists 78 other newspapers and magazines catering to groups

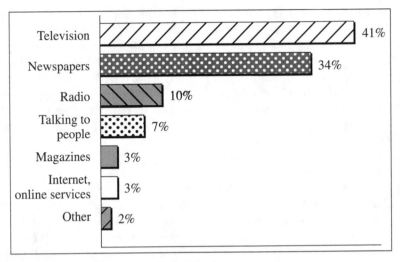

FIGURE 6.1 Political information sources in California

When asked, "Where do you get most of your information about what's going on in politics today?" Californians respond this way. *Question:* What mix of media do you use to keep up with California politics?

Source: Mark Baldassare, *The Changing Political Landscape of California: Statewide Survey* (San Francisco: Public Policy Institute of California, April–May 1998).

including African Americans, Arabs, Armenians, Cambodians, Chinese, Hispanics, and Koreans.

Despite readership declines, many Californians still depend on newspapers for state and local government news. How much knowledge they receive depends on the paper. The *Sacramento Bee* reports state politics heavily because its readers include not only elected officials but thousands of state employees. Sacramento is, after all, a "company town." The *Los Angeles Times* can afford a sizable Sacramento bureau, and their reporting reflects it. Most California newspapers depend on wire services (Associated Press) and direct government sources (press releases) rather than doing their own investigative reporting. Smaller newspapers focus on local news, often leaving state politics to larger papers.

How politically influential are newspapers? First, as we find with media in general, they often report examples of political corruption, mistakes, verbal miscues, or botched public policy. Compared to the past, today's reporting has a harder edge to it. According to the

editors of the *California Political Almanac,* "Gone are the times when most of the Capitol's reporters and politicians ate, drank, and caroused together, and neither group judged the other too harshly."[3] Second, while newspapers are fond of endorsing candidates and propositions, the effectiveness of those endorsements is questionable. Endorsements can be influential in local elections where other voter cues are absent. Some observers believe that the long-term editorial stance of newspapers appears to be more influential than specific election-eve endorsements. According to journalist and author Peter Schrag, "I don't think any newspaper has any great influence on a quick decision. My feeling is where we make the biggest difference is in setting the climate for the debate."[4]

TELEVISION

The popularity of television has diminished the political influence of newspapers, especially among certain groups. When asked in a 2000 survey where Californians get most of their news about the governor and the legislature, 44 percent of all respondents cited television; for Latino respondents, this figure jumped to 66 percent. Although 35 percent of all respondents listed newspapers as their primary source, only 17 percent of Latinos did.[5] Given its pervasiveness in much of California's political life, television falls far short of its potential as a linkage institution. The reasons are several.

The linkage power of television stems from the fact that it communicates in pictures. To a news producer, a political story is not inherently interesting unless it is visually interesting. According to one, his colleagues are interested in "slash, flash, and trash. They want the [story] to bleed, scream and yell."[6] In response, public officials deliberately employ symbols, stunts, or pseudo-events to make their messages visually interesting. One legislative hearing on the problem of vicious dog attacks featured visibly maimed victims. Celebrities sometimes serve as telegenic witnesses and camera magnets. Legislators claim such measures are necessary to inform the public and shed light on the state's problems. Television pictures also can be misleading. Research shows that local station portrayals of street crime create the impression that blacks and Latinos break the law in greater numbers than is in fact the case.[7]

Given its power, complaints about the media are commonplace. One is that the media are biased, that they treat the news in a partial, unfair manner. Some see an *ideological bias* where the media tend to favor Republicans or Democrats, conservatives or liberals. California journalists think this may be in the eye of the beholder. People want to see a story reported in a predetermined way and find fault if it is not. According to former Associated Press writer Doug Willis, "Republicans think I am a left-winger and Democrats think I am a shill for a fat-cat publisher. These things

balance out." California reporters do examine what policymakers say and do and compare the differences. As journalist Steve Scott says, "We have a low threshold for hypocrisy." Public officials who claim to be friends of environmentalists and then accept campaign contributions from oil companies will likely be challenged on the possible inconsistency.

Television in particular exhibits a *structural bias*. That is, television as a business is structured to minimize news coverage of government and politics. It tends to focus less on politics and more on human interest stories: entertainment, crime, sports, the weather—anything but politics. As television columnist Howard Rosenberg put it, the only way to attract media attention would be to "have the four leading candidates chase each other on a freeway."[8]

At a deeper level, television coverage tends to be not only sparse but shallow. News stories themselves tend to be brief—very brief—due to the inherent limitations of commercial television. The result is a lack of analysis—why events, political or otherwise, happen. For example, one study of California television news showed that violence dominated local news coverage. Furthermore, the emphasis was on the specifics of particular crimes, not on the underlying social conditions that contribute to violence.[9] Coverage of state politics has a similar quality to it, to the extent it is covered at all. This is bad news for the politically attuned, but the news is not all bad. Local Sacramento stations occasionally contribute news stories to their network affiliates in Los Angeles and San Francisco. The Northern California News Satellite sells its state politics stories to client stations. Furthermore, the California Channel enables some 5 million cable TV households to view floor sessions, committee hearings, news conferences, and other related programming. It has become California's version of C-SPAN for the politically thirsty.

Given its limitations, why does television news still hold promise as a linkage institution in California politics? In a word, size. The state has nearly 70 television stations (second in number only to Texas) and more cable subscribers than any other state. Ninety-five percent of the state's households own television sets. More important, more than 85 percent of them live in only four media markets: greater Los Angeles, the San Francisco Bay Area, Sacramento, and San Diego. Access to those markets is a precious, costly commodity for public officials, election candidates, and interest groups. The sheer size of the Los Angeles market (reaching more than 50 percent of the state's voters) skews California politics by favoring those officials who have had prior exposure in that part of the state.

Television is also essential for political communication. Political advertising is prolific because it is the only realistic way candidates can reach voters. As a result, candidates often inundate newscast commercial time with messages unmediated by editors, reporters, and producers. The messages get through. Focus group research suggests that Californians are more likely to remember a candidate's television commercials than straight news about the candidate.[10]

THE INTERNET

Many observers believe the Internet has vast potential to revolutionize U.S. and California politics. Indeed, the California numbers are impressive. Of the nation's 50 "most wired" cities, 7 are in California. Fully 70 percent of California voters say they use computers at work, home, and school. The number of California campaigns with Web sites swelled from only one in 1994 to 300 in 2000. One California political consultant tells his clients, "If you don't have a web site, it makes you look like a dinosaur."[11]

How important is the Internet? Less than meets the eye. So far, the Internet seems to have attracted those well-informed Californians already inclined toward politics. Furthermore, until more Californians use their computers to become more politically literate, many candidates will spend their money elsewhere. Still, Web-based communication is increasingly the norm and seems to be the wave of the future. Most state agencies, all members of the legislature, and many local governments disseminate information and receive feedback by way of the Internet. Furthermore, some initiative entrepreneurs regard the Internet as a promising tool. For example, a March 2000 school voucher initiative drive was launched on the Web.

Political Parties

In addition to the media, *political parties* also link citizens to their government. Parties are organized groups that (1) possess certain labels, (2) espouse policy preferences, (3) both nominate and work to elect candidates for public office, and (4) help frame government's postelection policy agenda. In American politics, they are found at all levels—federal, state, and local—though not in equal measure. Political parties come in three forms.[12] The *party in the electorate* refers to voters who hold partisan affiliations; this group was discussed in

Chapter 5. The *party in government* refers to partisan elected officials and institutions, such as the legislature, which organize around party labels. The *party organization* means the formal party apparatus: its structure, staff, budget, rules, and processes for achieving its goals. As a linkage institution, we will discuss the party as organization.

POLITICAL PARTIES: CALIFORNIA STYLE

Like the United States as a whole, California has a two-party system. Democrats and Republicans dominate at least partisan elections. But California's system is one of weak parties. To curb machine bosses like San Francisco's Abe Ruef and corporate elites like the Big Four, the Progressives established elements of a weak party system. *Direct primaries* allowed voters themselves to nominate candidates; *cross-filing* allowed the candidates themselves to run as Democrats, Republicans, or on occasion both; and *nonpartisan elections* blurred affiliations of judges and disallowed parties from endorsing or assisting local officeholders.

A more recent reform occurred in 1996 when voters approved the Open Primary Law (Proposition 198). It created a *blanket primary,* which allowed voters to cross party lines and vote for any candidate, regardless of party label. This innovation allowed more than 1.7 million "decline-to-state" voters a chance to vote for partisan candidates. But in late June 2000, the U.S. Supreme Court on a 7–2 vote overturned the law, claiming it violated the First Amendment associational rights of political parties. According to Justice Antonin Scalia, "Proposition 198 forces political parties to associate with . . . those who, at best, have refused to affiliate with the party, and at worst, have expressly affiliated with a rival."[13] As a compromise, major parties now allow "decline to state" voters to vote in their respective primary elections if they request to do so. With that exception, California has returned to a closed primary system.

Third or *minor parties* widen voter choice at least for some voters. What does it take for a minor party to be included on a California ballot? Two routes are possible: (1) signing up 77,389 registered voters (1 percent of the total votes cast in the 2002 gubernatorial election), or (2) getting 773,883 registered voters to sign a petition seeking party qualification (10 percent of the total votes cast in the previous gubernatorial election). The first option is relatively easy; the second has never succeeded. To repeatedly appear on a statewide ballot, minor parties must maintain a list of at least 86,212 registered voters or have one of their major candidates garner at least 2 percent of the votes cast in the last gubernatorial election. California's officially recognized minor parties include the American Independent Party, the Green Party, the Libertarian Party, the Natural Law Party, and the Reform Party.

HOW THE PARTIES ARE ORGANIZED

Because the state elections code dictates how California parties are organized, party structures look very similar. The lowest level is the *county central committee.* California parties do not have precinct-level organizations common in "strong party" states. Most voters elect these committee members in primary elections without really knowing who they are. These local committees do not "run" local party affairs, have few if any funds to disperse, and must compete for influence with elected officials and unofficial party clubs.

The *state central committee* is the key organizational unit for both Republicans and Democrats. Numbering in the hundreds, its membership is a hodgepodge of party leaders, elected officials, and appointees from the ranks of activist party members. Every two years, state central committee members meet to discuss policy issues, select party leaders, hear elected officials and major candidates speak, "network" each other, and rally the party faithful. These party gatherings showcase, for better or worse, the current diversity that exists within both major parties. In the Democratic Party, liberals, moderates, and various caucus groups fight among themselves. In the Republican Party, fiscal conservatives, social issue conservatives, and more pragmatic moderates vie for influence over education, abortion, gun control, gender issues, and gay rights. Full-time party chairpersons are selected to staff the state central committees. Their job includes raising funds, serving as party spokespersons, and refereeing intraparty squabbles.

SURROGATE "PARTIES"

If political parties are considered important linkage institutions in a representative democracy, what happens in states where parties are destined to be weak? In California, surrogate institutions have been created to replicate strong party functions. For example, a group of moderate Republicans in 1943 formed the California Republican Assembly. This grassroots group of 5,000 members and 100 local chapters claims to be the "conservative conscience" of the state Republican Party and usually endorses social issue conservatives.

In 1953, Democrats organized the California Democratic Council (CDC). This 10,000-member group calls itself the "conscience of the state Democratic Party." These surrogate "parties" hold less meaning for the electorate today than once was the case.[14] The rise of political action committees, candidate-centered campaigns, and media-driven elections have combined to limit party influence where it matters most: picking candidates and winning elections.

ENDORSEMENT POLITICS

Arguably the most important test of a strong party organization is its ability to select nominees for public office. Short of hand-picking nominees, parties should be able to at least endorse them. In their quest for nonpartisan-

ship, California's Progressives banned that practice in 1913. The results can be embarrassing as when San Diego area voters once nominated for Congress a Ku Klux Klan Grand Dragon over party objections. In the 1980s, the U.S. Supreme Court declared California's ban on party endorsements unconstitutional, arguing that such bans violated the parties' rights to spread their views and the voters' rights to inform themselves about candidates and issues.[15]

Despite their power to do so, California's major parties appear skittish about making endorsements even in partisan elections. At times, party activists hesitate to pick sides in competitive primaries. At other times, endorsements reveal and publicize deep schisms inside the party. At the party's 2002 winter convention, California Republicans endorsed conservative businessman Bill Simon over former Los Angeles mayor and ideological moderate Richard Riordan. Many of the party faithful claimed Riordan was not a "true" Republican.

If parties cannot or will not endorse candidates, other options are available, namely *slate mailers*—large, colorful postcards listing "endorsed" candidates and propositions (see Photo 6.1). Note the quotation marks. In many cases, distributors of these mailers are actually campaign-oriented businesses. Candidates and proposition sponsors must pay to play. What do these mailers cost a campaign? Payments may range from a few hundred dollars for a city council race to $75,000 or more in statewide proposition contests.[16] Although such mailers may seem deceptive, they would be less necessary if political parties could fully support "their" candidates.

Elections

No matter how weak, American political parties and elections are intertwined, linking average citizens to their government in profound ways. Public officials are to be held accountable peri-

Improving Neighborhoods For California's Families
Election Recommendations from Parents' Ballot Guide

PROPOSITION 35   **YES ***
PUBLIC/PRIVATE PARTNERSHIPS
• Use of private sector architects/engineers
• Earthquake retrofit schools on-time/on-budget
• Supported by schools and taxpayer groups

PROPOSITION 36   **YES ***
Drug treatment for nonviolent offenders
Saves money, reduces crime

PROPOSITION 37   **YES ***
STOP HIDDEN TAXES
Stop Higher Taxes on Gas and Utilities

PROPOSITION 38   **NO ***
SCHOOL VOUCHERS
• State PTA Agrees: Prop 38 Hurts Our Kids
• Abandons Our Public Schools
• Has No Accountability to Taxpayers
• Will Cost California Taxpayers Billions
Prop 38...Another Expensive Experiment Our Children Can't Afford

PROPOSITION 39   **YES ***
FIXES SCHOOLS • PROTECTS TAXPAYERS
Teachers, parents, PTA, AARP ask you to vote for
Prop 39. Fixes the way schools spend money, fixes
our schools, adds accountability, protects taxpayers!

Cast Your Ballot ... with an eye toward our future.

PHOTO 6.1   **Campaign Mailer**
This slate mailer was prepared and distributed by the Parents' Ballot Guide in Torrance, California. In the fine print is this disclaimer: "Appearance is paid for and authorized by each candidate and ballot measure which is designated by an *." *Question:* How influential are slate mailers such as this? How influential should they be?

odically for what they do and say. This practice is a key feature of the nation's political culture. Elections are important to policymakers too because they provide some measure of government *legitimacy*. In other words, voters grant officials they choose credibility and authority to act on their behalf. Policymakers occasionally misinterpret their own election victories as *mandates* to do something in particular, especially if they win by wide margins. Aware of the complex factors that constitute election results, political scientists tend to discount the mandates so often claimed by election winners.

Californians are peppered with elections. Partisan elections are scheduled for every other even-numbered year. The primary election is the first Tuesday in June, and the general election is the first Tuesday after the first Monday in November. Presidential election years from 2000 on are exceptions. California has instituted an early March presidential primary election to give the state greater clout in the selection of delegates committed to specific presidential candidates. Nonpartisan elections for judges appear within that cycle as do ballot propositions. Local elections (county, city, special district, and school district offices) may be combined with the primary or general elections or may be scheduled by the local entity for a separate time altogether. As a linkage institution, the election process surely provides California voters with a channel of influence only imagined in many parts of the world.

CAMPAIGN PROFESSIONALS

To run a candidate or proposition in California requires a variety of campaign consultants: campaign managers, fund-raisers, media experts, pollsters, lawyers, accountants, and computer experts. General campaign managers range from solo practitioners (found in smaller communities) to large firms located in Sacramento, San Francisco, or Los Angeles. They advise candidates on all aspects of campaigning, coordinate the use of specialists, and control the technology used in the campaign. Given the cost of campaigning in California, public relations firms adept at fund-raising are a must. They do direct mail or stage expensive dinners featuring "drawing card" celebrities, such as Democrats Barbara Streisand and Tom Hanks or Republicans Arnold Schwarzenegger and Bruce Willis.

Media specialists divide California into media markets, not electoral districts. Because politicians or would-be politicians do not think in those terms, media consultants are essential. They work with candidates and initiative campaigns to produce newspaper advertisements and broadcast commercials. All these media are tailored to specific markets and audiences. Because San Francisco voters are different from Fresno voters, appeals are customized based on geographic, demographic, and ideological differences. Candidates use television ads not only to hype their own qualifications but to criticize opponents. Some are simple "comparison" ads; others are full-blown attack ads. For example, in 2002, the Gray Davis campaign highlighted opponent Bill Simon's legal difficulties, inexperience, and pro-life views. One ad on behalf of Simon simply concluded: "Had enough? Fire Davis."

Polling specialists ask voters what they think about the issues and the candidates. The most helpful polls are tailored to particular campaigns. *Benchmark polls,* taken before a campaign begins, tell a candidate what issues are important, plus what the voters think of the candidate. *Tracking polls,* taken during the course of the campaign, reveal how the campaign is progressing and whether or not particular strategies are working. *Focus groups* test the reactions of a relative handful of voters to commercials and other political stimuli. All these techniques help pollsters measure the intensity of voter feelings and the impact of candidate messages. Lawyers, accountants, and computer experts are also essential. State regulations require candidates to report campaign spending and to disclose personal income, which in turn requires legal analysis and careful bookkeeping, especially in the larger races. Webmasters are now essential to create and maintain campaign-based Web sites.

Increasingly, California's campaign professionals work to pass or defeat various initiatives. From a consultant's point of view, issue campaigns are more lucrative; there are no spending limits on the "independent expenditure committees" that fund such efforts.

Furthermore, issue campaigns are more impersonal; in working with interest groups, consultants avoid the headaches of candidate emotions and family pressures. As consultant Steve Hopcraft puts it, "Groups don't have a spouse."[17]

Do election professionals make a difference in elections? Yes, in certain situations, but less so than many people think. Other factors such as incumbency, issues, and candidate personality play significant roles. Win or lose, consultants appear to contribute to escalating campaign costs. This is a function of consultants raising and spending campaign cash and then taking a percentage of whatever is spent. As one Ohio consultant put it, "Outside California, we call it the Californication of politics."[18]

THE ROLE OF MONEY

In an era where California campaigns seem awash in money, the money itself has become an issue. Candidates and officeholders complain about escalating campaign costs but seem ready to raise and spend whatever it takes to win. Indeed, Governor Gray Davis raised an average of $1 million a month during his first term in office. To be sure, television ads and direct mail are costly, previous campaign debts need to be retired, and future races must be planned. How much is too much? Candidates bent on winning rarely ask the question.

Where do candidates raise campaign cash? *First,* from themselves. Wealthy candidates are allowed to spend unlimited amounts of their own money. But wealth does not assure victory. For example, in 1994 Michael Huffington lost to U.S. Senator Dianne Feinstein despite spending nearly $30 million of his own fortune. In 2002, Bill Simon poured $11 million into an unsuccessful campaign against Gray Davis. *Second,* in order to signal broad-based support, candidates use direct mail, email, or other means to attract small "grassroots" contributions. *Third,* to bring in larger contributions, candidates seek contributions from the state's *political action committees.* PACs, the election arm of interest groups, are the largest source of campaign funds for legislative and statewide races. Claiming that they simply want access, PACs commonly contribute to incumbents and to those legislators who control legislation of interest to them.

Contributions to candidate campaigns are strictly monitored in California. The *Political Reform Act of 1974* (Proposition 9) requires disclosure of campaign contributions and expenditures, regulates the organization of campaign committees, limits entertaining by lobbyists, and prohibits conflict of interest by local officials. The *Fair Political Practices Commission* (FPPC) monitors all nonfederal elections, issues advisory opinions, and conducts random audits. It also investigates charges of wrongdoing and fines candidates for missing filing deadlines, submitting inaccurate reports, sending deceptive mailers, and laundering contributions.

Given what some regard as the undue role of money in elections, calls for reform are frequent but usually unsuccessful. State legislators, regardless of party, have resisted campaign finance reforms, thinking they would help challengers. Several initiatives have bypassed the legislature, presenting reforms directly to the voters. Most have been rejected by the courts as an unconstitutional infringement of free speech. The most recent was Proposition 34, passed in 2000. Unlike earlier measures, it set contribution limits so high ($3,000 for legislative races, $5,000 for statewide races, and $20,000 for gubernatorial races) that reformers believe it will do little to alter big-money politics in California. In addition, so-called *soft money* has entered California politics. These are unregulated, unreported contributions to political parties for party-building and get-out-the-vote efforts. In fact, they are also used to attack opposing parties, candidates, and views. To get around Proposition 34, interest groups are now forming their own independent ex-

penditures campaigns that need not conform to the proposition's limits. Like water, campaign money seems to flow around any reform obstacle in its path.[19]

CALIFORNIA ELECTIONS AND NATIONAL POLITICS

Elections in California play an increasingly important role in national politics. Four factors help explain this presence.

1. As was noted earlier, voter-approved initiatives often engender similar efforts in other states. Proposition 13 (1978) spawned similar tax-cutting efforts elsewhere. California's rejection of affirmative action in public programs (Proposition 209) encouraged such efforts in several other states.

2. California is a significant source of campaign contributions sought by out-of-state candidates. As one presidential candidate put it, "I have my political director call New Hampshire. I have my finance director call California."[20] In the 1999–2000 election cycle alone, California donors (individuals and PACs) poured nearly $182 million into federal elections.

3. California candidates are compelling recipients of out-of-state campaign funds. National PACs join their in-state counterparts to swell campaign coffers. For example, in 1998, U.S. Senator Barbara Boxer received an unprecedented $1 million funneled through EMILY's List, a group founded to promote women's issues and candidates.[21]

4. To increase its clout in presidential primaries, the California legislature moved the state's quadrennial presidential primary election to early March. While other states have also engaged in "frontloading," the change in California has enormous consequences. Early on, candidates must raise huge sums of money to buy adequate amounts of television time. This favors already established and well-funded candidates as was the case in 2000 with the ultimate

major party nominees Vice President Al Gore and Texas Governor George W. Bush.

Interest Groups

It would be difficult to overemphasize the power and influence of interest groups in California politics, both state and local. An *interest group* is a body of individuals who share similar goals and organize to influence public policy around those goals. They are as old as the republic. Founder James Madison considered the potential problem of "factions" in America (his term for both groups and political parties) but thought the new republic could control them. By the 1830s, Frenchman Alexis de Tocqueville observed, "In no country in the world has the principle of association been more successfully used or applied to a greater multitude of objects than in America."[22] By the 1950s, political scientists considered the activity of interest groups central to politics. What strikes political scientists today is the hyperpluralistic expansion of groups and the splintering of interests—a process particularly evident in California.

Interest groups have an enormous impact on California politics and clearly contribute to its hyperpluralistic character. The Secretary of State's official *Directory of Lobbyists, Lobbying Firms, and Lobbyist Employers* is nearly 600 pages long. That is just at the state level. Other groups, sometimes local versions of statewide groups, operate below the state level to sway county governments, cities, special districts, and school districts. For example, local chambers of commerce often have government relations offices that monitor and influence local government decision making from a pro-business perspective.

CALIFORNIA GROUPS: WHO ARE THEY?

In contemporary California, interest groups are as diverse as the state itself. Together, they resemble the interest group system in the na-

tion's capital. This hyperpluralistic maze of groups can be divided into five categories based on primary interest or motivation:

1. *Economic Groups.* These groups are primarily motivated by money—income, profits, better salaries, or the economic health of a company or trade. In their view, business regulations, tax policies, labor/management issues, access to markets, occupational safety, and environmental rules can mean financial gain or loss. They range from individual companies to trade associations to employee groups. Examples include the Association of California Insurance Companies, the Western State Petroleum Association, and the California Manufacturers Association.

2. *Professional Groups.* Professionally motivated groups both provide member services and represent group interests in the policy process. They possess economic interests to be sure but are also concerned about the regulation of their profession per se. It is common for the state to both regulate entry into certain professions and oversee their conduct. Notable California examples include the California Teachers Association, the California Medical Association, the California Bar Association, and the California Trial Lawyers Association.

3. *Public Agency Groups.* These groups represent various units of government at the state and local level. Representative are the following: the League of California Cities, the California State Association of Counties, the California Special Districts Association, and the Association of California Water Agencies.[23] The state even lobbies itself; executive branch agencies routinely defend their own interests at legislative hearings.

4. *Cross-Cutting Groups.* These groups do not fit neatly into other categories even though they share some overlapping interests. Cross-cutting groups attract members from other groups due to social, ethnic, ideological, religious, or emotional ties. Illustrative are the

Did You Know . . . ?

In 2000, there were eight lobbyists for every California legislator. Lobbyist spending in the state totaled $180 million, three times more than second place New York State.

SOURCE: Center for Public Integrity.

Traditional Values Coalition, the Mexican American Political Association, and Handgun Control, Inc. Scholars and policymakers alike call some of these groups "public interest" groups because their policy goals are not solely economic or professional in nature.

5. *Miscellaneous.* This catch-all category simply means some California groups defy reasonable classification. Where do you place the Americans for Smokers Rights or California Trout, Inc.? Some groups are ad hoc or single issue in nature: they temporarily organize around a "hot" issue or a legislative bill or an initiative. When the issue dies, so do they. Others defy simple classification because public policy is only a minor concern.

6. *Local Groups.* Various local groups abound as well. Of course, some are local chapters of statewide groups such as the Sierra Club, the Chamber of Commerce, and local teacher union affiliates. They provide "on the ground" support for statewide policy positions and are available to lobby legislators during frequent district visits. Others focus only on local issues; in the Bay Area they include the Bay Area Transportation and Land Use Coalition, People on the Bus, Say NO to BART!, and Marin Advocates for Transit.

HOW INTEREST GROUPS ORGANIZE

Interest groups in California have found there is no best method of organizing to function as linkage institutions. The following patterns are common. Most involve legislative advocates or lobbyists, those individuals who represent groups in the policy process.

In-House Lobbyists

Some businesses find that policymaking so affects their interests that hiring their own "in-house" lobbyists is the most effective route to adequate representation. For instance, ARCO, Allstate Insurance Company, Ford Motor Company, and the City of Los Angeles represent themselves in the political process. For good measure, many of these interests hire lobbying firms to augment their own employees.

Associations

Many individual entities join together around common goals. The Sacramento Yellow Pages under "Associations" proves there is strength in numbers. One can almost fill in the blank: The California Association of . . . Nurserymen, Nonprofits, HMOs, CD-ROM Producers, Winegrape Growers, or Suburban School Districts. Groups like these link members to the policy process through numerous meetings, legislative briefings, and newsletters. The larger ones command substantial resources for lobbying and campaign activity.

Contract Lobbyists

Known as "hired guns" in the lobbying world, contract lobbying firms represent multiple clients often in the same general subject area such as education, health, or insurance. For instance, Birdsall, Wasco, and Associates represents more than 20 school districts and other like-minded groups. Some contract lobbyists are former legislators, legislative staff members, and administration officials who rely on their vast contacts and governmental expertise.

"Brown Bag" Advocates

These modestly funded groups may be associations or individuals. What sets them apart is their lack of the financial resources of the lobbying firms and associations. Large campaign contributions and lavish receptions—tools of the trade for large groups and big firms—are out of the question for groups like JERICO: A Voice for Justice. Instead, they rely on networks of intense believers. For instance, the Children's Lobby (representing child-care providers, educators, and parents) combines grassroots activism, a telephone network, and "white hat" issues to provide what clout they have.

WHAT INTEREST GROUPS DO

When interest groups come to mind, the image is of lobbying—testifying at committee hearings or entertaining legislators. But interest group representation is more complex than that. Several tactics are employed to link group members to the political system.

Public Relations

Interest groups want the general public to know that their respective goals are similar. For instance, companies may pay for televised public service announcements, "sponsor" public television programs, or "adopt" public school classrooms to further their image in the community and throughout the state.

Supporting Candidates

Once regarded as risky business, interest groups now work both to elect their friends and to defeat their enemies. The development of political action committees has allowed all manner of groups to contribute to legislative campaigns through essentially paper organizations registered with the FPPC. Some cannot afford to contribute (the brown baggers) or legally cannot (government groups, such as the League of California Cities). In recent years, the largest campaign contributors have been medical doctors, trial lawyers, state employees, insurance companies, and bankers.

Influencing Propositions

As noted earlier, interest groups can sponsor or support various statewide ballot measures. Some of these efforts combine altruism with traditional self-interest. For instance, the California Building Industry Association worked closely with the legislature to craft a massive $9.2 billion school facilities bond measure— Proposition 1A. It passed in November 1998 with more than 62 percent of the vote. What was in it for the homebuilders? Lesser known provisions in "1A" included limits on school fees charged to developers and other pro-developer provisions. The builders in turn pumped $2.5 million into the winning campaign.[24] Money and clout do not always persuade voters. In 1998, the tobacco industry outspent its opponents $29 million to $7 million to defeat Proposition 10, a tax hike on tobacco products. It passed, but barely.

Lobbying

Lobbying is what interest groups do to influence policymakers. It includes monitoring legislation, drafting bills for legislators to introduce, testifying at public hearings, and contacting individual members and/or their staff. Lobbyists also pay attention to the executive branch, where agencies issue rules and otherwise implement legislation. Their most important asset is credible, albeit one-sided, information on how a legislative bill or an agency decision will impact their group. Under term limits, they have to restate their positions over and over again as neophytes replace veteran lawmakers in the legislature. According to lobbyist Jack Gualco, with high turnover "You've got to start new every two years."[25] Further discussion on lobbying can be found in Chapter 7.

Litigation

Interest groups often find the courts making policy through interpreting the state constitution, legislative statutes, and administrative rulings. Therefore, in many situations, the most effective method of participation by an interest group is to litigate. For instance, after passage of Proposition 1A, the Indian gaming measure, California's card room operators filed suit to halt its implementation. In 2001, the California Medical Association fought in court new financial disclosure regulations established by the state's Department of Managed Health Care. If interest groups do not qualify as litigants, they can file *amicus curiae* (friend of the court) briefs to explain their position in court cases. This is done at every level of California's legal system.

Conclusion: Competing for Influence

California's linkage institutions indeed connect Californians with their policymakers. The media are daily conduits of political and governmental news, if readers, listeners, and viewers bother to pay attention. During election campaigns, California's television stations link candidates and issue campaigns to voters through paid political advertising. The Internet promises to play an increasingly important role as an emerging linkage institution.

Political parties link partisan voters and their candidates through election activity, but a variety of constraints—legal and otherwise—weaken their efforts to do so. Parties are augmented by "surrogate" parties, for-profit "endorsers," and an army of political consultants who work on behalf of both candidates and issue campaigns. The most formidable competitors to California's political parties are a plethora of interest groups. These groups seemingly represent every agenda, population segment, economic interest, social value, or walk of life in the state. Increasingly, the diversity of the Golden State is mirrored in and represented by these groups. In a sense, California politics today is a hyperpluralistic mix of interest groups clamoring for influence and power.

KEY TERMS

mass and elite media (p. 61)

ideological and structural bias (p. 63)

political parties and minor parties (pp. 64–65)

blanket primary (p. 65)

county and state central committees (p. 65)

surrogate parties (p. 66)

slate mailers (p. 66)

political action committees (p. 69)

Political Reform Act of 1974 (p. 69)

Fair Political Practices Commission (FPPC) (p. 69)

interest groups (p. 70)

lobbyists (p. 71)

REVIEW QUESTIONS

1. Illustrate the concept of linkage with each institution in this chapter.
2. Evaluate various forms of media as linkage institutions in California.
3. How are the major parties organized in California, why are they so weak, how do public officials cope with those weaknesses?
4. Why are campaign professionals important in California's electoral process?
5. To what extent do interest groups mirror the diversity of the state and contribute to hyperpluralism?

WEB SITE ACTIVITIES

Fair Political Practices Commission
(www.fppc.ca.gov/)
This site describes the work of the FPPC and provides access to all California campaign regulations, conflict-of-interest laws, and enforcement decisions.

Political Parties and Interest Groups
(www.calvoter.org/parties.html/ and
www.calvoter.org/interestgroups.html/)
The California Voter Foundation provides up-to-date links to California's political parties and to many interest groups.

Rough and Tumble
(www.trumble.com/)
Updated daily, this site links you to California newspaper articles and columns dealing with state and local government and politics.

INFOTRAC COLLEGE EDITION ARTICLES

For additional reading, go to InfoTrac College Edition, your online research library, at http://infotrac-college.com/wadsworth

If It Bleeds

Southern Strategy: Meet Gary South

Effective Slate Mailers

NOTES

1. "Linkage" was first coined by V. O. Key, *Public Opinion and American Democracy* (New York: Knopf, 1961), chap. 16.
2. Kay Lawson, *Political Parties and Linkage: A Comparative Perspective* (New Haven: Yale University Press, 1980), 1–24.
3. A. G. Block and Claudia Buck, *California Political Almanac* (Sacramento: State Net, 1999), 559.
4. Quoted in Bob Forsyth, "Newspaper Editorials: Do They Really Matter?" *California Journal* 22 (January 1991): 31.
5. Mark Baldassare, *Californians and Their Government: Statewide Survey* (San Francisco: Public Policy Institute of California, January 2000), 18.
6. Steve Scott, "Tube Dreams," *California Journal* 30 (May 1999): 29.
7. T. L. Dixon and D. Linz, "Overrepresentation and Underrepresentation of African Americans and Latinos as Lawbreakers on Television News," *Journal of Communication* 50 (Spring 2000): 131–154.
8. Quoted in Lou Cannon, "Bleeders Sweeping Leaders Off California TV," *Washington Post,* May 23, 1998, A6.
9. Lori Dorfman et al., "Youth and Violence on Local Television News in California," *American Journal of Public Health* 87 (August 1997): 1131–1137.
10. Mark Baldassare, *California in the New Millennium: The Changing Social and Political Landscape* (Berkeley: University of California Press, 2000), 40–42.
11. Claudia Buck, "Coming of Age on the Web," *California Journal* 31 (September 2000): 14.
12. See Frank J. Sorauf and Paul Allen Back, *Party Politics in America,* 6th ed. (Boston: Scott Foresman/Little Brown, 1988), 10.
13. *California Democratic Party v. Jones,* 530 U.S. 567 (2000).
14. Richard Bergholz, "Hard Times Befall Once-Influential Groups," *California Journal* 16 (August 1985): 322–324.
15. *Eu v. San Francisco County Democratic Central Committee,* 489 U.S. 214 (1989).
16. Jon Matthews, "Slate Mailers Anger Some Voters, Confuse Others," *Sacramento Bee,* November 5, 2000.
17. Quoted in Noel Brinkerhoff, "Course Correction," *California Journal* 28 (December 1997): 44.
18. Quoted in Noel Brinkerhoff, "Consultants and Campaigns," *California Journal* 31 (November 2001): 10.
19. Bill Ainsworth, "Cash Flow," *California Journal* 33 (February 2002): 54–57.
20. Quoted in Beth Fouhy, "Here Come the Democrats," *California Journal* 34 (March 2003): 40.
21. Eric Lichtblau, "Group to Add $1 Million to Boxer Campaign," *Los Angeles Times,* October 26, 1998.
22. Alexis de Tocqueville, *Democracy in America* (New York: Alfred A. Knopf, 1945), 191.

23. The magnitude of the governmental lobby is revealed in Curtis Richards, "Government Lobbyists: California Spends Millions to Influence Itself," *California Journal* 22 (August 1991): 377–380.

24. Cynthia H. Craft and Kathleen Les, "School Bonds," *California Journal* 29 (November 1998): 28–35.

25. Quoted in John Borland, "Third House," *California Journal* 27 (February 1996): 30.

Legislative Politics

O U T L I N E

**Introduction: The Road
to Proposition 140**

**California's Legislative
History**
The Early Years
The Progressive Era
Stagnation Amid Change
Reform
The Golden Years
Inching Toward 140
The Post-140 Legislature

What the Legislature Does
Policymaking
Representation
Executive Oversight
Civic Education

**Getting There and
Staying There**
Recruitment
Why They Stay: Rewards of
Office
How They Stay:
Reapportionment Politics
The 2001 Reapportionment

Organizing to Legislate
The Role of Leadership
The Committee System
The Staff

The Legislative Process

The Third House

Conclusion
Key Terms
Review Questions
Web Site Activities
InfoTrac College Edition Articles
Notes

Introduction:
The Road to Proposition 140

Question: Which state pays its legislators far more than any other state but forces them to leave office as soon as they gain valuable experience?

Answer: California.

Indeed, the California state legislature is an anomaly. It makes statutory policy for the largest state in the Union, incubates political leaders, and is an enviable place to act on behalf of the public interest. It was once regarded as the most professional of all state legislatures and, in many ways, it still is. But today's challenges are sobering. Member tenure is term-limited, campaigns are exorbitantly expensive, and the policy stakes are higher than ever. The legislature is an easy target of criticism.

California's Legislative History

Criticism of the California legislature is as old as statehood. In fact, the institution has always reflected the state's different political eras. Its history includes the early years, the Progressive era, stagnation amid change, reform, the golden years, and life after Proposition 140.

THE EARLY YEARS

In the mid-1800s, the state legislature was an amateur body dominated by farmers and beholden to the Southern Pacific Railroad (SPR). People considered the members of the legislature to be dishonest drunks—the legislature of "1,000 steals" or "1,000 drinks." In 1849, it consisted of 16 senators and 36 assemblymen. By the second constitutional convention in 1878, it had grown to its current size, 40 senators serving four-year terms and 80 assembly members serving two-year terms. The combination of frequent elections, part-time politicians, and domination by the SPR's Political Bureau led to a corrupt "political machine" atmosphere and fueled the rise of the Progressives.

THE PROGRESSIVE ERA

Under the righteous indignation of the Progressives, Hiram Johnson assumed the governorship in 1911. New constitutional language limited legislative duties and even the number of days the legislature could meet. The initiative, a reform that would eventually compete with the legislature for policymaking power, was instituted. During this period, the voters did resist six different referenda to create a unicameral (one-house) legislature—an idea some Californians still favor.

STAGNATION AMID CHANGE

From the 1920s to the 1960s, California experienced tremendous growth and change. Urban and suburban populations surged as did the economy. The Depression and World War II brought federal programs and dollars to California. The legislature did not fully reflect these changes; in fact, it resisted them. Like the Congress, representation in the lower house (the Assembly) was based on population; in the upper house (the State Senate), it was based on area. No county could have more than one senator (the so-called *Federal plan*). The result was skewed representation. In fact, as late as the 1960s, San Diego, Los Angeles, and Alameda counties claimed half the state's population but sent to Sacramento only one senator each. As a result, policymaking was factionalized more by region than by partisanship.[1]

REFORM

In the 1960s, two events led to substantial legislative reforms. First, a legislatively appointed Constitutional Revision Commission recommended a series of constitutional amendments allowing the legislature to govern most of its own affairs (such as setting salaries and determining calendars). In short, the legislature would become more professionalized. Due to the unflagging efforts of then Assembly Speaker Jesse Unruh, voters approved Proposition 1A by a 3 to 1 margin. Second, federal courts ruled against California's "Federal plan" in 1965. Both houses in a state legislature would have to be reapportioned on the basis of "one man, one vote."[2] The post-reapportionment election of 1966 produced immediate change. Compared to the old guard, the new members were younger, better educated, possessed more professional backgrounds, and represented more minorities. They also seemed more partisan in their dealings with each other.

THE GOLDEN YEARS

The 1960s and 1970s ushered in still more reform such as the two-year session adopted in

1972. This innovation allowed bills to survive beyond the first year, avoiding time-consuming reintroductions. A robust economy enabled the legislature to spend generously on both public policy and itself. Staffs and salaries grew steadily. All was not well, though. Proposition 9 (1974) addressed what the public considered an all-too-cozy relationship between legislators and lobbyists. It limited campaign finances and lobbying practices and disallowed campaign work by state-paid legislative staff. Those elected after Proposition 13 passed in 1978 seemed more ideologically rigid than their veteran colleagues. The breakup of the postwar bipartisan consensus (favoring active government and greater spending) appeared complete.

INCHING TOWARD 140

Voter approval of term limits (Proposition 140) in 1990 was the culmination of several developments. First, divided government (Republicans controlling the governor's office; Democrats, the legislature) became routine and led to well-publicized policy gridlock. Second, while some voters were gradually "dealigning" from their respective parties (considering themselves to be independents), legislators were becoming *more* partisan in their dealings with each other. Third, the media began to spotlight how campaign funds were raised. Then Assembly Speaker Willie Brown doled out excess campaign funds of his own to loyal colleagues.[3] Members readily sought out service on so-called *juice committees* because the industries they regulated readily contributed to committee members' campaigns.[4] In the wake of several bribery scandals, the public's general regard for the legislature plummeted.

THE POST-140 LEGISLATURE

By 1996 and 1998, California had experienced 100 percent turnover in its legislature and the revolving door continues. Proposition 140 has profoundly impacted the legislature in one area after another. Compared to the past, post-140 legislators are younger, and fewer are former staff members. Latinos, women, and those with local government experience have increased in number. Legislative turnover has also resulted in less experienced staff. In addition, power has shifted in various ways. The Senate has gained influence as veteran but termed-out assembly members and staffers join the Senate. The governor has gained more power at the expense of the legislature. Lobbyists are as knowledgeable as ever but must work harder to get legislators' attention both in Sacramento and in the members' districts.[5]

What the Legislature Does

Amid all this change, the California legislature still remains at the core of politics in the Golden State. As with all legislatures, its functions are varied. Let's look at four broad and overlapping ones: policymaking, representation, executive oversight, and civic education.

POLICYMAKING

The first function of a legislature is policymaking. California's legislature addresses a stunning variety of policy issues each year. Among the 1,168 laws that took effect on January 1, 2003, were bills that did the following:

• Authorized the use of stem cells for research purposes

• Imposed restrictions on so-called greenhouse gases from future automobiles

• Allowed homosexuals the same inheritance rights as heterosexual couples

• Entitled tenants to 60- rather than 30-day notice to move

In California, there are three types of legislation: bills, constitutional amendments, and

TABLE 7.1 The Legislature at a Glance, 2003–2004

	Senate (40)		Assembly (80)
Democrats	25		48
Republicans	15		32
Women	11		25
Latinas	(6)		(6)
Latinos	4		12
African Americans	2		4
Asian Americans	0		6
Former Assembly Members	37	Former Senate Members	4
GLBT*	0		5

Note: *Gay, Lesbian, Bisexual, Transgendered

resolutions. *Bills* are proposed statutes (laws at the state level) and can be introduced only by legislators (see Table 7.1). Even the governor's budget (itself a bill) must have a legislator's name on it.[6] *Constitutional amendments* are changes to the state constitution and require a two-thirds vote from both the legislature and the voters. *Resolutions* are merely statements representing the collective opinion of one house or both on miscellaneous subjects. They may commend individual Californians, praise a champion sports team, or express a popular opinion on some fleeting issue. The most important bill and most important policy the legislature adopts each year is the state budget.

REPRESENTATION

A second legislative function, *representation,* sounds simple enough. In a representative democracy, legislators ideally express the will or act upon the wishes of those who elect them. In reality, representation is very complex and operates on a variety of levels.

1. The first level of representation is geographic. Forty senators and 80 assembly members represent the particular interests of their home districts. Given the state's diversity, from densely urban districts near the coast to sparsely populated districts in the interior, a multitude of geographic perspectives translate into a multitude of policy perspectives and priorities.

2. Legislators often represent the characteristics of constituents back home. Overall, legislators usually approximate their districts in terms of race, religion, or ethnicity. While legislators arguably seek out the good of California as a whole, Latinos may be more interested in immigration or bilingual education issues than their non-Latino colleagues, blacks more interested in civil rights issues, female legislators in health issues, and gays in same-sex partner benefits. Yet compared to their districts, they tend to be better educated, more male, more involved in their communities, and more successful in their previous occupations.

3. Individual constituents sometimes need specific representation, that is, individual attention. This constituent service activity or "casework" may help constituents deal with assorted state bureaucracies such as the Departments of Motor Vehicles or Social Services. District office staffers, including college and university interns, do the bulk of this work. Occasionally, some policy ideas come from this process, but it usually means troubleshooting for specific constituents.

4. Functional representation refers to the specific policy interests and preferences legislators bring to Sacramento. For example, former teachers or school board members and farmers may logically gravitate to the education and agriculture committees. Others may wish to represent key industries in their districts, such as computer technology. As Table 7.2 portrays, the legislature's policy committees

TABLE 7.2 California's Standing Legislative Committees

Assembly (30)	Senate (25)
Aging and Long Term Care	Agriculture and Water Resources
Agriculture	Appropriations
Appropriations	Banking, Commerce, and International Trade
Arts, Entertainment, Sports, Tourism, and Internet Media	Budget and Fiscal Review
Assembly Legislative Ethics	Business and Professions
Banking and Finance	Constitutional Amendments
Budget	Education
Business and Professions	Elections and Reapportionment
Education	Energy, Utilities, and Communications
Elections, Reapportionment, and Constitutional Amendments	Environmental Quality
Environmental Safety and Toxic Materials	Governmental Organization
Governmental Organization	Health and Human Services
Health	Housing and Community Development
Higher Education	Insurance
Housing and Community Development	Judiciary
Human Services	Labor and Industrial Relations
Insurance	Legislative Ethics
Jobs, Economic Development, and the Economy	Local Government
Judiciary	Natural Resources and Wildlife
Labor and Employment	Public Employment and Retirement
Local Government	Public Safety
Natural Resources	Revenue and Taxation
Public Employees, Retirement, and Social Security	Rules
Public Safety	Transportation
Revenue and Taxation	Veterans Affairs
Rules	
Transportation	
Utilities and Commerce	
Veterans Affairs	
Water, Parks, and Wildlife	

are organized around a rich diversity of functional interests.

5. A last level is perceptual representation. Legislators themselves perceive their representational roles in different ways. *Trustees* rely primarily on their own best judgment when voting on legislation rather than the less-informed wishes of their constituents. *Delegates* lean primarily on those constituent wishes and deliberately seek them out. As a practical matter, most legislators are *politicos;* that is, they combine these roles depending on how controversial specific issues are locally.[7] These perceptions are not static. A recent study of the California Assembly suggests that, over

time, legislators change their role perceptions. Why? It could be that legislators vote inconsistently or do not think about whether they are trustees, delegates, or politicos.[8]

EXECUTIVE OVERSIGHT

A third function of California's legislature is executive branch *oversight*. The state constitution mandates some of these oversight activities. For instance, the Senate must confirm various gubernatorial appointments to commissions (such as Fish and Game, Public Utilities, and the University of California Regents), and both houses confirm gubernatorial appointments to fill vacancies in constitutional offices. Like Congress, the legislature can impeach and remove statewide officeholders and judges. General oversight of state agencies is aided by a Joint Legislative Task Force on Government Oversight, which reviews the effectiveness of state programs.

A routinely used oversight tool—"power of the purse"—involves the annual budget process. In the *authorization process,* the legislature gives authority for an agency program to exist. In the *appropriation process,* the legislature creates spending authority, thereby allowing the agency to implement the program. The budget process allows the legislature to evaluate agency performance, set its own spending priorities, reward its friends, or punish its enemies. The legislature does not engage in oversight by itself. It receives help from the independent Bureau of State Audits (formerly the Auditor General's Office), which conducts financial audits and program reviews, sometimes exposing executive branch waste and inefficiency. This bureau, in turn, is overseen by another watchdog group, the Milton Marks Commission on California State Government Organization and Economy (the Little Hoover Commission).

CIVIC EDUCATION

The final legislative function involves the *civic education* of constituents. Legislators are ex-pected to educate people about the legislative process and California politics generally. In Sacramento, they meet with students from the district, professional lobbyists, and many interest group members who visit the Capitol. Legislators explain their version of how the process works and why pet legislation is so difficult to pass or afford. Back home, they may write guest editorials, speak to service clubs and community gatherings, issue press releases, hold "office hours," and confer with local chapters of statewide groups.

These four legislative functions commingle constantly. For example, a constituent complaint about the Department of Motor Vehicles may lead to a member inquiry about how the department operates. Urban and rural legislators sit side by side on committees, learning to appreciate the geographic diversity they bring to their work. Minority legislators bridge geographic differences by creating bicameral caucuses that highlight their commonalities.

Getting There and Staying There

Why people seek *any* public office is an interesting question to political scientists. What motivates people to give up their privacy, normal family life, career continuity, and, for some, substantial income. Because being a California legislator is a full-time job (and then some, legislators say), a member must maintain two residences, even if one is a small Sacramento apartment. Family dislocation (Where do you put the kids in school? What about a working spouse?) and frequent travel to the district create stresses most Californians can only imagine. What about resuming a career after a legislative stint? Is that even possible? Yet the price is worth it to many members, who attempt to convert their beliefs into public policy.

RECRUITMENT

The initial decision to run for the legislature is determined by both personal desire and requests by others. Three patterns of candidate recruitment have emerged in California. *First,* some candidates are self-starters. They include local government officials whose jurisdictions are affected by state policies, professionals who are impacted by state regulations, legislative staffers who what to try out "their own wings," and the independently wealthy who believe that their business acumen would be an asset in Sacramento. *Second,* some legislative candidates are sponsored by or recruited to run by others. In California, this sponsorship comes not so much from local party officials but from legislative leaders in Sacramento. In recent years, the Assembly speaker and Senate president pro tem as well as partisan caucus staffs have provided both encouragement and campaign funding to promising candidates. They generally seek winnable candidates who will be good legislators *and* who will support them in future leadership battles. In contested primaries, these Sacramento benefactors often wait to support the primary winner in the general election campaign.

In recent years, many legislative races have featured a combination of self-starting and sponsorship. Given the entrepreneurial nature of California politics and the historically weak local political parties, many candidates need self-starter qualities, such as a burning ambition to run and win. Yet these people alone cannot marshal the resources needed to win. Remember, California's legislative districts are the largest in the nation—roughly 875,000 people per Senate district and 437,000 people per Assembly district. As a result, face-to-face voter contact in some districts necessarily gives way to costly political advertising. Unless a candidate is wealthy, outside help is essential. In California, some candidates will not receive sponsorship if there is a contested primary. Once nominated (winning the pri-

mary), many resources are mobilized, including party assistance, Sacramento sponsorship, PAC contributions, and soft money expenditures. As with Congress, most legislative incumbents win.

WHY THEY STAY: REWARDS OF OFFICE

Given the frustrations of the legislative life in California (hyperpartisanship, gridlock, term-limited tenures, incessant travel, and family pressures), why do legislators hunger to stay and hate to leave? For instance, why do they run for the Senate when their Assembly terms expire? The reasons are several.

First, many legislators relish making policy in their beloved state. Serving on just the right committees and moving into leadership positions on those committees are paramount to these policy achievers. Post–term limit members bring a sense of policy urgency, knowing they have only a few years to enact their preferences into law. *Second,* the material benefits of legislative service are impressive. In 1998 an independent citizens' commission set members' annual salaries at $99,000, making them by far the nation's highest paid state legislators. Legislative leaders receive still higher salaries. In addition, members each receive a tax-free $121 each day their house is "in session." This can amount to another $30,000 for a typical nine-month session. Other expenses include an automobile, cell phone, health insurance, trips to the district, and funds to hire staff and rent office space. Critics call these expenditures unwarranted "perks," but others consider them the normal cost of running the nation's largest state. *Third,* legislative service brings a great deal of psychic satisfaction. Staff members do the members' bidding, and lobbyists, constituents, and seemingly all others pay them deference.

Historically, California's legislature was a hothouse for political careers. The power of incumbency and relatively safe districts assured some job security, and relatively generous pay and perks encouraged longevity. Considered a dead end in many other states, legislative service in California allowed rapid advancement and rewarded political ambition and policy entrepreneurship. California lawmakers viewed and used their positions as springboards to higher office.[9] Proposition 140 has affected careerism in two ways. For some members, it effectively aborts long-term careers as elected officials. For others, it alters their routes to higher office. In what has been called the "term limits shuffle," legislators constantly cast about for other offices—federal, state, and even local—to extend their public careers. On occasion, departed legislators land appointments to administrative posts. For example, Governor Gray Davis appointed former state senator Steve Peace as his $131,412 a year finance director. Former state senator Robert Presley runs the Youth and Adult Correctional Agency.

HOW THEY STAY: REAPPORTIONMENT POLITICS

Willingness to stay in office is not the same as staying; ask any incumbent who loses a reelection bid. If elections give the voters a chance to select their legislators, redistricting gives the voters a chance to choose those voters. For many members, the very boundaries of a legislative district can spell victory or defeat. How are these boundaries drawn? After each decade, the U.S. Census Bureau counts the population and gathers other demographic data. In a practice called *reapportionment,* the legislature redraws district lines for the U.S. House of Representatives, the State Assembly, and State Senate to reflect population growth and movement within the state. As with other bills, the governor must sign any reapportionment plan. The California Constitution requires that any plan consider to the extent possible the "geographic integrity" of existing city and county boundaries.

But population shifts and communities of interest are not the only factors in redrawing district boundaries. Reapportioning districts for partisan or other advantage is a common practice called *gerrymandering.* There are three types: (1) *Partisan gerrymandering* splinters or packs voters in such a way as to favor or disfavor the election of Republicans or Democrats. (2) *Incumbent gerrymandering* protects incumbents regardless of party. (3) *Racial gerrymandering,* once used to dilute the strength of racial minorities, has been used to concentrate minority voting strength—thereby advantaging minority candidates.

THE 2001 REAPPORTIONMENT

In the past, some reapportionment efforts have resulted in political warfare, pitting Democrats against Republicans, the legislature against the governor, and, on occasion, the California Supreme Court against numerous incumbents, as took place in the early 1990s. The 2001 reapportionment was an altogether different experience. With little or no debate, the state Senate approved the new maps on two votes: 38 to 2 and 40 to 0. The Assembly approved the maps on a bipartisan 58 to 10 vote.

What happened to the rancor of earlier battles? First, sizable voting majorities in the Assembly and Senate (50 to 30 and 26 to 14, respectively) gave Democrats a substantial advantage in redrawing the maps; Republicans were at their mercy. Merely maintaining the status quo was something of a victory for them. Second, although California's ethnic minorities had been growing in the 1990s, plan drafters were not sure they could eek out substantially more "minority-majority" districts. They were able to maintain and strengthen numerous Latino-majority districts and add a heavily Latino congressional district in Los Angeles County. Several other districts were redrawn in such a way as to benefit Latino electoral chances in the future. The plans seemed satisfactory to

Latino incumbents—23 of 26 Latino legislators supported them. A few incumbents complained publicly and privately that their reelection chances or opportunities to seek other offices were doomed; some had sought to make their *next* seats safe ones. In the end, the 2001 reapportionment process was a classic incumbent protection effort. As a result, it locked in (to the extent redistricting can) Democratic majorities and prior gains made by the state's minorities. It also locked into place the minority status of California's Republican lawmakers (see Figures 7.1a and 7.1b).[10]

Organizing to Legislate

Reapportionment aside, making laws is still the legislature's primary task. Nearly 5,000 bills are introduced during each two-year session of the California legislature. On paper the process of making laws seems straightforward enough. In reality, it is complex and fraught with both intrigue and, on occasion, chaos. The members themselves sometimes say, "Never watch laws or sausages being made."

The California Constitution requires a bicameral legislature, consisting of a lower house (an 80-member Assembly) and an upper house (a 40-member Senate). Assembly members serve two-year terms; senators, four-year terms. Under Proposition 140, assembly members are limited to three terms; senators to two. Although both houses behave similarly in many respects, there are differences. The state Senate is more prestigious due to its smaller size and longer terms. Senators tend to be more politically experienced; many gained that experience in the Assembly. Senators can seek still higher office in the middle of their terms without losing their seats—a "free ride." Compared to the Speaker-dominated Assembly, senators are more independent. Each finds publicity easier to attain. As a body, the Senate can more easily challenge a governor by not confirming gubernatorial appointments that require Senate confirmation. Also, the Senate seems quieter and more deliberative than the rough-and-tumble Assembly.

How does the legislature itself organize to do its work? The process in both houses leans heavily on leadership, a committee system, and professional staff.

THE ROLE OF LEADERSHIP

Groups large and small need leaders to manage what they do. Legislatures are no different. In his study of state legislative politics, Alan Rosenthal listed six different leadership tasks: organizing for work, processing legislation, negotiating agreements, dispensing benefits, handling the press, and maintaining the institution.[11] California's legislative leaders perform each of these tasks. Let's look at some of the tasks for those in key positions.

Assembly Speaker

The Assembly Speaker used to be called a "self-inflicted dictatorship." Once elected by the entire Assembly, recent speakers have been chosen by the majority *party caucus* (its total assembly membership). Speakers sometimes must court minority party votes when majority control of the Assembly is marginal. Speakers balance power and policy—perpetuating their own power while using it to achieve policy goals. In part, this is done by controlling committees: determining the number and titles of committees, assigning all members to committees (with the exception of the Rules Committee), controlling the selection of other leadership positions within the Speaker's party, managing floor action, enforcing Assembly customs, and assigning office space and some staff. Under Jesse Unruh's leadership in the 1960s, the Assembly became a powerful policymaking force in state government. San Francisco's Willie Brown was the first African American to hold the post, and he served longer than any predecessor (1980–1996). Recent speakers have included Democrats Cruz Bustamante (the state's first Latino speaker and now lieutenant governor), Antonio Villaraigosa, and Robert Hertzberg. Early in 2002, Hertzberg was succeeded by fellow Democrat Herb Wesson of Los Angeles. Highly regarded for his people skills, Wesson is a prodigious fund-raiser, soliciting contributions from gambling, tobacco, and alcohol interests regulated by the committee he chaired—Government Organization.[12] Under term limits, speakers have a fundamental problem. Once they become known as speaker "material," they have roughly two years to actually *be* speaker. Wesson himself calls the position "a temp job at best."[13]

Other Assembly Posts

A number of other leadership posts round out the legislative elite in the Assembly. The *speaker pro tempore* is a member of the Speaker's party and exercises the powers of the Speaker in the latter's absence. The speaker pro tem usually presides during floor sessions, allowing the Speaker to mingle with other members. The *assembly majority* and *minority leaders* are selected from their respective party caucuses. They represent caucus interests on the Assembly floor; the latter communicates minority wishes to the Speaker. The Assembly Rules Committee exercises institutional leadership by selecting many legislative staff, studying legislative rules, and referring bills to committees. Its nine members include four members each from the Democratic and Republican caucuses; the Speaker appoints the chair.

Senate Pro Tempore

In the U.S. Senate, the vice president can preside and vote in case of a tie, but rarely performs either function. In the California Senate, the lieutenant governor has comparable powers but also rarely uses them. Day-to-day leadership is in the hands of the *president pro tempore* (pro tem for short). Although the entire Senate votes to fill this post, the majority party invariably chooses one of its own. Recent pro tems have included David Roberti (1980–1994), Bill Lockyer (1994–1998), and John Burton (1998 to the present). Burton is a colorful, longtime political operator who brings passion, emotion, intensity, and integrity to the job. By itself, this post is less powerful than the Assembly speakership. Smaller, "quieter," and less partisan of the two houses, the Senate exhibits a more consensual leadership pattern. Much of the pro tem's power stems from chairing a five member *Rules Committee*. The other four members consist of two senators from each party caucus. Its powers are comparable to both the Assembly Speaker and the Assembly Rules Committee.

THE COMMITTEE SYSTEM

To carry out their policymaking responsibilities, modern legislatures must organize into committees—much like Congress does. The committee process recognizes that screening legislation takes specialization and division of labor. California's legislature is divided into numerous committees. Combined, they form a *committee system:* the web of relationships among a number of committees required to enact policy.

Several kinds of committees constitute the committee system in California's legislature. The job of permanent *standing committees* is to process legislation. In other words, they formulate public policy (see Table 7.2 for a complete list of these committees). Members seek assignment to certain policy committees because of former occupations, current policy interests, or the possibility of receiving campaign contributions. Some women legislators have preferred to serve on committees dealing with human services issues such as children and welfare.[14] Already noted is a preference for "juice" committees (e.g., the Senate Insurance

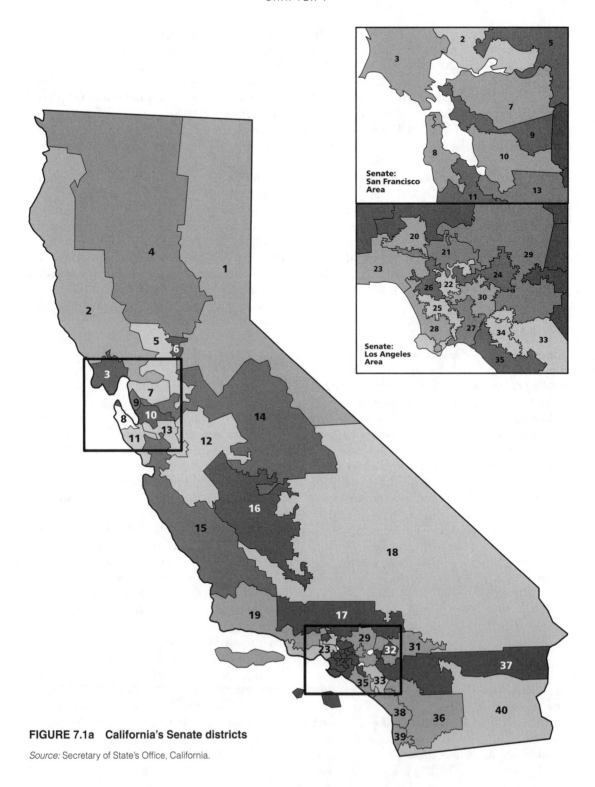

FIGURE 7.1a   California's Senate districts

Source: Secretary of State's Office, California.

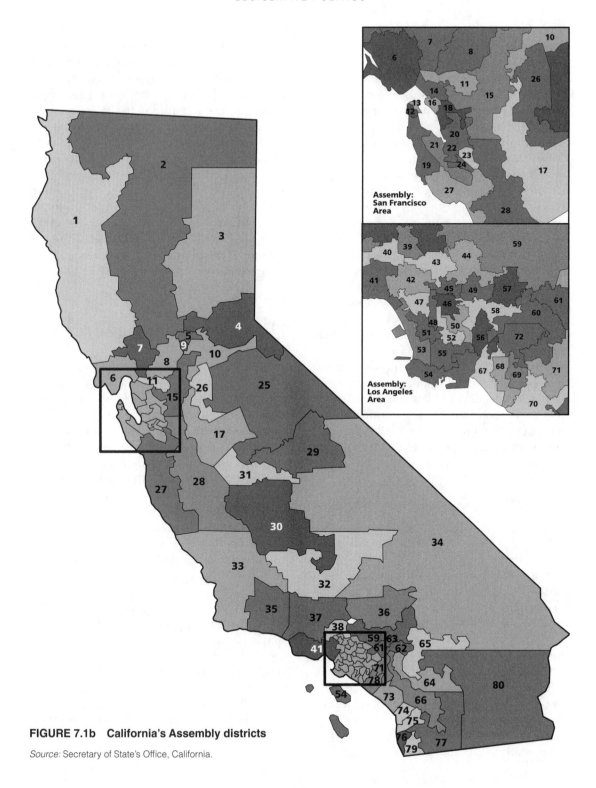

FIGURE 7.1b   California's Assembly districts

Source: Secretary of State's Office, California.

Committee) that control legislation of interest to potential campaign contributors.

Several other committees deserve mention. *Fiscal committees* handle bills that require the spending of money. Both houses have appropriations and budget committees devoted to this task. Members seeking power, prestige, or institutional importance covet these assignments. *Conference committees* are convened if the two houses produce different versions of the same bill; their job is to iron out the differences and send unified bills back to both houses for final passage. *Select committees* study various issues facing California with long-term solutions in mind. The Assembly alone has 64 of them. They cover topics ranging from aerospace, horse racing, and wine to California-Mexico relations, gun violence, and mobile homes. *Joint committees* include members from both houses and consider matters of common concern. Examples include fisheries, the arts, and school facilities.

Why all these seemingly extra committees? They can give needed visibility to emerging issues such as border conflicts and school safety. Also, they create added chairmanships and additional staff to hire. They too blend politics and policy in ways that benefit both members and constituents.

THE STAFF

To do its work, the legislature requires considerable staff support. Before the California legislature became full time in the 1960s, a few staff offices met its needs for information and analysis: the Legislative Counsel of California (created in 1913 to help draft bills), the California State Auditor (established in 1955 to provide fiscal oversight of state agencies), and the Legislative Analyst's Office (created in 1941 to give nonpartisan advice on fiscal and policy issues). In some ways, these offices have been islands of objectivity in a sea of subjective, partisan wrangling.

As committees grew in number, so did committee staff. In Sacramento, professional committee staff members are called "consultants." Given the many policy hats members must wear, the expertise these consultants provide is essential to the committee system. They may earn as much as or more than their elected bosses. In addition to the consultants, each house maintains separate staff to analyze pending bills and to do long-range research. Leadership staff assist the house officers for both parties. Party staff assist the respective party caucuses. In addition to secretaries and clerks, both houses employ undergraduate- and graduate-level interns to perform a variety of tasks. Some interns land full-time jobs as a result. More than a few have eventually become legislators.

The Legislative Process

In truth, passing most legislation requires neither vision nor political courage. Constituents back home could hardly care less about many bills; most are minor changes to existing law, business regulations, and policies affecting the relative few. But all bills, large or small, even the budget bill, must survive the same process. As Figure 7.2 shows, the flow of legislation is quite simple—on paper. An idea for a law can come from any number of sources, such as staff, lobbyists, executive agencies, constituents, and the member's own experience. For example, one legislator decided lasers should not be sold to minors after learning his own son played with one. In the process, he learned what trouble these gadgets can cause. The Legislative Counsel's office drafts the necessary legal language. The legislator who formally submits a bill is its author and is expected to shepherd it through the process; coauthors or cosponsors lend their names as supporters but do little else. In both houses, the respective Rules Committees assign bills to committees for hearings. The very fate of a bill may hinge on which committee hears it. Managing

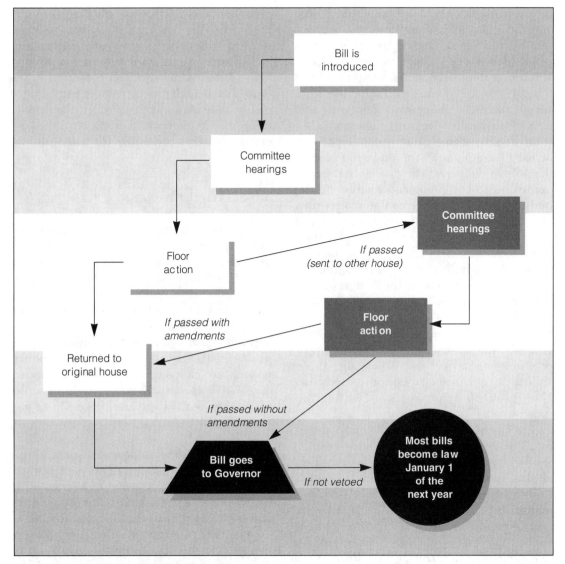

FIGURE 7.2   The legislative process in brief

Source: Legislative Counsel of California (www.leginfo.ca.gov/bil2lawd.html).

enough votes for a "do-pass" recommendation can be tricky business. A majority of committee members is required regardless of committee attendance when a vote is taken. Given multiple committee memberships, hectic schedules, and the sheer number of bills, simply getting supportive members to be there at the right time is a challenge. Ways to kill a bill include assigning it to more than one committee or calling for a committee vote when supporters are absent.

On each house floor, garnering enough votes is equally challenging. Majorities of 41 in the Assembly and 21 in the Senate are required to pass legislation, even if there is only a bare quorum at the time. A two-thirds vote is necessary on the annual budget as well as emergency bills (those taking immediate effect). Yet during floor debate, amendments to the bill may be offered and voted upon by only a simple majority *of those present*. Because it is so easy (numerically speaking) to amend a bill compared to passing it, floor amendments can be used to substantially modify a bill even to the point of killing it. The process that began in the house of origin repeats itself in the second house. A conference committee resolves interhouse differences. If its members cannot agree with the conference report, the bill dies. If it passes, the governor may sign it (making it law), do nothing (making it law without a signature), or veto it. Like the Congress, a vetoed bill then requires an extraordinary two-thirds vote of both the Assembly and the Senate for it to become law. Even a threatened veto can halt a bill's progress long before it reaches the governor's desk. In reality, there are many "veto" points or opportunities to say "no" throughout the process. Most bills die somewhere along the way.[15]

The fate of legislation also depends on timing. The beginning of a term moves rather slowly. By the end of a legislative session (usually late summer), the pace becomes frenetic. At that point, the textbook process becomes fiction as legislators amend or completely rewrite hundreds of bills without the committee hearings that would have been essential a few months earlier. During the closing days and weeks, some legislators try to slip through local or special interest bills (benefiting individual constituents or single groups). Upwards of 1,500 bills may be considered during those final weeks.

As you reflect on the legislative process in California, remember that the job of the legislature is to both pass and *not pass* legislation. Bills fail for various reasons. They may lack widespread support or be unacceptable to the governor. But less obvious reasons also exist.

Some members introduce bills but do little more, knowing that mere introductions seem to satisfy the concerns of some constituents and groups. Legislators may be ambivalent about dubious bills they feel pressured to author. If such a bill dies, a member can breathe easier while blaming committees, the leadership, "special interests," a media blitz, the governor, or budget constraints for its defeat.

The Third House

In many ways, the legislative process requires lobbying by interest groups. In a representative democracy, interest groups would have to be invented if they did not already exist. Chapter 6 outlined the role of interest groups as linkage institutions in California politics. They organize in different ways to express their policy preferences and serve their members. The professionals they employ to affect the policy process are called *lobbyists*. There are more than 1,000 registered lobbyists in Sacramento who influence the legislative process in six distinct ways:

1. *Making campaign contributions.* Contributing to campaigns is not lobbying per se. But since so many fund-raisers occur in Sacramento, lobbyists are expected to attend. Legislators and lobbyists alike agree that this practice is used more to "buy" access rather than votes on specific bills. Because contributions are made on a year-round basis, lobbyists sometimes make them—and worse yet, legislators sometimes solicit them—at the same time their bills are being considered.

2. *Simply being there.* If a physical presence was unnecessary, many groups would locate elsewhere than Sacramento. But because timing is so important in the legislative process, lobbyists need to be on hand to monitor or "watchdog" bills as they proceed through the legislative labyrinth. Being there also includes

making friends and establishing numerous contacts with legislators and their staffs. Capitol hallways, elevators, the sixth floor eatery, and members' offices all serve as contact opportunities.

3. *Knowing the process.* Simply being there is not enough. An intimate knowledge of the process as well as the personality quirks of members and staff is essential. Any legislature is a parliamentary labyrinth characterized by a host of written and unwritten rules. The written rules involve the intricacies of the legislative process discussed earlier. Unwritten rules may encompass everything from how members address each other to what they wear. This is why so many successful lobbyists have been former members or staffers.

4. *Providing information.* The most important role a lobbyist can play is giving legislators, committees, and staff accurate, detailed information on a bill, especially its impact on their clients. Lobbyists should be and often are masters of the subject encompassed by a bill. Observers believe term limits will likely increase the informational power of lobbyists. According to political scientist Charles Price, "Without veteran legislators around to 'remember when,' lobbyists will possess the institutional memory, shaded no doubt, to reflect the interests of their clients."[16]

5. *Coalition building.* Many groups believe there is strength in numbers. Accordingly, they develop coalitions with each other to help craft policy, but it takes tenacity for this to succeed. For example, in 1998 two environmental and business coalitions forged an agreement to reinstitute a toxic cleanup "Superfund," only to have two lobbying powerhouses—the California Manufacturers and the California Chamber of Commerce—persuade legislators to oppose it. All sides worked to reestablish it the following year.

6. *Grassroots lobbying.* An increasingly common lobbying technique is the use of *grassroots*

pressure. Because legislators of necessity pay attention to constituents back home, grassroots efforts help mobilize them and connect them with their representatives on specific policy issues—even single bills. Modern technology and the presence of term limits makes "farming the membership" both feasible and effective. According to public relations executive Katherine MacDonald, "Grass-roots efforts work more now because new legislators tend to be more grass-roots based and less Sacramento based."[17] As a result, they respond to organized phone call, letter, fax, and email campaigns. A variant of grassroots lobbying is *crowd lobbying*. Members of some interest groups may gather in Sacramento for briefings and to play "lobbyist for a day" as they roam statehouse hallways. That said, not all constituents are equal or equally significant to legislators. Successful lobbyists know how to cultivate those constituents closest to legislators or how to help their clients become significant constituents.[18]

In short the lobbyists, or the third house, represent one point of a legislative triangle. The other two points are legislative committees (both members and staffs) and executive branch agencies (their legislative liaison offices). These triangles or issue networks exist on every subject of permanent interest in state government. They best portray the three-way communication and influence pattern characterizing the legislative process.

Conclusion

Arguably, the California legislature has faced daunting challenges in recent years. This has been due largely to the anger of California voters who passed term limits. In fact, the entire initiative process competes with and even threatens the traditional representative function of the legislature.[19] Future challenges may well center around the state's growing diversity. Although legislatures are intended to represent the people of a state, representation in modern California is no easy matter. As noted, California is becoming increasingly diverse in every sense of the word—culturally, ethnically, socially, and economically. Pluralism is giving way to hyperpluralism. The legislature is increasingly a place where conflicts between diverse groups unfold. Historically, the legislature has best represented the social, economic, and political upper tiers of California—those who can afford to organize. Occasionally, it represents the problems faced by the relatively poor or powerless. In political theory, it is an institution designed potentially to represent pluralistic interests, but, in reality, it most effectively represents the state's

elite. For instance, despite revenue declines in recent years, business interests received additional tax breaks from legislators, ostensibly to create new jobs. Other groups will need to amass political power to match their growing numbers if they are to have comparable clout in the state capital.

Due to Proposition 140, reapportionment, and the newfound electoral clout of Latinos, a new generation of legislators has begun to emerge. Some of these newcomers will bring fresh ideas and zeal to "get things done" within their limited terms of office. Others will likely bring inexperience to a complex legislative process. Will they surmount a process that has frustrated so many in the past? Time will tell.

KEY TERMS

Federal plan (p. 77)

juice committees (p. 78)

bills, constitutional amendments, resolutions (p. 79)

trustees, delegates, politicos (p. 80)

executive oversight (p. 81)

authorization and appropriation processes (p. 81)

reapportionment and gerrymandering (p. 83)

partisan, incumbent, and racial gerrymandering (p. 83)

party caucus (p. 89)

assembly minority leader, speaker pro tem, president pro tem (p. 85)

standing, fiscal, conference, select, and joint committees (pp. 85, 87)

grassroots lobbying and crowd lobbying (p. 91)

REVIEW QUESTIONS

1. Briefly survey California's legislative history.
2. Describe the functions legislatures perform and the roles legislators perceive.
3. How are legislative candidates recruited? Why and how do they manage to stay?
4. Describe the power of the Assembly Speaker and other leadership posts.
5. Explain how the committee system represents both a diverse state and ambitions of legislators.
6. As a lobbyist, how would you most effectively deal with today's legislature?

WEB SITE ACTIVITIES

California Assembly and Senate (www.assembly.ca.gov/ and www.senate.ca.gov/) These sites provide current schedules, district finders, member directories, and links to legislation, committees, caucuses, and other California government Web sites.

Legislative Analyst's Office (www.lao.ca.gov/) Here you have access to the same policy expertise available to the legislature.

Legislative Counsel of California (www.leginfo.ca.gov/) This is an excellent gateway site leading you to bill information, state laws, legislative information, and related publications.

INFOTRAC COLLEGE EDITION ARTICLES

For additional reading, go to InfoTrac College Edition, your online research library, at http://infotrac-college.com/wadsworth

The Next Generation of Legislatures

Out of the Frying Pan

Time's Up: Under Term Limits, California's Legislative Engine Sputters

NOTES

1. For more on this period, see William Buchanan, *Legislative Partisanship: The Deviant Case of California* (Berkeley: University of California Press, 1963).

2. *Reynolds v. Sims,* 377 U.S. 533 (1964).

3. See Richard A. Clucas, *The Speaker's Electoral Connection: Willie Brown and the California Assembly* (Berkeley: University of California Press, 1995).

4. See A. G. Block and Stephanie Carniello, "Putting on the Squeeze," *California Journal* 18 (April 1987): 178–180; and Delia M. Rios, "Squeezing the Juice from Committee Assignments," *California Journal* 12 (March 1981): 109–110.

5. This parallels the national experience with legislative term limits. See John M. Carey, Richard G. Niemi, and Lynda W. Powell, *Term Limits in the State Legislatures* (Ann Arbor: University of Michigan Press, 2000).

6. This "author system" is described in William K. Muir Jr., *Legislature: California's School for Politics* (Chicago: University of Chicago Press, 1982), chap. 3.

7. A classic study of legislative roles can be found in John C. Wahlke et al., *The Legislative System: Exploration in Legislative Behavior* (New York: Wiley, 1962).

8. Kent C. Price, "Instability in Representational Role Orientation in a State Legislature: A Research Note," *Western Political Quarterly* 38 (March 1985): 162–171.

9. Two related articles on this subject are Peverill Squire, "Career Opportunities and Membership Stability in Legislatures," *Legislative Studies Quarterly* 13 (February 1988): 65–77; and "Member Career Opportunities and the Internal Organization of Legislatures," *Journal of Politics* 50 (August 1988): 726–744.

10. Carl M. Cannon, "California Divided," *California Journal* 33 (January 2002): 8–14.

11. Alan Rosenthal, *The Decline of Representative Democracy: Process, Participation, and Power in State Legislatures* (Washington, DC: CQ Press, 1998), 162–177.

12. Alex Gronke, "Herb Wesson," *California Journal* 32 (November 2001): 20–24.

13. Quoted in Miguel Bustillo, "Taking His Father's Advice to Heart, and to Head the Assembly," *Los Angeles Times,* February 4, 2002.

14. Although gender differences are not dramatic, men and women do have different policy priorities including committee preferences, according to a multistate study that included the California legislature. See Sue Thomas and Susan Welch, "The Impact of Gender on Activities and Priorities of State Legislators," *Western Political Quarterly* 44 (June 1991): 445–456.

15. Some bills follow a tortured path, only to die for lack of a single vote. See William Trombley and Jerry Gillam, "How a Bill Twists in the Wind," *Los Angeles Times,* October 14, 1991.

16. Charles Price, "Advocacy in the Age of Term Limits," *California Journal* 24 (October 1993): 33.

17. Quoted in Laureen Lazarovici, "The Rise of the Wind-Makers," *California Journal* 26 (June 1995): 18.

18. For more on legislative strategies of interest groups, see Jay Michaels and Dan Walters, *The Third House: Lobbyists, Money, and Power in Sacramento* (Berkeley: Berkeley Public Policy Press, 2002).

19. For an analysis of the representational challenge faced by state legislatures in general, see Rosenthal, *The Decline of Representative Democracy.*

Executive Politics

OUTLINE

Introduction

How Governors Lead

**The Governor's Duties
and Powers**
Executive Powers
Budget Leadership
Legislative Power
Judicial Powers
Other Powers

**The Plural Executive:
Competing for Power**
Lieutenant Governor
Attorney General
Secretary of State
Superintendent of Public
Instruction
Insurance Commissioner
Fiscal Officers

**California's Bureaucracy
and the Politics of Diversity**
Functions of Bureaucracy
Power Sharing and Clout

Conclusion
Key Terms
Review Questions
Web Site Activities
*InfoTrac College Edition
   Articles*
Notes

Introduction

"He hasn't gotten credit for what he's done and he gets blamed for things that are not his fault," said John Mockler, an education official in Governor Gray Davis's administration. That could be said of any California governor but it seemed especially true of Davis who won re-election over businessman Bill Simon in 2002 only to face a recall effort one year later. Once called the "best trained governor in waiting," Davis began his first term with a focus on the state's troubled education system. As the energy crisis of 2001 hit, the "Education Governor" became the "Energy Governor," and later the "Oracle Governor"—after an overpriced, no-bid computer software contract awarded to Oracle Corporation was linked to a $25,000 donation to the Davis reelection campaign. Over the course of his first term, Davis became as well known for his obsessive quest for reelection campaign funds and his thirst for publicity and media exposure as for his substantive policy leadership.[1] Early in his second term, a

PHOTO 8.1
Governor Gray Davis reveals the proposed budget cuts that will be necessary to bridge the state's serious revenue shortfall for the next fiscal year.

record 67 percent of California voters rated his job performance unfavorably.[2]

During the 2002 campaign, Davis aired a television commercial that spelled out his vision for California. "We must continue fighting to improve our schools. We must invest in transportation to move people and goods more efficiently. We must protect our quality of life with affordable health care, a cleaner environment, safe streets, and safe working conditions. Together, we can make California even better." Notice the word "we." Indeed, California governors do not and cannot act alone in governing the nation's largest state and most comprehensive state government. Their powers are not exhaustive. They must compete for influence in a system full of

checks and balances. Let's examine the political and administrative setting in which California governors operate.

How Governors Lead

The governor operates in a complex pattern of executive leadership. On one hand, California's governor is at the apex of the political system—more powerful than any other single individual. The entire executive branch exemplifies the themes of this book. It deals with virtually every group or issue in the state, in effect mirroring the diversity that is California. It also exhibits its own form of hyperpluralism: diluted and shared power, politically independent offices and agencies, and many avenues for interest group influence. Only the governor can provide statewide political leadership, but the state's diversity and fragmented political system present numerous roadblocks to leadership.

Experience with colonial governors on the East Coast taught the original colonies a lesson: To prevent autocratic governors, constitutionally weaken their offices. As newer states copied older state constitutions, they also limited gubernatorial power. California did so too, even though it experienced relatively weak colonial governors under Spain and Mexico.

Lengthy service as governor is a recent phenomenon. Earl Warren served more than two terms, and governors from Pat Brown to Pete Wilson each served two four-year terms. Presumably, eight years gives a governor ample time to form an agenda, exercise leadership, and implement priorities. Ironically, the records of very recent governors suggest that lengthy tenure alone does not necessarily guarantee effective leadership.

The governor's annual salary of $175,000 is among the nation's highest and would seemingly reflect the office's leadership role. In reality, a number of California public employees including public health administrators, top public university administrators, and many local government managers earn more.

Like other elected executives, California governors do not exercise power in a political vacuum. Borrowing heavily from research on the American presidency, Robert Crew identified five variables that affect gubernatorial leadership.[3] These variables can be applied to gubernatorial politics in California. They include the governor's personality, political skill, political resources, the overall political environment or context, and strategic considerations:

1. *Personality.* Highly personal factors such as motivation, behavior, and character affect how governors approach the job, relate to staff and legislators, and communicate with the public—in short, how they lead. Tenacious, persuasive, competent, confident, active, gregarious, flexible, cool, aloof, stubborn, tough, and pragmatic are just some of the terms used to describe the state's various governors.

2. *Political skill.* California governors need extraordinary political skill to push their priorities through the legislature and the state's bureaucracy. These skills involve working successfully with legislative leaders, political party operatives, the media, and interest groups.

3. *Political resources.* Such resources come from inside or outside the governor's office. Internal resources include the amount of time, information, expertise, and energy a governor has. External resources include party support in the legislature, public approval, electoral margins, and professional reputation.

4. *Political context.* "Context" refers to factors in the external environment that affect a governor's performance. California's economy is one such factor. When the economy is strong, governors are able to propose new spending programs and tax cuts. When the economy falters, revenues sag, forcing governors to propose painful and unpopular cuts and various tax and fee increases.

5. *Strategic considerations.* Given the factors mentioned, each governor must craft a strategy to achieve desired goals. This involves a game plan to deal with the legislature as well as methods to gain interest group and popular support. Previous strategies in California have involved large-scale, ambitious programs such as water projects and the master plan for higher education. Pete Wilson took office espousing "preventative government," and Gray Davis emphasized education reform, echoing public concern over the state of public education. Often these big-picture strategies give way to smaller scale, incremental changes in public policy.

Timing is an important strategic consideration for governors. Relatively few windows of opportunity exist—times when governors can pursue a policy agenda with some hope of success. These windows are determined by routine political cycles, such as the election calendar and the annual budget process. As with presidents, California governors normally have brief "honeymoons" of popularity and support early in their administrations. Windows of opportunity often close during election years, especially on tax-related bills. During recessions, those windows may never fully open. Since so many policy issues depend on adequate funding, revenue levels themselves open and close windows of opportunity.

The Governor's Duties and Powers

Whether resources are in their favor or not, California governors possess a wide range of duties and powers. In terms of public expectations, their responsibilities to lead the state outstrip their actual, formal powers and stem from both the Constitution and political necessity. They are both visible and invisible to the general public. Some powers the governor must share with the legislature or other executive branch agencies. Others are relatively unchecked by competing forces.

EXECUTIVE POWERS

The governor is first and foremost the chief executive officer of the state. In constitutional language, the "supreme executive power" of the state is vested in the governor. "The Governor shall see that the law is faithfully executed."[4] Although this is much easier said than done, the governor possesses a number of powers to achieve this goal.

Organizing a Personal Staff

The governor's *inner circle* consists of a chief of staff and a variety of assistants called "secretaries," assigned to legislative matters, adminis-

tration, the press, appointments and scheduling, and legal affairs. Gray Davis's appointments exemplified a common pattern: a blend of relative youth (schedulers and press aides) and experience (numerous department and agency heads). In addition, Davis pulled together a political brain trust by means of daily conference calls.[5]

Making Appointments

Although most of California's 278,000 executive branch employees belong to a civil service system, the governor appoints some 2,500 individuals to various posts. These people include high-level administrators, various commission posts, and judgeships. Through these appointments, governors can diversify their administrations, reward their friends and allies, and extend their own policy priorities. As Davis once put it, appointees should "think like I think."[6]

Managing the Executive Branch

In addition to immediate staff, California governors have their own versions of presidential *cabinets*. They include secretaries of these major agencies: State and Consumer Services; Business, Transportation, and Housing; Environmental Protection; Child Development and Education; Food and Agriculture; Health and Welfare; Resources; Trade and Commerce; Veterans Affairs; and the Youth and Adult Correctional Agency. Also included are the Director of Finance, the Director of Industrial Relations, and the Director of Information Technology. Many of the subagencies (Caltrans, the Highway Patrol) operate like semiautonomous fiefdoms, well outside the governor's routine attention span. As a group, the governor's cabinet is less a policy body than a collection of executive branch appointees.

Issuing Orders

The "executive power" of California's governor also includes the ability to take action independent of the legislature. A primary vehicle to do this is the *executive order.* Such orders usually contain this language: "Now, therefore, I, Gray Davis, Governor of the State of California, by virtue of the power and authority invested in me by the Constitution and the statutes of the State of California, do hereby issue this order to become effective immediately." Intended to bypass the time-consuming legislative process during times of emergency, Davis issued a spate of such decrees during the state's recent energy crisis.

BUDGET LEADERSHIP

Although the constitutional language "supreme executive power" sounds impressive, what requires the governor's constant attention is the state's budget. The California Constitution requires the governor to submit a budget to the legislature within the first 10 days of each calendar year. A tremendous amount of preparation goes into the submission of that "budget bill." The state budget is the premier policy statement for California, and governors want their priorities reflected in it.

The process is twofold. The *internal budget process* (within the executive branch) begins the previous July when the governor, through the Department of Finance (DOF), submits a "budget letter/price letter" to all executive agencies and departments. The budget letter relays the governor's policy priorities, and the price letter contains fiscal assumptions (like the rate of inflation) used to determine budget baselines. During the rest of the year, departments and the DOF haggle over which figures will emerge in the governor's January budget.[7] The *external budget process* pits the governor against the legislature. This part of the process is the most visible to the public and clearly the messiest from the governor's standpoint. At this stage, the governor shares budget power primarily with the Assembly Budget Committee, the Senate Budget and Fiscal Review Committee, and the Legislative Analyst's Office. When stalemates occur, a so-called Big Five (the governor and the two caucus leaders each from the Assembly and Senate) emerges to force some consensus.

The Constitution also requires that the legislature enact the budget bill by June 15 and for the governor to sign it by June 30, the last day of each fiscal year. It also mandates an extraordinary two-thirds legislative vote on the budget, an increasingly difficult political feat to achieve. In 2002, it took nearly two months after the July 1 deadline to pass the budget. While these stalemates make the headlines, less publicized conflicts occur regularly, and it is easy to see why. When revenues are down, budget makers argue over where to cut spending; when revenues are up, they argue over new spending ideas versus new tax cuts.

An approved budget is not the end of the story. During the fiscal year, additional spending requests plus new revenue projections require further adjustments. Although the governor's budget power seems to dissipate during legislative debate on the budget bill, the governor's power over an approved budget is substantial. The most formidable tool the governor has at this point is the *item veto.* This refers to the governor's ability to reduce or reject any item in an appropriations (spending) bill (see Figure 8.1). Forty-two governors, including California's, have this power.

A final word on the governor's budget powers is in order. Some parts of the overall budget are outside the effective control of the governor *and* the legislature. They include separate spending decisions made by voters through initiatives (Proposition 98's funding requirements for education), revenues dedicated to certain uses (gas taxes for highway expenditures), or automatic spending increases called COLAs (cost of living adjustments).

LEGISLATIVE POWERS

California governors must deal constantly with the legislature and not just on the annual bud-

> *Item 0450-101-0932—For local assistance, State Trial Court Funding. I reduce this item from $2,082,060,000 to $2,081,310,000 by reducing:*
>
> *(1) 10—Support for operation of the Trial Courts from $1,773,533,000 to $1,772,783,000.*
>
> *I am deleting the $750,000 legislative augmentation to establish a truancy court pilot project in Los Angeles County. Actions related to truancy, family issues, and juvenile crime are already within the responsibility of the established family court system. It is not clear that further delineation of areas of responsibility within the courts is necessary, and such delineation could result in inefficiencies and duplication of efforts.*

FIGURE 8.1 Line item veto

In 2001, Governor Gray Davis "blue penciled" a large number of expenditures, including Senate Bill 739. The governor's veto message totaled 85 pages. On page 2 was this item. *Question:* Can you see from this example why U.S. presidents would love to have the line item veto power?

get. They must exercise legislative leadership to achieve a host of other policy goals. This is not an easy task because governors and legislators bring profoundly different perspectives to their respective policy roles. Four of them are highlighted here.

• *Party differences.* The most telling source of conflict occurs when the governor is of one major political party and the legislature is controlled by another major party, what political scientists call divided government. In some years, Republican governors and Democratic legislative majorities have clashed on taxes, welfare spending, and many other issues. That said, same-party control of the governor's office and the legislature does not guarantee a smooth working relationship. Gray Davis and the heavily Democratic legislature had to work together to temper demands by party liberals for an activist agenda the public might not support.[8]

• *Constituency differences.* At times, differences in perspective between a governor and the legislature can be traced to constituency differences. Legislators represent individual, more homogeneous districts, whereas the governor represents the entire state population, as diverse as it is. The needs of the whole state may not square with the constituent views of a particular Assembly or Senate district. For instance,

a governor must balance the water needs of the entire state, not just those of farmers or city dwellers, as individual legislators might.

• *Interest differences.* Legislators are particularly responsive to the views of individual interest groups, as noted in Chapter 7. Governors try to represent the larger "general interest" of the state and, in doing so, seem more willing to step on interest group toes in the process. For example, Gray Davis received a great deal of electoral support (campaign contributions and votes) from labor unions but resisted demands by unionized government workers for substantial pay increases.

• *Responsibility differences.* When California legislators want to diffuse blame, they can easily point their fingers to committee chairpersons, legislative leaders, or insensitive colleagues from elsewhere in the state. Governors cannot spread the blame for failure nearly as far. If they try, their own leadership ability is questioned. Furthermore, the public tends to lay singular responsibility on the governor. The highly respected California Poll measures the *governor's* popularity, not each legislator's.

Governors employ several resources in dealing with the California legislature: an overall legislative program, the general veto, calling special sessions, and personal relations. This is how each works.

- *Legislative program.* Each January, the governor presents a "State of the State" speech, much like the president's "State of the Union" speech. This is an opportunity to fashion a coherent set of policy priorities by which legislation might be evaluated. As previously noted, Gray Davis initially focused on education. To reinforce their legislative program, California governors often stage symbol-laden media events, as Davis did when he appeared in a school classroom to read *The Little Engine That Could.*

- *General veto.* As noted earlier, the item veto allows the governor power to "blue pencil" a particular expenditure contained in an appropriations bill. A *general veto,* like the president's veto power, allows the governor to reject an entire nonspending bill. Like line item vetoes, the governor's veto message briefly summarizes the bill's content and explains the refusal to sign it.

- *Special sessions.* In the past, when the legislature was not in session, governors called *special sessions* to deal with pressing matters. Modern legislative sessions are virtually year round, and fewer special sessions are needed. But governors still call them now and then. Davis's 1999 special session on education reform ran concurrently with the new regular session begun in December of 1998. That is not as redundant as it sounds; laws enacted during special sessions take effect in 60 days, not the following January 1, as is usually the case.

- *Personal relations.* One of the governor's most potent but underrated legislative tools is good interpersonal relationships. For example, Ronald Reagan cultivated the press corps. Earl Warren and Pat Brown were known for their warm relations with legislators, whereas Jerry Brown, George Deukmejian, and Gray Davis were more distant and cool.

JUDICIAL POWERS

Gubernatorial power also involves the judiciary or can be essentially judicial in nature. For instance, the governor's appointment power extends to the judicial branch, as explained in Chapter 9. When a vacancy occurs on the California Supreme Court or the Courts of Appeal, the governor makes the appointment. Governors even appoint superior court judges when vacancies occur between elections. These appointments can add up. By the end of Governor Deukmejian's two terms, he had appointed nearly two-thirds of all state judges.

Like U.S. presidents and appointments to the U.S. Supreme Court, governors can leave their imprint on state supreme courts. Deukmejian's appointments were moderate conservatives with pro-business credentials. Jerry Brown's appointments reflected his desire to create opportunities for minorities and to shake up the legal system. His selections included several firsts: Chief Justice Rose Bird (the first woman), Cruz Reynoso (the first Latino), and Wiley Manuel (the first African American). Once appointed, appellate justices must face the voters every 12 years. Both Bird and Reynoso and another justice, Joseph Grodin, were ousted in 1986, in part because they opposed the death penalty.

The governor's purely judicial powers involve *clemency* (or acts of mercy). First, the governor may *pardon* an individual convicted of a crime. This means releasing someone from the consequences of a criminal conviction. Second, the governor may *commute* or reduce a sentence. Third, the governor may issue a *reprieve* (the postponement of a sentence). Recent governors have steadfastly refused to use this power in capital cases. Fourth, the governor may *reverse parole decisions* by the Board of Prison Terms. This relatively new power was granted by the voters in 1988. Considering himself tough on crime, Gray Davis rejected numerous parole decisions made by a unanimous Board. Fifth, the governor may *extradite* a fugitive to another state from which the fugitive has fled.

A related task is more legal than judicial in nature. Governors largely determine which court cases the state pursues at the appellate level. For instance, Pete Wilson decided to appeal a federal judge's ruling that Proposition 187 (the anti-immigrant measure) was unconstitutional. His successor, Gray Davis, opposed 187 and eventually dropped the appeal, rendering much of 187 dead.

OTHER POWERS

During times of crisis and public disorder, the governor's role as *commander in chief* of the National Guard (the state militia) comes into play. The scenario usually involves some disturbance or disaster, the inability of local police to maintain order, a local request for National Guard assistance, and the deployment of guardsmen to restore order. Guardsmen were deployed during the 1965 Watts riot, the 1994 Los Angeles riot, and the 1994 Northridge earthquake.

Lastly, governors are *chiefs of state*. As such, they greet foreign dignitaries, address interest group conventions, accompany presidents who are traveling in California, cut ribbons on public works projects, and process a huge volume of mail. Schoolchildren write governors assuming they exercise far more power than we have discussed. Consider this one: "Dear Governor Reagan: I wrote you once before about having to go to school on my birthday—and nothing happened. My next birthday is a month away and I am wondering what your plans are. Let me hear from you soon. Jeff."[9]

The Plural Executive: Competing for Power

As considerable as the governor's powers are, they are circumscribed in some profound ways. A significant limitation is called the *plural executive*—an array of executive officials with cabinet-sounding titles who are separately elected and politically independent of the governor. Unlike the president's cabinet, which serves at the pleasure of the president, many comparable state officeholders are elected directly by the people. This reflects a historic mistrust of gubernatorial power. Although one would think this would hinder a governor's leadership role, the duties of some of these elected officials are largely administrative in nature; independent political power is often neither required nor even possible.

LIEUTENANT GOVERNOR

The least threatening office of the group is lieutenant governor. California governor Friend W. Richardson (1923–1927) never held the post but sized it up succinctly: "to preside over the senate and each morning to inquire solicitously after the governor's health." In 1998, former Assembly Speaker Cruz Bustamante won this office by a 53 to 39 percent margin over state senator Tim Leslie (R–Tahoe City). In succeeding Gray Davis, he became the first Latino elected to statewide office since 1871. His annual salary is $131,250. In 2002, he faced Republican state senator Bruce McPherson and won by a 49 to 42 percent margin.

Since lieutenant governors consider presiding over the California State Senate a waste of time, and modern governors tend to be quite healthy, what do they do? First, they sit on various boards and commissions, including the Regents of the University of California, the Trustees of the State University System, and the State Lands Commission, and chair the Commission for Economic Development, an agency intended to attract new business to California. Second, the lieutenant governor becomes acting governor the minute the governor leaves the state. This is problematic when the two are of opposing parties. For instance, when Democratic Governor Jerry Brown traveled the nation running for president, Republican Lieutenant Governor Mike Curb hastened to appoint a judge before Brown could return.

Ironically, while sitting California governors are often mentioned as possible presidential candidates, they can ill afford the absenteeism required to wage a national campaign.

Politically speaking, the lieutenant governor is in a "Twilight Zone" of sorts. The responsibilities assigned to the office rarely embrace the great issues facing California. The media all but ignore the office, giving its occupants few opportunities to communicate with the voters who elect them. The office is a slippery stepping-stone at best. In California's history, only 6 of 30-some lieutenant governors have become governors. Reformers would like to either abolish this post or, at minimum, require the governor and the lieutenant governor to run on the same party ticket (a requirement in 23 other states). Yet polls show that most Californians favor the status quo.

ATTORNEY GENERAL

In contrast to the lieutenant governor, the state attorney general is quite powerful. In fact, the attorney general is the second most powerful position in California's executive branch. This office oversees the state's Department of Justice, which employs 5,000 people, including 1,000 attorneys. Historically, the "A.G." has truly been a stepping-stone to higher office. Attorneys General Earl Warren, Pat Brown, and George Deukmejian each became governor. Candidates for attorney general have come from the ranks of Congress, the state legislature, and politically active district attorneys. The position pays $148,750 per year.

In criminal matters, the department conducts investigations, argues all appeals above the trial court level, and nominally oversees local district attorneys and county sheriffs. In civil matters, the attorney general and his army of lawyers advise other state agencies and litigate on their behalf. The office's advisory opinions are legally binding until replaced by a court's decision. The attorney general also defends the state in various lawsuits but is not obligated to do so if the A.G. disagrees with the state's position in a case. Upon taking office in 1999, former Democratic state senator Bill Lockyer vowed to aggressively pursue civil rights claims and environmental protection. In 2002, he won reelection over Republican state senator Dick Ackerman with 51 percent of the vote.

SECRETARY OF STATE

In terms of discretionary power, the secretary of state stands in stark contrast to the attorney general. Whereas the nation's secretary of state is essentially a minister of foreign affairs, California's secretary of state is essentially a clerk of records and elections. As archivist, this official maintains all current and historical records. This $131,250 per year post also possesses many election-related duties (preparing and distributing statewide voter pamphlets, processing candidate papers, certifying initiative petitions, publishing election results, and tracking campaign donations and expenditures).

Historically, the position of secretary of state was so routine and uncontroversial that it was held by a father/son team (Frank C. and Frank M. Jordan) for nearly all of the period between 1911 and 1970. Recent secretaries of state include Jerry Brown who used the position to push for campaign reform, March Fong Eu, the first Asian American elected to California's plural executive, and Bill Jones, who championed term limits, the blanket primary, and various voter registration and election reforms.[10] In 2002, he sought the Republican nomination for governor but lost to Bill Simon. In the general election, Democratic assembly member Kevin Shelley faced former assembly member Republican Keith Olberg. Shelley won with 46 percent of the vote.

SUPERINTENDENT OF PUBLIC INSTRUCTION

One of the most fragmented arrangements in California's executive branch is the superintendent of public instruction. Several features of this $148,750 per year post set it apart from other statewide elective offices. First, unlike other members of the plural executive, the position is officially nonpartisan, reflecting the notion that education and "politics" should not mix. Second, the superintendent shares responsibility for the 1,200-employee Department of Education with a gubernatorially appointed 11-member Board of Education. Third, even though 80 percent of school funding flows through this department, the actual task of education takes place locally in more than a thousand school districts. This governance structure has been a perfect formula for policy fragmentation and diffusion of educational responsibility. As Davis's former education secretary, Gary Hart, put it, "Everybody is bumping into everyone else."[11] Consequently, in hyperpluralistic fashion, governors, *their* education secretaries, superintendents, the state board, legislators, educators, and interest groups continually battle over education policy and funding. In 2002, state senator Jack O'Connell won election to the post. As did his predecessor, Delaine Eastin, he vowed to use the position as a bully pulpit for education.

INSURANCE COMMISSIONER

In 1988, California voters "pluralized" still further the executive branch by approving Proposition 103. They authorized auto insurance rate reductions and established an elected rather than an appointed insurance commissioner. This is the only member of California's plural executive created by the initiative process. The commissioner heads the state's Department of Insurance, which regulates the insurance industry in California, and is paid $149,000 annually. In 1990, state senator John Garamendi became the first commissioner to win election to the post. He returned from private life to win election to the office a second time in 2002.

The insurance commissioner writes industry regulations, levies fines for unfair business prac-

tices, and controls proposed insurance rate increases. From 1994 to 2002, Republican Chuck Quakenbush held the post. Facing certain impeachment, he resigned in disgrace after diverting and misspending insurance funds intended for Northridge earthquake victims.

The Quackenbush scandal raised some larger issues surrounding this post. For years, consumer groups viewed the department as little more than a cheerleader for the politically powerful insurance industry. Making the post elective rather than appointive may have worsened the problem. Most campaign contributions come from insurance industry political action committees, calling into question how supportive the commission would be to the interests of insurance consumers. In reaction, Garamendi declined such funding in his 2002 campaign.

FISCAL OFFICERS

Although all members of California's plural executive are elected and therefore require campaign funds, the very job descriptions of some of them center around money: collecting it, investing it, and dispersing it to pay the state's bills. These offices are the controller, treasurer, and Board of Equalization.

• *Controller.* As the chief fiscal officer of the state, the controller pays all bills, monitors all state accounts, and earns $140,000 per year. In addition, this official sits on a staggering 63 boards, committees, and commissions, including the Franchise Tax Board (which collects the state's income tax) and the Board of Equalization (which collects other taxes). Gray Davis, who served from 1986 through 1994, used his membership on the State Lands Commission to oppose oil drilling and toxic waste dumping, a popular stance among California's environmentalists. Kathleen Connell served from 1994 through 2000. In 2002, former Ebay executive Democrat Steve Westly won a tight race over Republican state senator Tom McClintock.

• *Treasurer.* If the controller writes the state's checks, the treasurer handles the money while it is in the checking account. Because there is a lag between when revenue is received and when it is spent, the treasurer invests it in the interim. Obviously the goal is to obtain the highest possible interest rates for moneys on deposit. Another important responsibility is to auction state bonds (a form of borrowing discussed in Chapter 11). Because this revenue funds major construction (such as water projects, school construction, and affordable housing) and must be paid back with interest to large financial institutions, the treasurer tries to obtain the lowest possible rates. In 2003, the treasurer oversaw the investment of $56 billion in public moneys and sat on pension boards that invested another $225 billion in the world economy. Because the treasurer decides who gets to resell revenue bonds to investors, investment firms have contributed to treasurers' election campaigns, a questionable practice given their economic stake in the office. Nonetheless, New York City, home to many of those firms, does appear to be a predictable campaign stop for state treasurer candidates. In 2002, Philip Angelides won reelection to this $140,000 per year post over former utilities commissioner Republican Greg Conlon.

• *Board of Equalization.* The last fiscal office in California's plural executive is the Board of Equalization, consisting of four elected individuals plus the state controller, who serves ex officio (without vote). The four are elected by districts and represent more than 8 million people each. These four, who earn $131,250 per year, are largely invisible to average Californians, even when campaigning. The Board administers and collects roughly $31 billion in sales taxes, excise taxes, and fees each year. This organizational relic was placed in the 1879 Constitution to assess Southern Pacific Railroad's property, a needed reform at the time. To this day, the Board directly assesses utility company property. Efforts to fold this outmoded body into the Franchise Tax Board have failed.

California's Bureaucracy and the Politics of Diversity

Any large, diverse state with a complex economy and a comprehensive state government will possess a substantial bureaucracy. California boasts one of the nation's largest. According to the *California Political Almanac,* "There is virtually no aspect of life in California that is not in some way touched by the state bureaucracy and its work force."[12] About 278,000 employees work for a host of departments, agencies, boards, and commissions. Although this seems like a lot, the ratio of state employees to the state's overall population has been declining in recent years. About 90,000 are governed by the tenure and hiring practices of the University of California and State University systems. Most of the rest operate under *civil service*—the idea that permanent employees should be hired and evaluated on the basis of merit, not politics. This means competence and expertise rank higher than political connections and clout. California's civil service system, like those of other states, was modeled after the federal Pendleton Act of 1883 and Progressive era opposition to patronage. The *State Personnel Board* administers the overall civil service system, hears appeals from disciplined employees, and spearheaded the state's affirmative action program before Proposition 209 abolished it.

FUNCTIONS OF BUREAUCRACY

Even the briefest survey of California's bureaucracy demonstrates the magnitude of government and the diversity of its work. About 7 out of 10 state employees work in higher education, corrections, transportation, 24-hour care institutions, and public safety.

© Tom Myers Photography

PHOTO 8.2 The growth of California's bureaucracy
Sacramento's downtown skyline is increasingly dominated by high-rise state government office buildings,
not the picturesque Capitol itself. *Question:* In what
ways is state policymaking a partnership between those
who work in the Capitol ("the building") and those who
work in all of those executive branch office buildings?

The primary purpose of California's bureaucracy is implementation—carrying out
policies and laws approved by the legislature
and even the voters (through initiatives). Most
of the myriad day-to-day activities of bureaucracies are required to implement policy. The
following sampling of various state agencies illustrates some of these activities. The Highway
Patrol *patrols* state highways and *monitors* school
bus transportation. The Department of Alcoholic Beverage Control *licenses and regulates* the
manufacture, sale, purchase, possession, and
transportation of alcoholic beverages. The
State Banking Department *protects* Californians against financial loss at state-chartered

banks. The Integrated Waste Management
Board *promotes* recycling and composting. The
California Department of Transportation *builds,
maintains, and rehabilitates* the state's roads and
bridges. The Department of Fair Employment
and Housing *enforces* the state's civil rights laws
that ban various forms of discrimination. The
Department of Health Services *manages* numerous health programs. The Air Resources
Board *establishes* clean air standards and *re-
searches* antismog approaches.

To the extent the various layers of government in California contribute to hyperpluralism, the same can be said about California's
bureaucracy. Virtually all state agencies, departments, offices, and boards coordinate their
activities with similar local government efforts,
or they may actually direct those efforts. For
example, local school districts interact with
state agencies on funding, curriculum, standards, testing, and teacher credentialing.

All these functions and activities have produced mountains of paperwork in the Golden
State. No matter where one turns, there are
regulations to follow, forms to fill out, and fine
print to read. The title of one Little Hoover
Commission report on California's bureaucracy summed it up—*Too Many Agencies, Too
Many Rules.*[13] Critics of California's bureaucracy would do well to remember this: Given
the state's size, complexity, and diversity, California's bureaucracy is bound to be large,
complex, and diverse.

POWER SHARING AND CLOUT

California's bureaucracy also shares power
with the federal government. Most federal aid
to California passes through state agencies.
For example, the portion of federal gas taxes
returned to the state funnel through the Department of Transportation (Caltrans) to various state or local transportation improvements.
Certain state agencies also share power with
local governments. For example, counties actually deliver many state services and have

some, albeit limited, discretion over their provision. Administration of welfare programs is one example.

The clout of California's public employees comes not only from what they do but from their ability to organize. Borrowing labor practices from the private sector, most state employees are organized into more than 20 different bargaining units, represented by 12 unions. The largest is the California State Employees' Association, representing nearly 141,000 active and retired civil servants. There are also specific unions representing specific professions in state government. For instance, about 25,000 prison guards belong to the California Correctional Peace Officers Association (CCPOA).[14] As union members, state employees deal with many personnel-related issues such as collective bargaining rights and sexual harassment, plus the administration of pension plans.

Conclusion

The themes of hyperpluralism and diversity emerge from a review of California's executive branch. Executive leadership in California is a diffused phenomenon. Power is shared between the governor, other statewide elected officials, plus a huge bureaucracy. California governors, as elsewhere, can employ a number of resources to enhance their leadership potential. Historians regard Hiram Johnson, Earl Warren, Pat Brown, and Ronald Reagan as gubernatorial giants. They clearly made the most of the power they had. But they governed in a simpler time over a smaller and less diverse California. Today's governors wield substantial formal powers, but even these are shared by the legislature, a plural executive system, and at times the voters themselves. The office's most singular duties are constitutionally mandated, such as submitting a budget, exercising veto power, and performing various judicial roles.

The vastness of California's bureaucracy in some respects mirrors the diversity of the state itself. Virtually every economic sector and demographic group is represented in and/or regulated by the executive branch. The state's bureaucrats can wield a great deal of power but commonly share it with the judiciary or legislature. Reformers increasingly believe the gridlock between the executive branch and the other branches is the source of California's governing problems. But given the enduring idea of checks and balances in American politics, others believe gridlock is a price worth paying to avoid unchecked executive and bureaucratic power.

KEY TERMS

political context (p. 96)

inner circle (p. 97)

cabinet (p. 97)

executive order (p. 98)

internal and external budget processes (p. 98)

item and general veto (pp. 98, 100)

special session (p. 100)

clemency and pardon (p. 100)

plural executive (p. 101)

civil service (p. 104)

State Personnel Board (p. 104)

REVIEW QUESTIONS

1. Apply Crew's gubernatorial leadership variables to Governor Gray Davis and other recent California governors.
2. Of the governor's duties and powers, which do you think are the most and least important?

3. What advice would you give California governors on how to maximize their budget powers?

4. In what ways does California's plural executive increase political fragmentation and encourage hyperpluralism?

5. If you wanted to use a statewide elective office as a stepping-stone to the governorship, which would you seek, not seek, and why?

6. In what ways can California's bureaucracy exercise power independent of the governor? Is the bureaucracy itself a function of hyperpluralism?

WEB SITE ACTIVITIES

Governor's Office
(www.governor.ca.gov/)
Aside from a "Governors' Gallery," this site features biographical information, speeches, press releases, executive orders, and volumes of other information related to the current governor.

State Agencies
(www.ca.gov/)
Click on "Government" and then on "California Agencies"; this will lead you to a stunningly long list of agencies, departments, divisions, boards, commissions, and other state entities. These links epitomize the scope and diversity of California's executive branch.

INFOTRAC COLLEGE EDITION ARTICLES

For additional reading, go to InfoTrac College Edition, your online research library, at http://infotrac-college.com/wadsworth

The State of Davis: California's Governor Is Less Golden, But Still Rich

Drivers Get Lost in California's Smoggy Bureaucracy

Consolidating California's Energy Bureaucracy

NOTES

1. For more on Davis's fund-raising prowess, see Cynthia Craft, "Gray Davis: Show Me the Money," *California Journal* 23 (May 2001): 10–15.

2. Mark Di Camillo and Mervin Field, "Voter Opinions of Davis Hit a Record Low," *The Field Poll, Release #2067* (April 15, 2003).

3. See Robert E. Crew Jr., "Understanding Gubernatorial Behavior: A Framework for Analysis," in Thad Beyle, ed., *Governors and Hard Times* (Washington, DC: Congressional Quarterly Press, 1992), 15–27.

4. California State Constitution, Article V, Section 1.

5. Mark Z. Barabak, "Daily Power Call Shapes Political Life of Gray Davis," *Los Angeles Times,* May 21, 2002.

6. Steve Scott, "Rating Gray Davis: His Administrative Style," *California Journal* 31 (August 2000): 34.

7. For more on the budget process, see Richard Krolak, *California's Budget Dance: Issues and Process,* 2nd ed. (Sacramento: California Journal Press, 1994).

8. Anthony York, "The New Legislature: Resisting Temptation," *California Journal* 30 (January 1999): 18–25.

9. Quoted in Helene Von Damm, *Sincerely, Ronald Reagan* (Ottawa, IL: Green Hill, 1976), 162–163.

10. For more on Jones, see Bill Ainsworth, "Bill Jones: From GOP Good Ol' Boy to Republican Renegade," *California Journal* 31 (May 2000): 30–33.

11. Quoted in Sigrid Bathen, "Who's in Charge?" *California Journal* 28 (June 1997): 16.

12. A. G. Block and Claudia Buck, eds., *1999–2000 California Political Almanac,* 6th ed. (Sacramento: State Net, 1999), 89.

13. To access reports like this, go to www.lhc.ca.gov/lhc.html.

14. For a profile of this powerful union, see Noel Brinkerhoff, "Guardians of the Guards, *California Journal* 28 (March 1997): 44–47.

C H A P T E R   9

California's Judiciary

OUTLINE

Introduction

**State Courts in
Our Legal "System"**

**How California
Courts Are Organized**
Trial Courts
Appellate Courts
Supreme Court

So You Want to Be a Judge
Entering the Profession
The Right Experience
Selection Mechanics
Judicial Discipline

How Courts Make Decisions
The Criminal Process
The Civil Process
Juries and Popular Justice

How Courts Make Policy
Trial Court Policymaking
Appellate Court Policymaking
Criminal Justice and
Punishment

Conclusion
Key Terms
Review Questions
Web Site Activities
*InfoTrac College Edition
    Articles*
Notes

Introduction

News item: Years after the fact, a customer sues a tattoo parlor for misspelling the word "villain" on his arm. The customer provided the incorrect spelling but considered the parlor at fault nonetheless.

With lawsuit stories like this, no wonder people believe we are a litigious society. Although scholars disagree about whether the frequency of lawsuits is outpacing population growth, they do agree on this: Americans increasingly view all manner of problems in legal

terms, and they have plenty of help in doing so. Of all U.S. lawyers, about one in seven practices in California. In 2003, there were more than 142,000 active attorneys in California, far more than in any other state. More lawyers likely mean more lawsuits. In fact, the crush of civil and criminal cases has bogged down California's busiest court systems. At any one time in Los Angeles County there are more than 1 million small claims and civil cases in process; resolving many of them can take years.

Given the role of law in California's political system, what courts, judges, and juries do affects all Californians. The judiciary has always shared power with the legislative and executive branches. Conflict among them is increasingly common. At times it seems judges have the final say; at other times, they seem only to contribute to the policy gridlock occurring in the nation's most populous and diverse state. This chapter examines California's legal system and its policymaking role as well as how it is organized and what its participants do.

State Courts in Our Legal "System"

I use the term "legal system" advisedly. The federal Judiciary Act of 1789 actually created a dual system of courts, national and state. The federal courts deal with matters arising from the U.S. Constitution, civil cases involving regulatory activity, plus a relatively small number of criminal offenses. Fifty separate state systems address matters arising from state constitutions, civil matters, and most criminal offenses. State courts handle the vast majority of all court activity in the nation.

California is only one of those 50 systems, but it is not simply a copy of the others. Each state's judiciary reflects to some extent its political culture and history. The independent spirit that characterized California's history was bound to be reflected in its legal system; in fact, its Supreme Court has developed a national reputation for independence from the federal judiciary. The state's "independent-state-grounds" doctrine assumed that when state and federal constitutional provisions are similar, California could interpret those provisions more expansively or liberally. For example, the California Supreme Court struck down the death penalty before its federal counterpart did and rejected the state's method of financing public education (a decision the U.S. Supreme Court refused to make).[1] This exemplifies *judicial federalism:* the ability and willingness of differ-

ent court systems to produce potentially diverse, fragmented, and contradictory policy.

California's independent-minded judiciary does not operate in a vacuum. Some people prefer to resolve their legal disputes at the federal level. California has four federal district courts located throughout the state. It is possible for state and federal courts to hear the same kinds of cases (civil rights and liberties), a phenomenon called "concurrent jurisdiction." As a result, Californians can "shop" for the level—federal or state—most likely to give them the desired result. Challenges to voter-approved initiatives are often filed in federal court. Examples include Propositions 187 (immigration) and 209 (affirmative action).

If decisions by the federal district courts in California are appealed, they go to the United States Court of Appeals for the Ninth Circuit. This court is famous for its own judicial independence. In fact, the U.S. Supreme Court has rebuked this circuit court for frustrating California's efforts to execute death row inmates. More than most federal appellate courts, the Ninth Circuit handles cases involving diverse populations and sweeping social changes. The judges themselves admit that California provides them with a variety of cutting-edge issues because of the state's size, diversity, and propensity to pass constitutionally vulnerable initiatives. For example, in 2001 they ruled unconstitutional a petty theft sentence under California's Three-Strikes Law. In that case, a repeat offender was sentenced to 25 years to life for shoplifting $154 worth of videotapes. In 2003, the U.S. Supreme Court reversed that decision, ruling that the sentence was not cruel and unusual punishment.[2]

How California's Courts Are Organized

California's judicial system is the largest in the world, consisting of more than 1,600 judicial positions divided into three tiers of courts.

TABLE 9.1 California's Court System

California Supreme Court
1 chief justice, 6 associate justices
• Hears oral arguments in San Francisco, Los Angeles, and Sacramento
• Has discretionary authority to review decisions of the Courts of Appeal and direct responsibility for automatic appeals after death penalty judgments

Courts of Appeal
105 justices
• 6 districts, 18 divisions, 9 court locations
• Review the majority of appealable orders or judgments from the trial court

Trial Courts
1,499 judges, 437 commissioners and referees
• 58 courts, one in each county, with from 1 to 55 branches
• Provide a forum for resolution of criminal and civil cases under state and local laws, which define crimes, specify punishments, and define civil duties and liabilities

Question: Should death penalty cases go directly to the Supreme Court or work their way through the Courts of Appeal like other cases?

Source: Judicial Council of California, 2002.

These layers divide the judiciary's caseload within the system while allowing ample opportunity for litigants to appeal unfavorable decisions (see Table 9.1). Let's briefly look at each layer, beginning where most cases start—at the bottom.

TRIAL COURTS

On the lowest rung of the judicial ladder are the state's *trial courts*. These courts are triers of fact; they determine who is right in civil disputes and who might be guilty in criminal cases. Depending on the county's size, trial court judges either hear a wide variety of civil and criminal cases or specialize in a particular

area of the law: juvenile, family, probate, or criminal. They are paid about $139,000 per year. At this level, cases may be decided either by juries or only by judges (*bench trials*). California's *Three-Strikes Law* (which imposes a minimum 25-years-to-life sentence for defendants with two or more prior felony convictions) has significantly increased the workload for some trial courts. Because many defendants prefer jury trials rather than guilty pleas, more time is spent by judges, juries, and staff who record and assess second- and third-strike data. Supporting the judges are professional court administrators who manage court personnel, budgets, and workloads. Because more than 30 percent of criminal arrests in California are illicit-drug-related, many counties have established "drug treatment courts" that combine the standard judicial process with community drug treatment services.

The volume of trial court cases in California is staggering. In 2000–2001, more than 8 million filings were handled by trial courts. Of these, 44 percent were criminal misdemeanor cases and 43 percent were civil cases. Although juvenile and criminal felony cases constitute only 13 percent of the total, they consume disproportionate resources due to frequent hearings, motions, and jury trials. To better cope with this workload and to equalize judicial services across the state, the 1997 Trial Court Funding Act transferred financial responsibility for the trial courts to the state. California has also increased court interpreter services and with good reason. On any given day, more than 100 languages may be being interpreted in the state's courts.

APPELLATE COURTS

District Courts of Appeal hear appeals from trial courts and quasi-judicial state agencies. Unlike trial courts, they normally decide questions of law, not fact. For instance, instead of deciding guilt or innocence in a car theft case, California's 105 appellate justices typically sit on three-member panels to determine if legal procedures were applied properly in that case. (Was the suspect informed of his or her rights? Did the judge instruct the jury properly?) If legal errors did occur, they can order a new trial. Although appeals are common, appellate courts dismiss most of them. Because the California Supreme Court also declines to hear most cases appealed to it, appellate court decisions are often final. In the 2000–2001 fiscal year, the Courts of Appeal processed more than 23,000 filings and disposed of 13,809 matters through written opinions. Appellate justices earn about $140,000 annually.

SUPREME COURT

The *California Supreme Court* is at the pinnacle of the system. Its purpose is to raise important constitutional issues as well as maintain legal uniformity throughout the state. When it speaks, other courts listen—not only in California but in other states and throughout the federal judiciary as well. Due to heavy volume, this court must be very selective in what it chooses to hear and what it chooses to say. In the 2000–2001 court year, the Supreme Court received nearly 9,000 filings but wrote only 103 opinions. Its seven justices spend most of their time in legal research and opinion writing. They hear oral arguments for only one week of every month they are in session. The court consists of a chief justice and six associate justices. The associate justices earn about $162,409; the chief justice earns somewhat more.

If the Supreme Court is so selective, what kinds of cases is it willing to hear? First, much of its work is civil in nature, reflecting the legal problems of California businesses. Second, all death penalty cases are "automatic appeals"; they bypass the appellate courts and must be heard directly by the Supreme Court. In 2000–2001, the Court considered 11 death penalty appeals and the backlog of such cases is growing. Most of these cases are 10 to 15 years old by the time they reach the court.

Third, some observers believe the widespread use of the initiative in California has skewed the court's workload toward initiative-related litigation, to the neglect of other worthy issues.[3] Examples include affirmative action, term limits, and illegal immigration.

So You Want to Be a Judge

A law school official once said that A-students become law professors, B-students become judges, and C-students become rich! A judgeship is a noble goal regardless of grade point average. Judges earn much less than senior corporate law partners, but the pay is reasonable; plus, a judgeship offers a level of prestige no law firm can match. A number of steps are required to become a judge. Given the number of judgeships and attorneys licensed to practice in California (2,000 and 190,000, respectively), only a small percentage will ever achieve this elusive goal.

ENTERING THE PROFESSION

To become a judge, one must first become a lawyer, but this was not always the case. In the past, nonlawyers could serve as justices of the peace, but times have changed. Today, virtually all California lawyers are law school graduates, and many of those from a plethora of California law schools. Who employs California's lawyers? A 2001 bar survey revealed that more than 75 percent are in private practice. The rest work in government or other contexts. As was the case across the nation, the profession historically has been male dominated. U.S. Supreme Court Justice Sandra Day O'Connor graduated from Stanford Law School only to discover that California law firms would only hire her as a legal secretary. That was in the 1950s. Today, about half of all law school students are women. Although 68 percent of the state's lawyers were still men in 2001, the profession is slowly moving toward gender equality.[4]

Access to legal representation in California to some extent depends on race and income. Nonwhite attorneys make up just 17 percent of the bar. Although they represent a third of the population, Latinos constitute only 3.7 percent of the state's attorneys; most of them work for government or in small or solo practices. African American trial judges are few in number, even in California's big cities. Judges and court officials are largely white. Furthermore, the poor experience much less access to legal representation than wealthier Californians. While progress has been made in recent years, California still lags far behind many other states in providing legal aid to its poor residents.[5]

THE RIGHT EXPERIENCE

What does it take to become a judge? A network of legal and political relationships helps. When asked what it took to become a California Supreme Court justice, former Justice Mathew Tobriner said to go to high school with someone who planned to become governor.[6] Although most lawyers settle into private practice or work for government, others become involved in local bar associations or dabble in partisan politics. Attending political fund-raisers helps, and contributing to a governor's campaign helps a great deal. Many judges appointed by recent governors have contributed to their campaigns. In the Davis administration, most successful appointees have been criminal prosecutors or have had civil law backgrounds. Few have been defense attorneys.[7] Because local district attorneys can boast of high conviction rates, they are considered prime candidates for judgeships.

SELECTION MECHANICS

The formal steps to becoming a judge vary, depending on the court level. All levels in California employ a version of the *Missouri Plan,* which combines both elections and appoint-

ments. This hybrid method is based on two assumptions: (1) Fellow lawyers can best assess the attributes of judicial candidates, and (2) in a representative democracy, ultimate accountability to the voters is important, even for judges.

Trial Courts

At the local, trial court level, voters elect judges for six-year terms in officially nonpartisan elections (once again, thanks to the Progressives). Reelection is virtually guaranteed. What lawyer wants to run against a judge, lose, and then face that judge in court? Some judges resign or retire from the bench between elections. When vacancies occur at the trial court level, the governor appoints a replacement, relying on local bar association recommendations and local political allies. Judges themselves can fill some vacancies by appointing commissioners, lawyers who act as judges on a temporary basis. These lawyers gain invaluable experience they can tout if a permanent judgeship opportunity arises.

How do otherwise dignified judges campaign for these posts? Traditionally, they have raised modest campaign support from fellow lawyers and the business community. They have rarely waged stereotypical election campaigns, but times are changing. Due to their own campaign inexperience, judges increasingly employ campaign management firms and spend sizable sums of money. In urban areas, county-wide judicial campaigns may cost upwards of $200,000 per candidate, even more in the big cities. Because of trial court consolidation, all judges must run on county-wide ballots. These county-wide judicial elections tend to dissipate the voting strength of ethnic minorities.

Appellate and Supreme Courts

The governor initially appoints all appellate and Supreme Court justices. At the next gubernatorial election, voters answer this question: "Shall Associate Justice Carlos R. Moreno be elected to the office for the term provided by law?" State Supreme Court justices face all California voters. Appellate justices face only the voters in their appellate districts. Once they win election, they serve 12-year terms. If they are filling an unexpired term, they serve only the remainder of that term. Justices rarely face opposition and never particular opponents in these retention elections. As a result, they usually retain their posts. A notable exception was the 1986 ouster of Chief Justice Rose Bird and Associate Justices Joseph Grodin and Cruz Reynoso over their opposition to the death penalty. More typical was the 2002 retention of three Supreme Court justices after virtually nonexistent campaigns for or against them.

How appellate or Supreme Court justices are originally appointed is intriguing. Although the governor makes the initial appointment, he shares that power with two other groups. First, the governor must consult a 25-member Commission on Judicial Nominee Evaluation. That rates the judicial fitness of potential nominees. Four grades are possible: exceptionally well qualified, well qualified, qualified, or unqualified. A second step is approval by a three-member Commission on Judicial Appointments, consisting of the chief justice of the Supreme Court, the attorney general, and the senior presiding justice of the court of appeals. Although this group normally approves a governor's choice, a split vote can embarrass the governor and spell future trouble for the nominee.

JUDICIAL DISCIPLINE

As we have seen, voters can, but rarely do, oust sitting judges. Does that mean lawyers and judges can do most anything they want? Not quite. The California Constitution provides for the impeachment of state judges "for misconduct in office."[8] This involves impeachment (an indictment of sorts) in the Assembly and a trial in the Senate. Aside from this rarely used method of judicial discipline, there is a complex system of judicial accountability involving not only the public but the legal profession as well. Judges are held to professional norms and are subject to peer review.

Professional Norms

Lawyers learn to think and behave like judges during law school, a process called *judicial socialization*. First, they learn about judicial ethics. For example, judges should "recase" themselves from cases in which they have a personal stake. Second, they learn to appreciate the rule of precedent—*stare decisis*. That is, judges are expected to make new decisions by relying heavily on previous ones, especially those of higher courts. Third, judges render decisions within certain limits such as sentencing standards, jury instruction rules, and uniform legal procedures. Whereas the general public cares primarily about verdicts, judges are equally concerned with procedures used to achieve verdicts. In a state and nation governed by the "rule of law," procedure is the all-important vehicle through which courts ascertain truth.

Peer Review

What happens when a judge yells at attorneys and their clients? Or calls two juvenile assailants "bitches"? Or takes five months to rule on a routine family law motion? These are the kinds of complaints handled by California's Commission on Judicial Performance. This independent state agency consists of nine members, including judges, attorneys, and lay citizens.

Its primary duty is to investigate charges of willful misconduct by judges, including intemperate courtroom conduct, financial or personal conflicts of interest, commenting publicly about pending cases, drunkenness, and using court resources for personal business. A *Code of Judicial Ethics* provides guidelines for right conduct with which all members of the judiciary must comply.

The Ballot Box

Although many voters pay no attention to disciplinary matters, they do react to well-publicized decisions they do not like. When judges consistently make decisions outside the broad political beliefs of Californians, sooner or later they may suffer the consequences at the polls, as those Supreme Court Justices did in 1986. At the local level, unpopular decisions can lead to recall efforts, even though these tend to be unsuccessful. For example, one Los Angeles judge who sentenced a shopkeeper to mere community service for killing a suspected teenage shoplifter spent $300,000 to fend off a recall attempt. She eventually resigned. An Orange County judge who allowed O. J. Simpson to reclaim his two children after his murder acquittal also battled a recall attempt. As a general rule, judges chafe at the notion of strict electoral accountability. Sacramento Superior Court judge Roger Warren echoed the paradox of judicial accountability: "We don't want judges who are totally immune and divorced from real life, and on the other hand we want them to be sufficiently independent so that they can make decisions based on principle."[9]

How Courts Make Decisions

In previous chapters, we examined how legislators and executives make policy and share power. Judges do both as well. But court decisions are different from policy decisions made in other branches. They result from pretrial and trial activity. As elsewhere in the nation, trials in California are based on the concept of *adversarial justice*. Determining truth and justice involves a contest between two conflicting sides. Each presents only information favorable to its side. Judges and juries find the "truth" in and around conflicting claims.

In any California courtroom, the process one sees is rather generic. The steps may vary somewhat depending on whether the case is criminal or civil. Criminal cases involve alleged wrongs against society (murder, armed robbery, and so on). That is why such cases are entitled "*People v. _____.*" Civil cases involve disputes between individuals in society (usually involving financial transactions, real estate, personal property, business relationships, family relationships, and personal injuries).

THE CRIMINAL PROCESS

Criminal cases feature numerous steps and decision points. We will examine what happens before, during, and after trials. Throughout the process, an enormous amount of discretion is available to virtually everyone but the defendant.

Pretrial Activity

The first decision is obviously the decision to arrest someone. Police exercise discretion at this point based on their own attitudes, the nature of the crime, the relationship between the suspect and the victim, and department policy. The second decision is the decision to prosecute. Prosecutors, called "district attorneys" in California, make that decision based on the quality of evidence and witnesses, office policy, and the availability of alternatives such as alcohol education programs. Which charges to file can vary depending on the locale. For example, "junk" crimes such as minor shoplifting and unreturned rental videos are rarely prosecuted in mega-counties like Los Angeles. San Diego prosecutors often return illegal immigrants to Mexico rather than press charges.

District attorneys play a dominant role compared to judges or defense attorneys. Contrary to the legal ideal—innocent until proven guilty—courtroom work groups (prosecutors, defense attorneys, judges, and other court officers) operate on an *assumption of guilt*. "If you are there, you are there for a reason," so the reasoning goes. This logic is based less on prejudice than on daily experience. During an *arraignment,* a judge informs the accused of the charges and the legal options available. In a felony case, a *preliminary hearing* determines if there is probable cause to hold a trial. That decision is called an *indictment.* In addition to district attorneys, grand juries sometimes issue indictments. These bodies are citizen boards, selected from auto and voter registration lists. These groups of ordinary citizens tend to be used in complex or sensitive cases and when witnesses need protection. Most criminal arraignments are accomplished with dizzying speed given the volume of cases judges must face. When people talk of "assembly line justice," they are usually referring to the arraignment calendar.

Defendants often bypass trials using *plea bargaining.* By pleading "no contest" or "guilty" to lesser charges, they avoid predictable guilty verdicts involving more serious offenses. Judges usually rubberstamp bargains negotiated by prosecutors and defense lawyers. Without plea bargaining (euphemistically called "case management"), judges and lawyers alike believe the criminal justice process would grind to a halt. In one Los Angeles study, 98 percent of the defendants pleaded guilty rather than face trial. District attorneys, who dominate the process, strike such bargains based on the strength of their cases, the seriousness of the alleged offenses, and defendants' criminal records.

The Trial

Criminal trials can be heard before a judge only (bench trials) or a jury made up of one's peers. Sometimes a defendant can choose which type. Bench trials are common for less serious offenses and constitute more than 20 percent of all criminal trials in California. Prosecutors and defense attorneys traditionally have played key roles in the selection of juries. Since justice means "winning the case" to

both sides, picking the right jury is essential. The process is both art and science. Jury selection experts believe that identifying prejudices is at the heart of jury selection. Proposition 115, passed in 1990, allows judges to question potential juries exclusively, eliminating repetitious questioning by lawyers. In some counties, judges now handpick all juries. On occasion a trial site is moved due to unfavorable pretrial publicity (a "change of venue"). In the famous 1992 trial of Los Angeles policemen accused of beating African American Rodney King, many legal experts believed the "not guilty" outcome was predetermined when the trial was moved to suburban Ventura County.[10]

Misdemeanor trials must begin within 45 days of arraignment, 30 days if the defendant is in custody. Felony trials must begin 60 days after arraignment unless the defense requests a delay. Judges usually grant such requests. Criminal cases thus take priority and force lengthy delays for civil cases, which have no such time constraints. In other words, the old rule of thumb "justice delayed is justice denied" does not necessarily apply to civil cases in California.

The steps of a trial are rather predictable. After opening statements by both sides, the prosecution presents evidence consisting of witnesses and various exhibits. The defense cross-examines the witnesses. The defense makes its case in much the same fashion. As the trial ends, both sides present closing arguments. The judge instructs the jury, if there is one; the jury deliberates and decides guilt or innocence. In felony cases, a 12-member jury is required and its decision must be unanimous. In misdemeanor cases, a smaller jury is possible if both sides agree.

The Verdict and Sentence

If there is a guilty verdict, a judge or jury determines the sentence. Jail and prison terms are set by the state legislature. Generally speaking, judges are guided by a determinate sentencing law that sets finite prison terms and gives judges less discretion than they once had. Within these bounds, judges do have discretion based on restitution to victims, the need to protect society, or other special conditions. For example, they may require juvenile offenders to clean up graffiti, not just pass the time in a Youth Authority facility.

THE CIVIL PROCESS

Most courtroom time is devoted to civil cases—disputes involving individuals, businesses, and government agencies. There are distinctive stages involving pretrial activity, the trial itself, and a judgment.

Pretrial Activity

First, an aggrieved party files a *complaint*. It consists of a specific claim (say someone breaks an ankle in a sidewalk hole) and a proposed remedy (usually a dollar amount to cover medical expenses and possibly pain and suffering). The defendant is informed of the claim and files an answer. The next step is called *discovery*, the gathering of information to prepare for a possible trial. This process can involve *depositions* (oral testimony under oath) conducted by the lawyers involved, *interrogatories* (written questions and answers), and research into various documents and materials. Every effort is made to settle the case before a trial actually begins. Sometimes the process is formal, involving ADR—*alternative dispute resolution*. It takes two forms. Generally speaking, *mediation* is voluntary and *arbitration* is determined by law or by prior agreement. An arbitrator's decision is legally binding. California requires a "mandatory settlement conference" as the trial date approaches. Out-of-court settlements can range from mutual apologies to millions of dollars. To avoid costly and unpredictable trials, some litigants use retired judges who charge up to $4,000 per day for their legal know-how and settlement experience.

The Trial

Trials are available for those who cannot or will not settle. The process in court is very similar to the process in criminal trials. In a jury trial, three-fourths of the jury must agree for there to be a verdict.

The Judgment

At the conclusion of a trial, the judge or jury decides whether a wrong was committed, who was responsible, and what damages, if any, should be awarded. Lawyers for the losing side may file posttrial motions asking to set aside or reduce any damages awarded. Judges may reduce damages they think are excessive.

JURIES AND POPULAR JUSTICE

As noted earlier, both criminal and civil cases can be decided by juries. Although juries are charged with deciding questions of fact and reaching appropriate verdicts, these bodies of laypeople do not necessarily research decisions as judges would. Microcosms of the local community, juries have been known to weigh facts selectively or interpret them in light of their own experiences. This has been called *popular justice*. The extreme of this has been called *jury nullification*—when jurors or juries ignore irrefutable facts, judges' instructions, the applicable law, or all of the above. For example, many Californians felt that O. J. Simpson was wrongfully acquitted of murder by a Los Angeles jury that ignored incriminating evidence. Fearing popular justice by juries, some defendants settle cases out of court, paying huge amounts of money in the process. Insurance companies commonly do this.

How Courts Make Policy

Courts not only make decisions, they make policy. Public policy is what governments choose to do or not do. Individual policy decisions can be made by a host of public officials, including those in the judiciary. Individual court decisions may not seem like broad policy statements; it depends on which level—trial or appellate.

TRIAL COURT POLICYMAKING

We think of trial judges as finders of fact, not makers of policy. Yet they do make policy in less obvious ways. First, they reflect policy preferences over time in many cases. This is called *cumulative policymaking*. Years of decisions in comparable cases reveal certain patterns, which vary from judge to judge. As a trial court judge, former California Chief Justice Malcolm Lucas was labeled "Maximum Malcolm" due to his typically harsh sentences in criminal cases. Second, judges generally reflect community norms. These norms are part of a community's local legal culture. Because these cultures vary from place to place, a form of judicial diversity results. For instance, charges of disturbing the peace, loitering, or obvious marijuana use may be treated differently in university towns than in wealthy residential enclaves. Third, trial judges' decisions reflect their own ideological leanings. Research shows that conservative judges tend to side with insurance companies in claims cases or with management in labor disputes; liberals with claimants and organized labor. Governors use this information when making judicial appointments. For example, Governor Gray Davis prefers jurists who favor the death penalty and abortion rights.

APPELLATE COURT POLICYMAKING

Unlike trial courts, California appellate courts decide matters of law, not fact. They can confirm, reject, or modify public policy with a single decision. Although guided by *stare decisis* (the rule of precedent), they are not wedded to it. They can enter the "political thicket" of partisan conflict or avoid it. The choice is theirs. When Californians think of judicial policymaking, they usually think of the California Supreme Court, and rightfully so. We will consider briefly this court as policymaker under three chief justices: Rose Bird (1977–1986), Malcolm Lucas (1986–1996), and Ronald George (1996–present).

The Bird Court

Rose Bird, a former public defender, presided over a court that viewed itself as change agent and problem solver. Remember, California courts have long assumed their independence from the federal judiciary. The Bird Court was both independent and active. It overturned numerous death sentences, widened opportunities for liability suits, nullified several initiatives, and generally favored environmental protection and the rights of workers, renters, women, and homosexuals.

The Lucas Court

The historic defeat of Bird, Reynoso, and Grodin in 1986 allowed Governor George Deukmejian not only to name their replacements but to shape the court's future policy role. A succession of appointments by Deukmejian and his successor, Pete Wilson, left the court with only one liberal, Stanley Mosk, a 1964 appointee of Pat Brown. Under Lucas, the court became less activist, less assertive, and less willing to use the state constitution to establish new legal doctrines. In contrast to the Bird Court, the Lucas Court tended to affirm guilty verdicts and death sentences.

The George Court

Under the leadership of Ronald M. George, the state Supreme Court has continued many of the trends and policies set by the Lucas Court. Possibly because the court is more diverse than it once was (two women, one African American, one Asian American, and one Latino), it cannot be neatly divided into ideological voting blocks. Different majorities align on a case-by-case basis. The court still retains its independent-mindedness relative to federal law and even state election trends. According to George, "the job would not be worth holding if you had to look over your shoulders to see which way the political winds were blowing."[11]

CRIMINAL JUSTICE AND PUNISHMENT

Any discussion of California's judiciary warrants a discussion of the state's incarceration policies. In this regard, the state's judiciary has been affected by sweeping social trends, changing sentencing laws, the perennial issue of capital punishment, and the state's investment in new prisons.

Social Trends

In many ways, court cases simply mirror broad social trends. They include changing demographics plus the widespread use of guns and drugs. First, those who statistically contribute more than their fair share of street crime tend to be young, minority males (see Table 9.2). For example, in 2002, 94 percent of California's prison population were men, 35 percent were Latino, and 30 percent were black. Experts attribute this to reduced employment opportunities, residential segregation, the presence of gangs, and the absence of positive role models in minority communities. Despite tough law-and-order, "build more prisons" rhetoric by elected officials, crime rates are largely dependent on these economic and demographic trends.

Second, the widespread availability of handguns and assault weapons also colors the crime picture in California. The statistics are sobering. Excluding law enforcement, there are about 26 million guns in California. Sixty percent of all homicides involve handguns. Gun-related homicides are extraordinarily high

TABLE 9.2 California's Prison Population

Male	94 percent
Race	
White	29.0 percent
Black	30.0 percent
Hispanic	35.6 percent
Other	5.5 percent
Drug-related offenses	37.9 percent
Average age	35
Average reading level	Seventh grade
From Southern California	58.6 percent

Question: What larger issues regarding incarceration in California does this prisoner profile raise?

Source: California Department of Corrections, 2003 (www.cdc.state.ca.us/).

among young, urban youth. Although handguns outnumber assault weapons, the latter are increasingly used against the police in drive-by shootings and by California's gang culture. In short, the state is awash in weapons.[12] In response, the state legislature has toughened its ban on certain assault weapons, limited handgun purchases, discouraged the manufacture of cheaply made handguns, and required trigger locks by 2002.[13] Third, drugs and alcohol figure in many of California's criminal cases. Because criminal cases take priority over civil cases, they have in effect swamped the courts. As we noted, the courts have responded by creating so-called drug courts to better manage this aspect of the overall workload of the judiciary.

Sentencing Mandates

Courts must also work with changes in sentencing policy. Before 1977, California judges worked with an "indeterminate sentence" policy adopted by the legislature. Convicts would stay in prison until "rehabilitated" or until the completion of a broadly defined term (say, 1 to 5, or 1 to 10 years). The only problem was that "rehabilitated" convicts returned to prisons at alarming rates (a phenomenon called *recidivism*). In 1976, the legislature passed the Uniform Sentencing Act, specifying narrower sentencing ranges within which judges can work. The Three-Strikes Law made sentencing even more uniform. It provided 25-years-to-life sentences for anyone convicted of a third felony, whether violent or not. At their discretion, prosecutors and judges may disregard certain "priors" (previous felonies). Critics of the law charge that people are being sentenced severely for petty crimes such as stealing cigarettes or, in one famous case, a slice of pizza. Defenders of it say Three-Strikes is fulfilling its intent—incarcerating habitual, repeat felons.[14] As mentioned earlier, in 2003 the U.S. Supreme Court upheld California's law.

California's diverse population seems to have an impact on sentencing decisions. One study concluded that, at almost every stage of California's criminal justice process, whites fare better than African Americans and Latinos. They are more likely to have charges reduced or receive rehabilitative placements versus prison time. Why the disparity? Researchers believe judges tend to follow probation reports, which weigh individual backgrounds in recommending sentences. Since many minorities come from lower socioeconomic backgrounds (a phenomenon associated with higher crime rates to begin with), many have prior records—a major factor in sentencing decisions. Also, whites plea bargain more often than minorities. If they are materially better off, they can more easily afford restitution to a victim, thereby avoiding jail or prison.[15]

Capital Punishment

The ultimate sentence is death. Age-old arguments over both its morality and its effectiveness have characterized its history in California. The penalty has been a political football in recent decades. In 1972, both the U.S. and California Supreme Courts ruled the death penalty unconstitutional due to its capricious and arbitrary use. In the federal case, *Furman v. Georgia*, Justice Potter Stewart regarded the death penalty as cruel and unusual "in the same way that being struck by lightning is cruel and unusual." In a 1973 bill authored by then Senator George Deukmejian, the legislature reinstituted capital punishment, citing the "special circumstances" under which it would be employed (such as killing during a robbery, multiple homicides, and murder of police officers). Thirty-four other states did the same. In 1976, the U.S. Supreme Court ruled in *Gregg v. Georgia* that such efforts to reduce the penalty's arbitrariness were permissible and that capital punishment was allowable where such measures were employed. By 2003, there were more than 600 inmates on death row—more by far than in any other state.

In the 1990s, California resumed actual executions. In 1992, Robert Alton Harris was the first person in 25 years to be executed in California. The gas chamber at San Quentin was the last stop on a 13-year odyssey of appeals. There have been only nine executions from 1978 to 2003. Officials allow and the condemned seem to prefer lethal injection. With this method, those slated for execution are strapped to a gurney and injected with a chemical cocktail. Today's executions in California, though relatively infrequent, seem to draw decreasing media interest and public attention.

California's death row inmates have many opportunities to appeal their fate. Appeals through the California state courts are slow, methodical, and time consuming; more so than in other states.[16] Furthermore, death penalty prosecutions vary considerably by county. Orange, Los Angeles, and San Bernardino counties regularly seek the death penalty, rural counties cannot afford to, and San Francisco never files capital charges. In effect, there are 58 death penalty "laws" in California.[17]

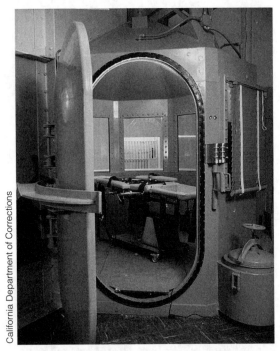

California Department of Corrections

PHOTO 9.1   California's lethal injection chamber, San Quentin State Prison

Question: To what extent should the imposition of the death penalty depend on different Supreme Court eras or on differences between states?

Prison Politics

Unlike their role in death penalty cases, California courts have been relative bystanders in the debate over prisons. For years, California prisons were able to keep pace with a growing state, but no more. Because of demographic factors, the rise of drug-related crimes, tougher sentencing laws, and vigorous prosecution efforts (such as large-scale drug sweeps instead of individual arrests), more people face prison terms. By 2003, nearly 160,000 Californians were housed in prison or other correctional facilities. Another 159,000 were on parole. About two-thirds of parolees return to prison for violating their parole, and the reasons are clear. According to one report, they tend to be unemployed substance abusers who lack basic survival skills. Contrary to public images, most California inmates are incarcerated for nonviolent offences such as drug use, property crime, and driving under the influence of alcohol.

Because of these factors, prison construction has become a growth industry in California. By 2003, California had 33 prisons, 38 work camps, 16 community correctional facilities, and 5 prisoner-mother facilities. The cost of warehousing convicts has become enormous. Prison construction can reach $50,000 per bed, and operating costs per prisoner are more than $28,000 annually.

Those convicted of lesser crimes or awaiting trial spend time in California's overcrowded county jails. The overcrowding is understandable. While there is some state funding for local jail expansion, it is not enough. Other local needs compete for precious county dollars. Furthermore, second- and third-strike inmates stay longer in jail while fighting long prison sentences. As a result of these factors and court-imposed limits on the number of people held at any one time, some jail officials have released nonviolent felons and advised the police to stop arresting low-level offenders. Jail demographics make matters worse. Race-based and gang-related violence, once the norm in state prisons, is increasingly commonplace in county jails.

Conclusion

California's judiciary manifests several trends in California politics. First, the legal profession in California certainly does not mirror the state's growing ethnic and cultural diversity. It remains largely white, middle class, and male in membership, though we see the entrance of more women. Second, in terms of workload, the judiciary is clearly impacted by the state's diversity. Criminal caseloads denote population changes plus widespread use of alcohol, drugs, and guns. Civil caseloads reflect a large, increasingly complex and regulated economy, plus an increasingly litigious society. Third, access to the judiciary is problematic, especially for the poor. Although public defenders, court appointed attorneys, and legal aid clinics provide low- or no-cost legal help, the poor in California do not enjoy the quality and quantity of legal assistance available to the middle and upper classes.

Fourth, in terms of governance, the judiciary carries out some vital functions (such as dispensing case-by-case justice) but also contributes to the "divided government" problem normally associated with the governor's office and the legislature controlled by different political parties. In one sense, the judiciary contributes to policy paralysis by allowing policy struggles like capital punishment to continue for years, even decades, in the courts. Yet judges can break the gridlock between the other two branches, as they have in areas such as reapportionment.

California's judiciary also reflects political fragmentation and hyperpluralism. Interest groups strategically use the courts to achieve policy preferences they could not obtain else-where in government. Judges themselves are relatively insulated from the electorate, rightly so in their view. Yet they can occasionally feel the pressure and even the wrath of volatile voters. But holding judges accountable is no easy task for voters. Trial court judges share power with policing agencies, courtroom work groups, and juries. On occasion, juries define facts, the law, and justice on their own terms. In making decisions, all judges respond to professional norms, statutory laws, conflicting interest group demands, and their own sociological and political backgrounds. In an age when voters seem to think that political parties make no difference, recent appointments to California's Supreme Court suggest the very opposite.

The policymaking role of California's judiciary will continue to be important and on some issues paramount. The courts will always be needed to validate, implement, or repair initiatives proposed by interest groups and passed by the voters. As the federal government continues to shift policy responsibility and accountability to the states, state courts will have no choice but to respond with policies that reflect each state's political culture and environment. California is no different.

KEY TERMS

judicial federalism (p. 109)

trial courts, district courts of appeal,
   the California Supreme Court (pp. 110–111)

Three-Strikes Law (p. 110)

Missouri Plan (p. 112)

judicial socialization (p. 113)

adversarial justice (p. 114)

assumption of guilt (p. 114)

arraignment, preliminary hearing, indictment (p. 115)

plea bargaining (p. 115)

complaint, discovery, depositions,
   interrogatories (p. 116)

alternative dispute resolution, mediation,
   arbitration (p. 116)

popular justice, jury nullification (p. 116)

cumulative policymaking (p. 117)

REVIEW QUESTIONS

1. How does the dual judicial system help explain judicial independence in California?
2. If you were a California appellate court judge, how would your workday differ from that of a trial court judge? How would you prepare for a judgeship?
3. Describe the workings of the civil and criminal process.
4. How do both trial and appellate courts make policy? How has state Supreme Court policy shifted in recent decades?

5. What issues affect criminal justice in California?

WEB SITE ACTIVITIES

Judicial Branch of California
(www.courtinfo.ca.gov/)
This site contains a wealth of data on California courts including opinions, procedures, administrative issues, latest developments, and links to other law- and court-related Web sites.

California Department of Corrections
(www.cdc.state.ca.us/)
To learn more about capital punishment in California, prison populations, or specific prison facilities, this site is helpful.

INFOTRAC COLLEGE EDITION ARTICLES

For additional reading, go to InfoTrac College Edition, your online research library, at http://infotrac-college.com/wadsworth

California Courts Address Perception of Racial and Ethnic Bias

California Juries Keep Handing Big Losses to Big Tobacco

Private Judges

NOTES

1. The relevant cases were *People v. Anderson,* 1972; *Serrano v. Priest,* 1971.
2. *Lockyer v. Andrede,* 01-1127 (2003).
3. Preble Stolz, "Say Goodbye to Hiram Johnson's Ghost," *California Lawyer* 10 (January 1990): 44–45.

4. "Survey Finds Bar Makeup Shifting, But Slowly," *California Bar Journal* (November 2001) (Available online at www.ca.bar.org/2dbj/01nov/).
5. California Bar Association, *The Path to Justice: A Five Year Status Report on Access to Justice in California* (California Bar Association, 2002). (Available online at www.calbar.org/).
6. David Balabanian, "Justice Was More Than His Title," *California Law Review* 70 (July 1982): 880.
7. Harriet Chaing, "Davis Shaking Up the State's Judgeships," *San Francisco Chronicle,* March 21, 2003.
8. Article IV, Section 18b.
9. Sheryl Stolberg, "Politics and the Judiciary Coexist, But Often Uneasily," *Los Angeles Times,* March 21, 1992.
10. Henry Weinstein and Paul Leiberman, "Location of Trial Played Major Role, Legal Experts Say," *Los Angeles Times,* April 30, 1992.
10. A.G. Block and Claudia Buck, eds., *1999-2000 California Political Almanac,* 6th ed. (Sacramento: State Net), 81.
11. John Borland, "The Arming of California," *California Journal* 26 (October 1995): 36–41.
13. Max Vanzi, "Where Does Gun Control Go Next?" *California Journal* 31 (March 2000): 8–15.
14. Janet Weeks, "Arguing the Third Strike," *California Lawyer* 19 (December 1999): 39–42, 78–79.
14. Greg Krikorian, "Study Questions Justice System's Fairness," *Los Angeles Times,* February 2, 1996.
15. David G. Savage, "State's Legal Morass Numbs Death Penalty," *Los Angeles Times,* May 31, 1998.
17. Maura Dolan, "California Death Row Shares Traits with Illinois'," *Los Angeles Times,* January 23, 2003.

CHAPTER 10

Community Politics

OUTLINE

Introduction
The Role of Community
The Limits of Community
Government

Counties
The Shape of California
Counties
How Counties Are Governed
County Troubles

Cities
How Communities Become
Municipalities
"Cities" Without "Government"
How California Cities Are Run

Special Districts
What Makes Them Special?
The Stealth Governments of
California
The Future of Special Districts

School Districts

Regional Governments
Regional Coordination
Regional Regulation

**Conclusion: Diverse
Communities, Diverse
Governments**
Key Terms
Review Questions
Web Site Activities
*InfoTrac College Edition
Articles*
Notes

Introduction

"Divorce L.A. Style" was the title of a *Newsweek* article on the desire of many in the San Fernando Valley to secede from the City of Los Angeles.[1] By the time of the November 2002 election, two divorce proposals were on the ballot: the San Fernando Valley and Hollywood. Los Angeles mayor James Hahn agreed with his successor, Richard Riordan, "Breaking Los Angeles apart is not the answer."[2] Although both proposals went down in defeat, California has in fact been breaking apart into

cities and other local governments since becoming a state. On that same election day, voters in the Northern California community of Rancho Cordova chose to incorporate, bringing the total number of cities to 478 (see Figure 10.1). Chapter 10 explains these community-level governments.

There are myriad local governments laid side by side and on top of each other across the state. Picture several jigsaw puzzles stacked one on top of the other. That is what local government looks like in the Golden State. Cities, counties, special districts, and various regional

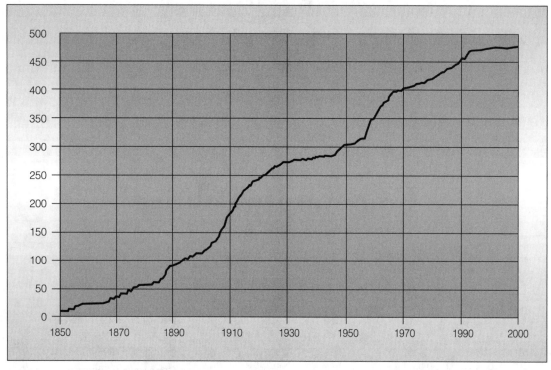

FIGURE 10.1   Growth of cities in California

Question: What do you think is the local impetus to incorporate, to form cities?

Source: Paul G. Lewis, *Deep Roots: Local Government Structure in California* (San Francisco: Public Policy Institute of California, 1998), p. 23; updated by author.

governments are the official local governments of California. There are also various "urban forms"—places that look and behave like cities but most definitely are not governed like them.

The two broad themes of this book, diversity and hyperpluralism, are vividly represented in California's local politics. The state's profound diversity plays itself out at the community level. It is in communities that people work, pursue various lifestyles, raise families, and educate their children. It is where neighbors do or do not get along, where California's polyglot of racial and ethnic groups live—in harmony or otherwise. From school board meetings to city hall hearings, it is in communities that values collide and cultures clash. At

this level, the struggle for power and control between individuals and groups is constant.

California communities also represent government at its most fragmented level and are one manifestation of hyperpluralism. Fifty-eight counties, 478 cities, nearly 1,000 school districts, and about 3,800 other special districts all present diverse approaches to community governance and have public agendas to defend. In addition to these, there are a growing number of quasi-governments such as neighborhood homeowner associations. Across the state, there are so many local governments that citizens are often unsure which government provides which service and whom to call when a problem arises. Hyperpluralism also suggests a host of public policy problems beyond the reach of governing institutions.

THE ROLE OF COMMUNITY

The late U.S. House Speaker Thomas P. "Tip" O'Neill once said, "All politics is local." A corollary could well be, "All politics begins at the community level." Local governments in California's communities perform three generic yet important functions. First, local governments provide various goods and services to their residents. These include education, garbage disposal, water, sanitation, building inspection, law enforcement, and fire protection. To some extent, each community can determine the mix and quality of services to provide. But most services are either fully expected by local residents (police) or flatly required by the state (welfare).

Second, local governments help socialize residents as community members. As most newcomers are assimilated into local society, they learn what behavior is acceptable and unacceptable. In diverse California, these norms can vary from community to community or even from neighborhood to neighborhood.[3] For example, simply "hanging out" in one place may be viewed as "loitering" elsewhere. Gang graffiti (called "tagging") may be quietly tolerated in some neighborhoods but vigorously opposed in others. Regulation of behavior by local government is called the "police power."

Third, local governments manage conflict among people and groups. Some conflicts are essentially arguments over policy such as service complaints, land use controversies, and budget allocations. Others reflect deep-seated social and cultural divisions in a community—divisions among racial and ethnic groups, rich and poor, home owners and renters, or newcomers and old-timers. The more heterogeneous a community population (large cities) or the more a community values extensive political participation (small towns), the more visible conflict will be. Such conflicts become political because local governments are expected to intervene. Political conflict is common in cities of all sizes.

THE LIMITS OF COMMUNITY GOVERNMENT

Despite expectations that local governments provide all three functions, California communities are limited in doing so. Three limits discussed here are the privatization of development, Dillon's Rule, and the myth of apolitical politics.

Privatization of Development

Historically, California's communities have been regarded as economic entities. Local growth is dictated by a tradition of *privatism*— an ongoing succession of private economic transactions. The role of local governments is to usually accommodate, assist, and at times subsidize those private interests. Because many local governments have continued this traditional role, they have remained largely ineffective in controlling private interests when public and private interests clash.

Dillon's Rule

In 1868, Judge John F. Dillon wrote, "Municipal corporations owe their origin to, and derive their powers and rights wholly from, the legislature."[4] The idea that states dominate and control local governments was adopted by the U.S. Supreme Court, other state courts, and, naturally, state legislatures. In California, this doctrine underlies all state–local relationships. While granting significant *home rule* (a measure of local self-government), the California Constitution stipulates local powers and even the very existence of local government. It should not come as a surprise that, during recent budget crises, state officials would tap the revenues of local governments over the protests of local officials.

Apolitical Politics

A final limit on local self-government in California is the enduring assumption that party politics corrupts governing. As noted in Chapter 4, the Progressives wanted to take "politics" out of government, meaning the corrupting influences of political parties and bosses. Their solutions included nonpartisan, at-large local elections, as well as professional city management. The Progressives believed good government meant the efficient provision of various municipal services. They underestimated government's contemporary role in reflecting and managing political conflict.

California's local governments are both numerous and richly diverse. We now survey the most common local governments in California: counties, cities, special districts, school districts, and regional governments.

Counties

One of the most diverse units of California local government is the *county*. California, as did other states, borrowed the county idea from British local government tradition. Originally, a county was a territory administered by a count. It was both a local government and a subdivision of a central government; counties retain this dual role today. As a "legal subdivision of the state" (Art. XI, Sec.1), the California legislature may delegate to counties any task belonging to the state itself.

THE SHAPE OF CALIFORNIA COUNTIES

In many ways, California's 58 counties reflect a bygone era. Consider the map in Figure 10.2. At the time of statehood, California had relatively few large counties. Southern California was one vast desert; much of it still is, as San

Bernardino County's boundaries attest. The Sierra foothill counties are elongated and relatively small for a reason. During the Gold Rush, it was thought that miners should be no farther than a day's horseback ride from a county seat where mining claims were filed. Those boundaries remain today.

In the late 1800s and early 1900s, new counties were formed, reflecting population and power shifts plus emerging local rivalries. Giant Mariposa County (encompassing much of Southern California) was subdivided into 12 counties. San Mateo broke away from San Francisco. Farmers and ranchers, fearing the early growth of Los Angeles, helped form Orange County in 1889. The last breakaway, Imperial County, formed east of San Diego in 1907. Despite vast demographic and economic change, the shape of California's counties has remained fixed since 1907. Local political cultures developed and calcified in that span of time, making further boundary changes difficult if not unthinkable.

As a result, there are tremendous disparities between California counties. San Bernardino is the nation's largest in area (20,000 square miles). It is 200 times larger than San Francisco County and embraces about 20 percent of the entire state. Los Angeles County teems with nearly 10 million people (larger than 42 other *states*) whereas tiny Alpine County is home to only about 1,200 people. Some counties have experienced uncontrolled growth while others have languished in California's economic backwaters. The state expects all 58 to perform similarly as units of government, yet their resources for doing so vary widely. Also, the counties vary significantly in per capita wealth. In terms of per capita income in 2000, San Francisco was the wealthiest county ($55,518) and Kings the poorest ($15,492).

HOW COUNTIES ARE GOVERNED

Legally speaking, there are only two types of counties: *general law* and *charter.* California's 45

FIGURE 10.2 California's counties

California's 58 counties come in all shapes and sizes; their boundaries have not changed in more than 90 years despite massive population growth and change. *Question:* How would you redraw these boundaries if given the chance?

general law counties adhere to state law as to the number and duties of county elected officials. Thirteen charter counties are governed by a constitution-like document called a "charter," which replaces some general laws and provides a limited degree of home rule. California's urban counties have charters, and

two-thirds of all Californians live in those counties. Both general law and charter counties are the primary units of local government in rural and some suburban areas.

Answering the classic question "Who governs?" at the county level is no easy task. Authority and responsibility—in short, power—is widely dispersed and shared among a number of decision makers.

Boards of Supervisors

In California, each county's legislative body is the board of supervisors. These boards are de facto city councils for those living outside of cities. Board members serve four-year staggered terms and are elected during primary elections in even-numbered years. If they do not garner a majority of votes (50 percent plus one), a November runoff is necessary. Although the elections are technically nonpartisan, informed voters likely know the partisan leanings of better-known candidates, especially incumbents. Once the domain of older, white men, today's boards include more women; in a few counties, they constitute board majorities. Over the years, service on a board of supervisors has been a stepping-stone to the state legislature or other elective posts.

What do these boards do? They adopt county budgets, determine some service levels, and make numerous decisions affecting unincorporated areas. The most contentious policy issues usually surround land use. Although county planning commissions make many land use decisions, supervisors hear various appeals and make final decisions. Where to locate shopping centers, housing projects, or unpopular industries (sometimes called LULUs—locally undesirable land uses) pit counties against cities, neighborhood against neighborhood, and occasionally neighbor against neighbor. Ironies abound. Citizens may pack a hearing over a small but controversial land use project while they virtually ignore large but invisible budget proposals. Boards of supervisors hire *chief administrative officers* or CAOs (called county managers in some places) to carry out board policy and administer county routines. Preparing and monitoring annual budgets plus preparing weekly board agendas consume a lion's share of a CAO's time.

Counties also provide for a variety of other elective officials. Together, they are California's local version of a plural executive. The exact arrangement of these positions varies from county to county. The most common elected officers are district attorneys, sheriffs, various fiscal officers, clerks, and school superintendents.

District Attorney

The lead prosecutor for the county is elected. As noted in Chapter 9, district attorneys can exercise a great deal of discretion in setting prosecution policy in a county. Some have become well known due to the cases they prosecute (for example, Los Angeles's Gil Garcetti and the O. J. Simpson case). Public defenders (who provide defense counsel for the poor) are not elected—making them potentially more dependent on a board of supervisors. District attorneys and public defenders can get caught in political battles between supervisors and judges.

Sheriff

The chief law enforcement officer for a county is an elected sheriff. This individual is usually an experienced, professional peace officer. Sheriffs administer an office, numerous deputy sheriffs, the county jail, and in some cases the coroner's office. The coroner conducts inquests of all questionable deaths. County sheriff departments often provide law enforcement services to cities that cannot or will not provide their own police departments.

Fiscal Officers

Several county officials, including auditors, treasurers, assessors, and tax collectors, handle the monies counties receive. This means they collect and count it, manage and invest it, and monitor its expenditure. Because their tasks are largely ministerial (administrative in nature with little room for personal discretion), they usually generate little controversy and few political enemies or opponents. However, in 1994, Orange County declared bankruptcy because its treasurer, Bob Citron, invested $1.7 billion of county funds in risky Wall Street securities.[5]

County Clerks

These individuals maintain county documents and records, such as real estate titles and transactions. They also act as voter registrars, supervising elections and maintaining voter lists. Voters rarely hear from clerks (except in the wake of some election snafu) and usually re-elect incumbents.

Superintendent of Schools

In some ways, this position is an oddity in county government. California's county school superintendents often respond to separately elected county boards of education, not boards of supervisors. They do not administer local schools because district-appointed superintendents do that. The offices headed by superintendents provide staff, payroll, training, and other support services to local school districts. Due to economies of scale, they can provide those services more cheaply than many local school districts acting separately. Although the California Constitution Revision Commission recommended that this office be abolished, there is little public concern one way or the other.

Other departments with unelected heads oversee local transportation, land use planning, public health, and welfare. In fact, California's counties play a critical role in administering CalWORKs—the state's version of the federal Temporary Assistance to Needy Families program (TANF), which is discussed in Chapter 11.

COUNTY TROUBLES

Several developments in recent decades have created substantial pressures for California counties, affecting their identity and their ability to govern at the local level. Let's look at a few of these issues. *First,* counties face increased funding pressures. In 1978, Proposition 13 cut property taxes, forcing cuts in many services. In recent years, counties have incurred additional pressures as state policymakers coped with massive revenue shortfalls. The problem is that counties cannot unilaterally cut just any program because they must administer a variety of state policies (welfare, environmental regulation, and public health policy). Some of these policy directives or *mandates* are fully funded; others are not. As one county association staffer put it, counties have had to fund assorted services with the fiscal equivalent of "bandaids, bailing wire, and bubble gum."[6]

Second, modern policy problems in California, such as smog, spill well beyond county boundaries. Regionwide population growth has swamped some urban and "urbanizing" counties with traffic jams on obsolete road systems. Some welfare recipients, crushed by housing costs along coastal California, have moved to less expensive areas of the state. This has transferred unanticipated welfare costs to county governments in those areas. The worst off counties are those with high levels of poverty, inadequate revenues, and high caseloads (of parolees, needy children, welfare recipients, and the ill).[7]

Third, counties are less politically responsive than democratic ideals would suggest. In smaller counties, boards of supervisors are often ideologically conservative and pro-growth regarding development. Even in the face of desperate need, some boards champion a low-tax, low-spending ideology. Size is also a problem. The state requires five-member county boards regardless of population size (San

Francisco is a combined city-county with an 11-member board plus a mayor). The Los Angeles board has been called the "five little kings" by critics who believe it is indifferent to the needs of most constituents. Some reformers argue that larger boards in larger counties would allow greater opportunity for minority representation and political responsiveness.

Cities

Today, more than 80 percent of the state's residents live in cities. California's earliest cities (San Diego, Los Angeles, Monterey, and San Francisco) were located along the coast, when passage by ship was one of the few travel choices available. Subsequent cities developed along major land transportation routes: roads, railroad routes, and later, freeways. All California cities needed adequate water to develop. Urban giants like Los Angeles and the Bay Area shipped it from great distances. Smaller urban areas developed local reservoirs to capture runoff water, tapped into agricultural water projects (like the Central Valley Project), or even built desalinization plants (converting coastal salt water into potable fresh water).

California's 478 cities have developed their own identities through economic specialization. Central Valley cities service surrounding farm areas. Large central cities are home to banking, legal, corporate, and information services. Other cities are manufacturing centers attracting many commuters. Still others in scenic locations (including coastal cities, mountain communities, and California's wine producing regions) attract tourists. Many suburbs are bedroom communities, offering housing and little else. Others have attracted "clean" industry, shopping malls, universities and/or recreation opportunities.

In short, California's cities defy overgeneralization. Together they now represent the state's economic and ethnic diversity. In some cases, cities have become homogeneous communities of either the wealthy or the poor, or single ethnic groups. In a growing number of cities, no single racial or ethnic group constitutes a majority of a city's residents. These are California's majority–minority cities.

HOW COMMUNITIES BECOME MUNICIPALITIES

If voters in a locale wish to incorporate, they usually initiate such a proposal via a petition. A *local agency formation commission (LAFCO)* studies fiscal and other impacts of the proposed city. LAFCOs (consisting of two city council members, two county supervisors, and one public member) were established in 1963 to foster the orderly development of local government and to prevent urban sprawl. After a favorable LAFCO decision, the voters decide whether or not to incorporate. New cities with fewer than 3,500 people must be general law cities. Larger ones can choose which approach to take. Only 107 California cities have their own charters. Some are quite detailed—Los Angeles's new charter con-

---

Did You Know . . . ?

California is a state of sizable cities. Fifty-eight of them are 100,000 people or more. Los Angeles is clearly the largest at 3.9 million. The smallest incorporated city is Vernon, with only 95 full-time residents. Because of its numerous factories, more than 50,000 workers commute there on weekdays.

SOURCE: Demographic Research Unit, California Department of Finance, 2001.

tains 10 articles and more than 1,000 sections. Like counties, California's general law cities operate under the statutes of the state.

"CITIES" WITHOUT "GOVERNMENT"

Some cities are not "cities" at all. So-called *urban villages* or *edge cities* are conglomerations of shopping malls, industrial parks, office "campuses," institutions, and residential housing. Orange County's urban village—the Costa Mesa-Newport Beach-Irvine complex—is considered California's third largest "downtown." In these "postsuburban" communities, a consumer culture predominates.[8] The development of such places rarely coincides with existing governmental jurisdictions. The impacts of urban villages elude cities and other local jurisdictions. Urban villages in Southern California and the Bay Area create similar impacts well beyond the reach of traditional cities.

Even at the neighborhood level, a growing number of middle-class Californians live in housing developments governed not by city hall but by *homeowner associations*. Today, about 6 million Californians live in 35,000 such nonprofit mutual benefit corporations. They are set up initially by developers, and all home owners are automatic members. Such groups have boards of directors in turn governed by assorted bylaws and documents called "CC&Rs" (covenants, conditions, and restrictions). In some respects, these documents are analogous to city charters. No wonder they have been called "shadow governments." Like cities, homeowner groups must obey various state statutes that set certain performance standards in areas such as budgeting and insurance. Their powers are both substantial and picayune—from maintaining private streets to dictating "neutral" window coverings and exterior paint colors.

HOW CALIFORNIA CITIES ARE RUN

Most California city governments consist of an elected council plus a mayor elected by the people or chosen by council colleagues. The council hires a city manager, a professional administrator who runs the day-to-day affairs of the city.

City Councils

These local legislatures adopt *ordinances* (local statutes), allocate revenue, determine the extent of public services offered, and make land use decisions. Except for California's largest cities (such as Los Angeles), city council work is part time. As with county supervisors, council members used to be primarily white, male, and middle class; but political times have changed. City councils today are more diverse—representing a wider range of economic interests, more ethnic minorities, and many more women. Most council members possess a volunteer ethic, a take-it-or-leave-it attitude toward their jobs. Many do little more than respond to city manager proposals. Some are elected on single issues and remain singularly focused. All in all, the primary power of most California city councils is to veto or second-guess the recommendations of professional city managers.

Mayors

California's largest cities have full-time mayors who often command more public and media attention than their powers would connote. Generally speaking, California mayors are weak—competing with elected councils and myriad commissions often possessing autonomous authority. Yet big-city residents perceive that mayors "run" their cities, and they hold them accountable for policy successes and failures. This is especially true regarding local economies. In the face of heightened responsibility but limited authority, California's big-city mayors must build coalitions among neighborhood associations, business interests, and other groups. They must be both visionary and results-oriented.

Voters in 157 cities directly elect the mayor. Many of these cities are medium-sized ones where the mayor's powers are even more circumscribed than those of large-city mayors. Mayors of medium-sized cities often serve as both mayors and council members. Although they preside over council meetings, in many ways they are equal to their council colleagues. They are expected to represent and lobby on behalf of their cities at various state and national meetings. Small city mayors are predominantly council members, often chosen by their colleagues after each election. This is the case in more than 300 of California's smaller cities. Although they preside at council meetings, they rarely possess a mandate to lead in any meaningful sense. Their mayoral duties are largely ceremonial: cutting ribbons, presenting resolutions to deserving citizens, and speaking at various social functions. When affairs in their cities go well, they rarely get the credit, but when community problems arise, they can easily become scapegoats.

City Managers

Professional administrators personify the ideal that "politics" and "administration" can be separated. City managers are directly responsible to the council. Although a growing number have long-term contracts, many city managers can be fired with little notice by a council majority. "Three votes on any Monday night and I am out of a job," said one. A primary responsibility of the manager is to build agendas for council meetings. Between meetings, managers hire and supervise department heads, provide budget leadership, study the city's long-range needs, and do whatever else the council wants. In recent years, they have had to devote growing chunks of time to finance. Some develop statewide reputations as fiscal wizards, able to generate revenue from unlikely sources. Furthermore, they must do all this and get along with at least five idiosyn-cratic council members and the fractious decision making that can result. Contrary to Progressive era thinking, good city managers *are* good politicians.

Commissions

Although they are easy to ignore, local commissions and boards play important roles in California cities. Large cities have many of them whereas small cities may have only a few. Some commissions may actually operate harbors, airports, or public works enterprises. Others merely advise or make recommendations to elected policymakers. The most common are planning commissions, which advise city councils on land use matters. They can exercise considerable power, as any developer can attest. Other boards provide advice on social services funding, libraries, the arts, and other matters. Service on these boards provides lessons in governing and occasionally that first step toward elective office.

Special Districts

They have been called America's "forgotten fiefdoms." There are nearly 30,000 of them across the country; they outnumber cities. California claims about 3,800, not including 994 school districts. Four counties have more than 200 of them; most counties have 50 to 200. They are special districts. Many of them were formed years ago to extend urban services to rural areas.

WHAT MAKES THEM SPECIAL?

California's special districts together provide 50 different services, but any single district typically provides only one service. Nearly 450 provide water; another 342 provide fire protection. Other services include community services, reclamation, sanitation, recreation, and even cemeteries (school districts are considered separately). Special districts do what general purpose local governments cannot or will not do. They can assess property taxes, issue bonds, and charge fees that are tied directly to the service provided. Not only do they spend vast sums on these services, they manage budget reserves of more than $19 billion.

A San Joaquin irrigation district was California's first special district. Created in 1887, its purpose was to provide steady water supplies at predictable prices to area farmers. Since that time, special districts have multiplied in the Golden State. They became attractive to communities that desired a particular service and local control over its provision. Cities and counties rarely resisted because these districts did not threaten existing political structures or boundaries; they simply added new, non-competing layers of local government.

California special districts are either *dependent* or *independent*. Dependent ones are actually subdivisions of cities and counties and are used, for example, to fund parking lots or street lighting. Counties also maintain more general service or maintenance districts in urbanized but unincorporated areas. California's 2,200 independent districts are separate legal entities providing and financing particular services noted earlier.

Special districts epitomize the diversity of local government in California. Some are tiny slivers of government quietly providing a specialized service at modest cost to relatively few people. Others are gargantuan. The Southern California Rapid Transit District and the Southern California Metropolitan Water District are two of the nation's largest. The latter's jurisdictional tentacles reach to the Eastern Slope of the Sierra Nevada—channeling precious runoff water to 6 million Californians in 27 client jurisdictions. Acting as a giant water wholesaler, this district maintains water supplies, determines water rates, establishes mandatory conservation programs, and levies fines against noncomplying client agencies.

THE STEALTH GOVERNMENTS OF CALIFORNIA

The largest special districts are powerful indeed. But most are virtually invisible and in many ways unaccountable to average Californians. They are the *stealth governments* of California. Special districts are governed by elected boards whose members serve rather anonymously. Meetings are poorly attended and are rarely reported in the local media. One cemetery district manager could not recall someone from the public *ever* attending a meeting. Special district elections are often the misnomers of democracy. Challengers are rare, and elections are sometimes canceled when no one steps forth. Voter turnout is typically low unless these elections are folded into California's primary or general elections. On occasion, lavish business trip spending makes news, but in many respects, special districts operate outside the limelight, much like private businesses. No wonder many citizens express a combination of ignorance and apathy regarding these stealth governments.[9]

THE FUTURE OF SPECIAL DISTRICTS

Political scientists view the plethora of special districts as organizationally messy—the height of governmental fragmentation. Why should the Bay Area have two dozen separate transportation agencies? Why should a patchwork of neighboring water agencies trip over each other providing a commonly scarce resource? Why shouldn't single purpose agencies have to weigh competing priorities like cities and counties do? Defenders of special districts disagree. To them, special districts foster home rule by providing particular services tailored to particular locales—customized government if you will. Furthermore, most special districts are quite efficient. As one district executive director put it, "We're lean, we're mean, and we do a better job than cities or counties could."[10]

California's special districts are poised to defend the status quo and fight for their share of both political clout and adequate revenue. In Sacramento, they are represented by the California Special Districts Association and numerous specialized groups including the California Association of Sanitation Agencies and the Association of California Water Agencies. Most of California's special districts have successfully resisted elimination, consolidation, or other reforms. A former state senator, Marian Bergeson, has called them "the closest thing to immortality you can get."[11]

School Districts

California's 988 school districts are different enough from other special districts to warrant separate consideration. As a group they, too, exemplify both diversity and hyperpluralism—our continuing themes. They range in size from the mammoth Los Angeles Unified School District with about 700,000 students to several hundred districts composed of single schools. As a group, these districts educate the state's children and youth, a growing segment of the state's population. Increasingly, they serve an ethnic rainbow in California—people from the four corners of the Earth.

Organizationally, school districts reflect the assumption that politics and education can and should be separate. With the exception of Los Angeles (which has a seven-member board), California's local school boards consist of five members. All run on nonpartisan ballots; some are elected at large and others are elected by district. Like other units of government, district-based boards must reapportion every 10 years and have been under pressure to better reflect California's minority groups. Boards typically meet several times a month. Many members receive only minimal fringe benefits. In contrast, the Los Angeles board members receive $24,000 per year, a modest sum given their workload. These boards have been a stepping-stone to higher office, especially for women. Of the eight former school board members in the 1999–2000 legislature, *all* were women.

Professionally trained superintendents head educational staffs—teachers, support personnel, and other administrators. Usually possessing doctorates in education, superintendents prepare board agendas, systemwide budgets, and various policy proposals. Although small districts may be "lean and mean," large districts employ huge numbers of administrators, often a bone of contention among lesser paid teachers.

Board members and administrators are destined to have conflicts. Elected board members represent accountability in a representative democracy. They bring to meetings the "commonsense" views of parents, taxpayers, and neighbors. By contrast, professional educators bring expertise including educational practices, trends, and jargon that may be foreign to their boards. A former superintendent once introduced to his board the subject of school-based management (making more decisions at the school level): "I said, 'Well, we need site-based management' . . . they all looked at me and said 'Site what? What's that?'"[12]

Unlike most other special districts, school districts operate under very close scrutiny—by parents, various interest groups, and the state government on which they heavily depend. The state's influence is pervasive. First, more than 60 percent of school funding comes from state aid (based on ADA, average daily attendance figures). Second, California's massive Education Code dictates in surprising detail what districts can and cannot do. Third, the state Department of Education also has an impact on local districts by administering statewide testing of various grade levels in various subjects, influencing curricula, approving textbook lists, and inspecting district performance. Even the federal government gets involved by funding or subsidizing certain programs (such as school lunches) and enforcing various civil rights laws. Compared to the state, federal influence is minimal because it supplies only 9 percent of K–12 funding in California.

Pressures on California school districts will mount in the future (see discussion on this in Chapter 11). Enrollment growth shows no signs of slowing. Education policy will continue to be a battleground involving ethnic, religious, and ideological groups—each demanding that their priorities be reflected in the curriculum and in education policy generally. At one level, school districts must cope with a host of social phenomena such as divorce, juvenile delinquency, drug abuse, and many inattentive parents. At another level, they are supposed to respond to a growing school-age population, parent demands for greater choice, state expectations for reform, ethnic diversity, and the usual assortment of local conflict and controversy.

Regional Governments

When policy problems spill beyond various local jurisdictions, regional approaches are needed. There are two models of regional governance in California: coordination and regulation.

REGIONAL COORDINATION

The coordination model is best exemplified by the state's 22 *councils of governments* (COGs). COGs are like small United Nations, groups of autonomous counties and cities in a region coming together to deal with issues of common significance. The federal government designates them as *metropolitan planning organizations (MPOs)* and requires them to draw up plans for transportation, growth management, hazardous waste management, and air quality. But they usually lack the legal authority to actually implement their plans. COGs also provide a forum for the member jurisdictions to communicate with each other. In the past, California COGs received large federal subsidies, but in recent years they have had to depend on member dues, transportation planning funds, and consulting fees usually paid by member agencies.

Of the nation's nearly 700 COGs, the Southern California Association of Governments (SCAG) is the largest—encompassing six counties, nearly 200 cities, and a population exceeding 15 million people. The Association of Bay Area Governments (ABAG) does planning for a nine-county, 100-city region. Numerous other COGs cover only one county (such as Kern, Humboldt, Fresno, Merced, San Diego, Sacramento, and Santa Barbara). Not only do COGs lack significant legislative authority, but their voting members (county supervisors and city council members) typically and understandably put local interests first. They resist giving a regional agency the power to dictate policy to member local governments. Yet to the extent knowledge is power, their ability to issue reports and studies often frames local policy debates.

REGIONAL REGULATION

Regional agencies employing a regulation model have the power to both write and to enforce various rules and regulations, usually in the field of environmental pollution. For example, the San Francisco Bay Conservation and Development Commission can veto any waterfront construction that threatens the bay itself. The Tahoe Regional Planning Agency has similar powers relative to Lake Tahoe. Of the state's 20 air quality districts, the South Coast Air Quality Management District (SCAQMD) is one of the more controversial. As other districts do, the SCAQMD studies problems, writes plans, and then issues rules. In the late 1980s, it proposed stringent air quality standards that had an impact on virtually every business and individual in Southern California. The regulations (which went so far as to ban barbecue starter fluid) triggered an avalanche of criticism but did illustrate the potency of the regulatory model.[13] Business and environmental groups argued over which is more important—clean air or jobs. These regionwide regulatory efforts usually involve complex trade-offs among various agendas, mandates, and organized interests.[14]

Regional government in California seems to be at a crossroads. Two contrary political forces explain the dilemma. On the one hand, some government officials and business leaders would like to strengthen or require regional approaches to admittedly regional problems. On the other hand, an opposite movement has been growing to empower grassroots groups and to strengthen home rule *below* the local government level. NIMBY (not in my back yard) and environmental groups have flourished by opposing land use projects of both local and regional significance. These contrary goals lock horns profoundly in an increasingly diverse and hyperpluralistic state.

Conclusion: Diverse Communities, Diverse Governments

California's local governments mirror the profound diversity of the state. Cities and counties come in all shapes and sizes. Special districts, the stealth governments of California, provide single services controlled by unpublicized boards. School districts educate children and youth through high school, and the state's 109 community college districts provide similar services to some high-schoolers, college students, and adults. Regional governments face the permanent challenge of coordinating other local governments and educating them to think re-

gionally. Private groups, such as homeowner associations, duplicate public governments but avoid (or think they do) the worst social, political, and economic problems at the local level.

Local government fragmentation mirrors a diverse state, but how problematic is fragmentation itself? Experts are not sure. Some governing problems are a function of size; some jurisdictions are too large or too small. The Los Angeles School District may be too large to serve its school-aged population well. In recent years, reformers have discussed breaking up this behemoth into smaller, more manageable districts—an idea people seem to support.[15] Other jurisdictions, especially some counties, are so small they cannot afford to provide even basic state-required services.

Is California overly fragmented? The layering of local governments across California's political landscape does seem to create voter confusion and the need for constant coordination. The state's regional governments help, but only help, in addressing local fragmentation. Nonetheless, local government fragmentation seems to be less of a problem in California than elsewhere. According to one study, California has fewer cities, counties, and special districts per capita than the national average. School districts have decreased in number as have the number of cities per 100,000 population. The result has been jurisdictional stability in a sea of fiscal, political, and demographic change.[16] A state-level Commission on Local Governance for the 21st Century suggested numerous reforms to address local government fragmentation and accountability issues in California, but few have been implemented.

KEY TERMS

privatism (p. 125)

Dillon's rule (p. 125)

home rule (p. 125)

general law and charter counties
   and cities (pp. 126–127)

chief administrative officers (p. 128)

mandates (p. 129)

incorporation (p. 130)

local agency formation commissions (p. 130)

urban villages, edge cities (p. 131)

ordinances (p. 131)

independent and dependent
  special districts (p. 133)

stealth governments (p. 133)

councils of governments (p. 135)

REVIEW QUESTIONS

1. What are the purposes of and limits to government at the community level?
2. Describe California's counties and why they seem to be in trouble?
3. Examine California cities and how they differ from counties?
4. Survey the special districts in your home county; are they stealth governments as this chapter suggests?
5. Review and illustrate the two major approaches to regional governance in California.

WEB SITE ACTIVITIES

California State Association of Counties (www.csac.counties.org/)
Information here includes the counties' lobbying activity, issues of interest to counties, county profiles, and links to all 58 county Web sites.

League of California Cities (www.cacities.org/)
The LCC site features legislative bulletins, association news, and links to hundreds of city home pages. Look up yours.

INFOTRAC COLLEGE EDITION ARTICLES

For additional reading, go to InfoTrac College Edition, your online research library, at http://infotrac-college.com/wadsworth

Divorce L.A. Style

Mayor Jerry Brown: Take II

SCAG, HOD Fight Over Housing Target

NOTES

1. Andrew Murr, "'Divorce, L.A. Style': The San Fernando Valley Wants to Secede from Los Angeles. Can This Marriage Be Saved?" *Newsweek* (May 13, 2002): 38.
2. Quoted in Jim Newton, "Mayor Attacks Secession, Urges School Reform," *Los Angeles Times,* April 8, 1999.
3. K. Connie Kang, "In This Ethnically Diverse State, One's Smile Is Another's Slight," *Los Angeles Times,* December 17, 2001.
4. Quoted in *City of Clinton v. Cedar Rapids and Missouri River Railroad Co.,* 24 Iowa 455, 475 (1868).
5. See Mark Baldassare, *When Government Fails: The Orange County Bankruptcy* (Berkeley: University of California Press and Public Policy Institute of California, 1998).
6. Quoted in Noel Brinkerhoff, "The Worst of Times," *California Journal* 28 (September 1997): 18.
7. Legislative Analyst's Office, *California Counties: A Look at Program Performance* (Sacramento: Legislative Analyst's Office, 1998).
8. For a thorough analysis of this phenomenon, see Rob Kling, Spencer Olin, and Mark Poster, eds., *Postsuburban California: The Transformation of Orange County Since World War II* (Berkeley: University of California Press, 1991).
9. See Little Hoover Commission, *Special Districts: Relics of the Past or Resources for the Future?* (Sacramento: Little Hoover Commission, 2000) (Available online at www.lhc.ca.gov/).
10. Ibid.
11. Quoted in Kevin Johnson, "America's Forgotten Fiefdoms," *Los Angeles Times,* May 26, 1993.
12. Beth Shuster, "Britton: L.A. Unified in Jeopardy," *Los Angeles Daily News,* April 5, 1992.
13. See Tom Waldman, "South Coast Air Quality Management District: A Colossus Astride Southern California," *California Journal* 21 (June 1990): 287–290.
14. See Wyn Grant, *Autos, Smog, and Pollution Control: The Politics of Air Quality Management in California* (Aldershot, UK, and Brookfield, VT: Edward Elgar, 1995).
15. Louis Sahagun, "Few Hold Positive View of L.A. School Board," *Los Angeles Times,* April 4, 1999.
16. Paul G. Lewis, *Deep Roots: Local Government Structure in California* (San Francisco: Public Policy Institute of California, 1998).

CHAPTER 11

Public Policy in California

OUTLINE

Introduction

**Budget Policy:
The Cost of Diversity**
California's Economy
State and Local Budget
Processes
State and Local Revenues
State and Local
 Expenditures

**Policies Stemming
from Growth**
Water Policy
Housing Policy
Transportation Policy
Energy and Environmental
 Policy
Larger Growth Strategies

**Policies Stemming
from Diversity**
Social Issues: Abortion and
Gay Rights

Education Policy
Higher Education Policy
Social Programs
Health Policy
California's Immigration
 "Policy"

Conclusion
Key Terms
Review Questions
Web Site Activities
InfoTrac College Edition Articles
Notes

Introduction

Although definitions abound, public policy is essentially what governments choose to do or not do. Chapter 11 describes the host of laws, programs, pronouncements, and other activities we call public policy. To avoid a disjointed discussion of dozens of major policies in California, I have grouped them into three categories: budget policy, policies stemming from growth, and policies stemming from the state's diversity.

Budget Policy:
The Cost of Diversity

• "Budget Cuts Deeply, Spares Few" (1992)

• "Budget Big on Schools, Jails, Kids" (1998)

• "Shrinking Budget Threatens Limit on Class Sizes" (2003)

These actual newspaper headlines epitomize budgeting in California. Because of its dependence on the condition of the economy, the budget process has a yo-yo quality to it. In economic bad times, revenues decline; the result is pessimistic debate over service cuts, denied pay increases, postponed projects, and possible tax increases. In economic good times, during times of revenue growth, there is rosy talk of service expansion, restored funding, pay increases, new programs, and possible tax cuts. But even in the good years, budgeting itself is not easy. The process is cumbersome, party politics infuses deliberations, interest groups clash, and numerous external constraints limit budget options. Budgeting in California increasingly reflects the state's hyperpluralistic character as diverse groups make claims on the public purse. How policymakers respond to those demands is characterized by conflicting interest group goals, the "tribalization" of interest group relations, and a budget process often colored or even paralyzed by the competing demands placed on it.

CALIFORNIA'S ECONOMY

To best understand the politics of budgeting in California, let's begin with this fundamental question: "Where does the revenue come from?" In short, the basic source of public revenue is the economy. Historically, California's diverse and resilient economy has been one of its strengths, heralding the state as a place of opportunity for all comers. As was noted in Chapter 1, modern California possesses a balanced economy consisting of numerous sectors: service occupations, retail, agriculture, tourism, manufacturing, and a plethora of "high-tech" activities such as computers, communications, and financial services. California's modern, trillion-dollar economy is both industrial and postindustrial—noted for innovation, sophistication, new ideas, new products, and the new jobs that follow.

Two aspects of California's economy ultimately affect the budget process. First, *California's bad times and good times seem to be either very bad or very good*. During the early 1990s re-

cession, California's unemployment rate was twice that of the nation's. By the late 1990s, California's economy was booming, but that was followed by another economic downturn in the early 2000s. Even prior to the terrorist attacks of September 11, 2001, state revenues had plummeted due to depressed foreign trade, rising unemployment, and steep declines in the U.S. stock market. Economic volatility leads to budget volatility.

Second, *the economic good times are not equally good for all Californians.* As noted in Chapter 1, there is in fact increasing socioeconomic fragmentation; income inequality is on the rise in California. In a technology-driven economy, many Californians are prospering beyond their wildest dreams, while others (immigrants, the poor, the unskilled, and the uneducated) are falling behind. As one researcher put it, "All boats have not risen and fallen equally with the California economic tide."[1]

Chapter 10 described the rich diversity of communities and local governments in California. There is also a rich diversity of local economies, which constitute the whole we call "the California economy." Some communities depend largely on only a few sources of income—logging, tourism, agriculture, a dominant regional shopping mall, a nearby military base, or even a single prison. Large cities and metropolitan areas are so diverse that troubles in one economic sector are largely compensated for by growth in other sectors. Local economies that are balanced and growing provide both needed jobs and needed revenue for local governments.

STATE AND LOCAL BUDGET PROCESSES

Whatever the state of the economy, California policymakers must agree to budgets every year. *The budget process is the institutional framework within which budget decisions are made.* The state budget process consists of several stages: planning, public debate, approval, and implementation.

Planning Stage

The governor and the bureaucracy dominate the planning stage, which takes about 18 months to complete. For example, the formal process to build the 2003–2004 budget (July 1, 2003 to June 30, 2004) began early in 2002 as agency budget planners developed spending estimates. Negotiations between the governor's office, agency staff, department heads, and the Department of Finance (DOF) take nearly a year. The end product is a budget the governor submitted to the legislature January 10, 2003. Incrementalism dominates the bureaucratic process. Projecting revenue is largely a guessing game as DOF officials must estimate future growth based on current trends. They may be on target or may not be. At this stage of the process, administrators provide continuity, given the comings and goings of elected officials, and form alliances among California's many interest groups. Masters of incrementalism, they can provide the most plausible reasons for retaining or increasing any agency's funding base.

While budget planning may have considerable power, their hands are tied in several ways. One constraint is *cruise-control spending;* that is, the relatively automatic nature of many spending decisions. For example, many portions of the state budget are spent on *entitlements*— payments to individuals who meet eligibility requirements established by law. CalWORKs (California's major welfare program) and Medi-Cal (California's version of federal Medicaid for the poor) are entitlement programs. Another constraint is the number of spending priorities established by various initiatives— so-called ballot box budgeting. For example, Proposition 98 required that roughly 40 percent of the state budget (in good times and bad) be spent on education.

Public Debate Stage

Once the governor submits the budget to the legislature, the process becomes much more public. Even so, it is leadership dominated in that the budget bills are submitted only to the legislature's two fiscal committees—the Assembly Budget Committee and the Senate Budget and Fiscal Review Committee. The two fiscal committees divide into subcommittees (such as Education and Health and Welfare) to study in depth portions of the overall budget. The Legislative Analyst's Office provides its own analysis of the governor's budget, sometimes challenging the governor's own budget assumptions (for example, what to expect in state revenues or federal aid). During legislative consideration, the governor proposes revisions, the most notable being the *May Revision.* Included may be new spending priorities and, more important, updated revenue estimates. In lean years, these revisions are usually bleak (revenues even less than anticipated), requiring policymakers to cut spending further, raise taxes, or dip into budget reserves.

While the public debate stage centers on the legislature, hundreds of interest groups express their views, mobilize their members, and provide revenue and spending alternatives of their own. Businesses may seek tax breaks, public employees may seek pay increases, and school systems may rally against contemplated spending cuts. Individual legislators may allocate funding for various pet projects back home.

Approval Stage

According to the California Constitution, a two-thirds vote in each house (27 in the Senate and 53 in the Assembly) is required to pass the budget. This vote is supposed to take place before June 15 of each year. The governor is supposed to sign the budget before July 1, the first day of the new fiscal year. Once the Budget Act is passed, *trailer bills* follow. These 16 bills implement the budget by specifying exact taxes, fee increases, and spending formulas in broad policy areas such as education or transportation. In the event this process breaks down, the Big Five (the governor, Assembly speaker, Senate president pro tem, and minority leaders in both houses) meet behind closed doors to hammer out compromises necessary to achieve the required two-thirds vote in each house. In recent years, protracted stalemates have become common and, as a result, on-time budgets have become only a sometimes occurrence.

The final, approved budget consists of three types of funds. The general fund is the largest and finances the bulk of ongoing state programs. Special funds encompass revenues for which spending is restricted by law such as transportation and the state's new Tobacco Settlement Fund (California's share of tobacco-related litigation). Bond funds consist of bond revenues used for capital outlays and other projects. Together, these funds support nearly 170 different departments and agencies as well as local governments and individual Californians.

Implementation Stage

After the budget is passed, programs are executed and monies spent throughout the fiscal year. The process reverts back to the executive branch departments where much of this spending occurs. During this time, the Department of Finance prepares monthly economic and cash revenue updates. This constant monitoring allows budget makers to anticipate future budget challenges.

Local Budget Processes

Given the diversity of local governments in California, only broad generalizations can be made about how they raise and spend money. First, local revenues depend on a host of factors including the nature of the local economy. The more diverse the economy, the more stable will be a community's revenue base. Second, local budgeting parallels state budgeting in many respects. California local governments normally use the same July 1 to June 30 fiscal year timetable. With some exceptions, they, too, use

annual budgets. The responsibility for budget leadership is executive in nature. During a four- to six-month process, budget responsibility falls to city managers, county administrative officers, special district managers, and school superintendents along with their fiscal staffs.

Third, the public is largely apathetic. Duly advertised budget hearings are often sparsely attended. Proposition 13 effectively eliminated the need for local governments to set property tax rates; as a result most voters lost interest in the subject. Exceptions include local interest groups such as chambers of commerce, taxpayer groups, or recipients of local grants. Fourth, the local budget process is at the end of a "fiscal food chain." The federal and state governments respectively monopolize the income tax and the sales tax. What is left for California's local governments? The answer is the property tax, assorted "nickel-and-dime" taxes, fees, and intergovernmental aid.

STATE AND LOCAL REVENUES

California's revenue system is a patchwork of taxes put into place during the 1930s. Experts regard the structure as complex and incomprehensible to average Californians. Specific revenues described here are shown in Figure 11.1.

Personal Income Tax

The largest source of state revenue is the personal income tax. Adopted in 1935, it largely parallels the federal income tax: taxpayers pay at different rates based on wages, salaries, stock options, and other forms of income. The state's rates range from 1 to 9.3 percent. It takes only $32,000 in annual income for an individual to reach the 9.3 percent rate; $65,000 for married couples or joint filers. While wealthy Californians pay a smaller percentage of their incomes in state taxes than less wealthy Californians, their taxes do constitute a large percentage of total income tax revenues. In 1999, the wealthiest 9.6 percent of

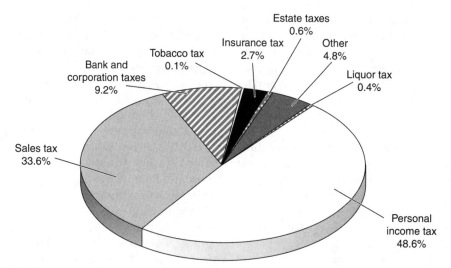

FIGURE 11.1 General fund revenues for 2003–2004

Question: If your intent as a legislator was to cut taxes in general or for specific groups, how might this graph inform you?

Source: California Department of Finance.

taxpayers—those with adjusted gross incomes over $100,000—paid 75 percent of the personal income tax. Therein lies a problem. The state's income tax has been buffeted by recent stock market downturns. For example, in 2001, state taxes from those making $1 million or more dropped nearly 50 percent, creating havoc for state budget makers. Today, it constitutes about 49 percent of the 2003–2004 general fund.

Sales Tax

The second largest source of state revenue is the sales tax. Constituting more than 33 percent of the 2003–2004 state general fund, it began in 1933 at a modest 2.5 percent tax on retail sales subject to the tax. The current statewide rate is 7.25 percent. Because it is inherently regressive, some necessities, such as food, prescription drugs, and utilities are not taxed. Internet purchases are not yet taxed, representing a growing loss in state revenue. Of the basic 7.25 percent, 2.25 percent goes to local governments for health, welfare, transportation, public safety, and other purposes.

In addition, voters in 24 counties and several communities have approved sales tax "add-ons" to fund local transportation or other projects. The actual effective sales tax is as high as 8.5 percent (San Francisco), making California's one of the nation's highest.

Corporate Taxes

California businesses pay a variety of taxes. The Bank and Corporation Tax is levied on all corporations doing business in the state. The rate is 8.84 percent of profits earned in California. The politically powerful insurance companies pay only a 2.35 percent tax rate on insurance premiums sold. Insurance taxes constitute only 2.7 percent of the 2003–2004 general fund; bank and corporation taxes 9.2 percent. Businesses and corporations can claim numerous deductions not available to individuals.

Excise Taxes

Numerous other taxes complement these larger sources of revenue. Excise taxes are assigned to particular items when they are made, sold, transported, or consumed. For example, California taxes tobacco products, alcoholic beverages, horse racing, and gasoline. They resemble sales taxes but are levied separately. While manufacturers have tried to keep California's "sin" taxes low on tobacco and alcoholic beverages, voters have raised the tobacco tax several times; it now stands at 87 cents per pack. Taxes on alcohol depend on the beverage but are quite low. For example, the tax on beer and wine is only 20 cents per gallon.

The 18 cents per gallon excise tax on motor fuels is added to the regular sales tax plus substantial federal excise taxes, all of which are included in the retail price at the pump. Gas stations collect it, and motorists rarely think about it. As with most excise taxes, the driving poor pay a higher share of their incomes on the gas tax than the wealthy do.

The Lottery

Joining many other states, Californians approved a statewide lottery in 1984. To sell voters on the idea, one-third of the proceeds were earmarked for education. The balance was reserved for winnings (50 percent) and administration (16 percent). As a source of state revenue, the lottery is small, unpredictable, inefficient, and, to some, ethically dubious. It amounts to less than 2 percent of all K–12 spending in the state.[2] California seems addicted to the lottery, as are more than 30 other states that have it. Just as the lottery has cut into horse racing revenue, expanded Indian casinos may well cut into lottery proceeds.

Debt

Some government policies require more money than current revenues can provide. Adding a new state park, prison, office building, or state university campus takes huge sums for land acquisition and construction costs. These capital improvements are normally funded through external borrowing. Although the State Constitution limits the debt the legislature can incur, it places no such limits on the voters. Therefore, when policymakers need to borrow for capital improvements, they seek voter approval to issue bonds. Two types of bonds are used in California: general obligation and revenue bonds. *General obligation bonds* are backed or secured by the "full faith and credit" of the state, meaning general revenues paid by taxpayers. They often finance schools, prisons, and highways. *Revenue bonds* are backed by the future revenue to be generated by the facility being financed, such as a toll road. While some Californians believe that the state engages in too much borrowing, bond approvals are understandable. Voters can anticipate tangible results without paying directly for them.

Another form of debt is when the governor and the legislature borrow internally (some say raid) from teacher and state worker pension funds or other special funds such as future tobacco settlement proceeds. This is a tempting practice because the funds are so large; it is also costly because pension loans must be paid back with interest.

Local Revenue

Traditionally, the property tax has been a distinctly local revenue source to pay for property-related expenditures. California's *ad valorem* (based on value) property tax is primarily governed by the provisions in Proposition 13, which limits the percentage of growth of that tax. The effects of this proposition have been gradually mitigated by significant increases in home prices, which, in turn, trigger new property tax assessments. Proposition 13 essentially restructured the fiscal relationship between local governments, notably counties and school districts, and the state.[3]

But Proposition 13 illustrates a more general axiom regarding revenue in California local government: *Revenue strategies in California communities are first and foremost dependent on factors external to local decision making.* These factors include the state of the overall economy, federal and state aid, voter initiatives, and interest rates. For instance, during recessions, people spend fewer dollars and therefore fewer sales taxes are collected. Federal aid to local governments has dwindled in recent decades. Proposition 13 cut property tax revenue, leaving a multitude of local governments to divvy up what was left. When the Federal Reserve Board cuts interest rates, local revenues on deposit earn less interest.

What do local governments do in response? Increasingly, they depend on assessments, service charges, and miscellaneous fees to balance their budgets. Many cities have attracted large shopping malls, which generate voluminous sales taxes. This practice of making land use decisions based on their revenue potential has been called the *fiscalization of land use.* Local governments have also aggressively pursued user fees associated with particular services (such as land use permitting, swimming pool use, recreation programs, and bicycle licenses). Some fees serve no purpose but to raise additional income (such as cable television franchise fees and business licenses).

STATE AND LOCAL EXPENDITURES

As the State of California and its communities divide policy responsibilities, spending policies result not only from clear policy choices but also from incremental, historical decisions that develop their own political momentum. The result is a complex mix of spending decisions and practices.

Occasionally newspaper reporters uncover legislators' spending ideas: $2 million for a San Francisco aquarium or $149,000 for a California trade office in Armenia. Although such projects may confirm voter suspicions about wasteful spending, they do not reflect where most state revenue actually goes. Figure 11.2 shows that about 90 percent of the 2003–2004 state general fund goes to education, health and human services, and prisons—the big three of state budgeting. California is quite typical of other states in this regard.

Education

Public education from kindergarten through community colleges consumes more than 43 percent of the general fund; Proposition 98 requires a minimum of about 40 percent. Spending for education remains enrollment driven. The school-aged population in California has been growing at a much faster rate than the general population. This requires more classrooms and more teachers in what will always be a labor-intensive government service. Higher education (including the University of California and the California State University system) consumes another 13.6 percent of the 2003–2004 general fund, up from 9.3 percent in 1994–1995. State funding for community colleges is governed by Proposition 98.

Health and Welfare

Addressing the health and welfare needs of California's poor, aged, blind, and disabled claimed 24 percent of the 2003–2004 general fund—down from 34.5 percent in 1993–1994. Caseloads have dropped somewhat in recent years due to job growth and welfare reform. Expenditures in this area largely represent direct payments to CalWORKs recipients, doctors, and hospitals. Within this portion of the budget, costs for Medi-Cal have recently soared due to rising medical care costs and federal requirements to serve more medically needy groups.

Corrections

California's prison system consumed 9 percent of the 2003–2004 general fund—up from 3 percent in 1969–1970. This dramatic increase is the result of a combination of factors: rising crime rates, increases in crime-prone

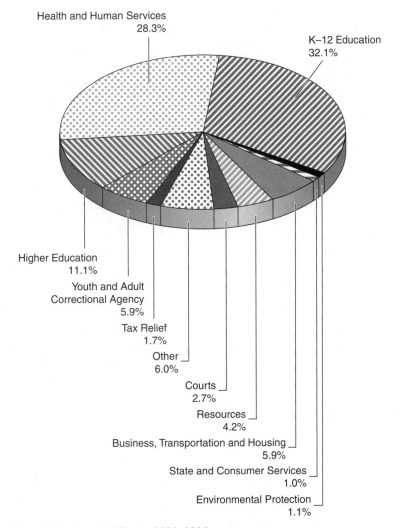

Health and Human Services
28.3%

K–12 Education
32.1%

Higher Education
11.1%

Youth and Adult
Correctional Agency
5.9%

Tax Relief
1.7%

Other
6.0%

Courts
2.7%

Resources
4.2%

Business, Transportation and Housing
5.9%

State and Consumer Services
1.0%

Environmental Protection
1.1%

FIGURE 11.2   General fund expenditures 2003–2004

Question: Aside from ideological concerns about the role of government, how does population growth affect the spending side of California's state budget? *Source:* California Department of Finance.

populations, and tougher sentencing policies (more prison time and less parole time). In recent years, the state's Three-Strikes Law lengthened sentences for some repeat felons. As a result, California's prison population jumped from 35,000 in 1983 to about 160,000 in 2003, making the state's corrections system by far the nation's largest and most costly.

What Is Left?

Traditional state operations (such as highways, environmental protection, resource management, business regulation, the state courts, and the legislature) plus tax relief receive the remaining 10 percent. Most of the executive branch agencies portrayed in Chapter 8 are reflected in the thinnest expenditure slices in Figure 11.2. Efforts to balance state budgets by cutting these government operations will always have limited success because they claim so little of the overall budget.

Local Expenditures

The two general purpose local government institutions in California are cities and counties. California cities vary greatly in size and in spending patterns, but on average they spend their revenues on these activities: public safety, public utilities, transportation, health, community development, culture and leisure, and general government. Public safety (police, fire and emergency services) consume on average 26 percent of city budgets.[4]

The spending patterns of California counties reflect the duties imposed on them by the state. For example, public assistance (Cal-WORKs and a few other programs) and public health activities respectively consume on average 35 and 17 percent of county budgets. Law enforcement, jails, and fire protection consume another 30 percent.[5]

Today, California's budget process itself seems to please no one. The California Constitution Revision Commission called it "crippled" and "dysfunctional." The California Citizen's Budget Commission claims "the budget process falls far short of today's needs." The California State Association of Counties calls a budget-related issue—the fiscal relationship between the state and local governments—"fundamentally flawed." A chorus of reform groups (including the California Governance Consensus Project, the Commission on Local Governance for the 21st Century, the Speaker's Commission on State and Local Government Finance, and the Governor's Commission on Building for the 21st Century) have recommended fundamental changes in the budget process. The following major reforms have been proposed:

- Use multiyear strategic planning to frame budget decisions

- Introduce multiyear budgets

- Require simple legislative majorities to pass budget bills

- Ensure prudent reserves for "rainy day" budgets

- Limit borrowing to cover budget deficits

- Keep the local property tax local

- Stabilize and simplify local revenues and state/local fiscal relations[6]

Policies Stemming from Growth

Many state and local policies in California stem from the state's incessant population growth. Here we consider the issues of water, housing, transportation, and the environment in terms of the population growth that makes them policy problems in the first place. The central question is this: How do California policymakers accommodate continual and inevitable growth without (1) degrading various qualities of life sought by diverse groups and (2) endangering the state's once-pristine environment?

Although rates of population growth in California fluctuate, this can be said: The state's long-term growth has been and will continue to be steady, if not relentless. The state's compound annual growth rate in the last 50 years has been more than twice the national rate. In 1940, California's population was 5.2 percent of the nation's; by 2003, it was 12 percent; by 2025 it will be 15 percent. At current rates, the state will add 4 million people—the size of Los Angeles—every six years. That translates to one new Californian per minute.

Growth rates have been high in some small rural counties, but the largest absolute numbers have been in the coastal and near-coastal counties of California. Los Angeles, San Diego,

Orange, Santa Clara, and Riverside counties experienced the highest numbers in the 1990s. The U.S. Census Bureau projects a population of 46 million by 2020—a 65 percent increase since 1990. In that span of time, California growth will far outpace even other high growth states.

WATER POLICY

One way or another, a variety of public policy issues can be traced to the drumbeat of growth in California. Some policies have made growth feasible, such as the provision of water throughout the state. Simply put, water drew people to the state and determined where they would settle. Since California is semi-arid and much of it is desert, this statement by itself is ironic. The availability of water was not as much a function of physical geography as it was a function of public policy. Over the years, policymakers figured out how to store and move this precious commodity in such a way as to defy the dictates of physical geography.

Winter precipitation is saved in three great storage systems, two of which are the Sierra Nevada snowpack and numerous underground water basins or aquifers (the airspace in soil and geological formations displaced by water). A third storage system is due to state and local public policy—the numerous manmade reservoirs that dot the California landscape. All three systems are monitored, regulated, and/or funded through state agencies, local governments, and water districts. These storage systems themselves face dangers from both periodic drought and overdemand.

One of the great public policy wonders in California has been the movement of water to otherwise arid portions of the state (see Figure 11.3). The evolution of water law and water rights encouraged the movement of water throughout the state. In time, localized irrigation projects including hand-dug canals were dwarfed by four immense projects that would forever change the face of California. The Owens Valley, Colorado River, and State Water Projects provided vast water supplies for Los Angeles and the rest of Southern California. The federally funded Central Valley Project provided cheap, plentiful, subsidized water for the state's farmers.

In recent years, several changes in water policy have occurred. *First,* many water districts have initiated mandatory rationing (during droughts) and permanent water conservation. *Second,* some communities sought alternatives to traditional water sources. Some built desalinization plants, converting sea water into potable water. To be sure, "desal" is expensive drought insurance, costing more than $1,000 per acre-foot—five times more than water from traditional sources. Others began to reclaim wastewater for irrigation and other nonpotable purposes. *Third,* a 1992 federal law required California to consider the needs of threatened fish populations, namely salmon and smelt. Future water allocations from the Central Valley Project would have to reflect the respective needs of farmers, city dwellers, and fish. This law allows surplus agricultural water to be sold ("transferred") to urban users during droughts. These new marketing approaches recognize water as a precious commodity, not a free resource for the taking.[7] *Fourth,* the state resolved to restore the integrity of the Sacramento-San Joaquin River Delta. A federal-state partnership (CALFED) was formed to balance the needs of a water-consuming public and the ecological needs of the Delta itself.[8] California's water future is still problematic. Water planners predict that by 2020 the state will experience water deficits from 2 million to 8 million acre-feet.

HOUSING POLICY

If providing water to a growing and thirsty state seems challenging, consider the Golden State's version of the American Dream—owning a home. Here we consider the challenge

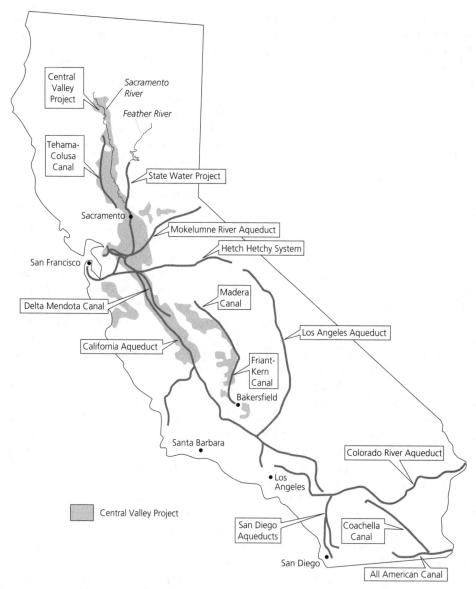

FIGURE 11.3 California's plumbing system

Question: Under what conditions, if any, would a massive public works effort like California's plumbing system be feasible today?

of providing adequate, affordable housing for all Californians.

Although the federal Housing Act of 1949 envisioned "a decent home and suitable living environment for every American family," governments (federal, state, and local) have not, nor ever will, build much housing. For the most part, it is a private sector activity. California's "policy" has mirrored the nation's: *Build housing for the haves and their housing will filter down to the have-nots. Filter down policy* assumes that, as people on the upper rungs of the economic ladder move up to better homes, the ones they vacate will be made available to those on the lower rungs. Private builders propose and construct the housing, private lenders finance its purchase, and local governments determine and enforce development standards. A smattering of government aid assists a small percentage of the have-nots in their quest for housing.

Does filter down work? Yes, if there is equilibrium between the supply of housing and the demand for it. But this equilibrium has been rare in California due to several factors. First, developers gravitate to politically acceptable, lower density, more expensive single-family housing. Second, California's constant population growth keeps demand for housing high, even where local governments are willing to approve more of it. This results in residential overcrowding, home sharing by both families and individuals, and an inability for some to move.

There is both good news and bad news in these housing trends. The good news is that home ownership has increased among California's ethnic groups. The largest gains in the last decade were among Latinos.[9] The bad news is that California still lags behind 47 other states in rates of home ownership. Simply put, demand outpaces supply. Given current population growth, about 250,000 housing units are needed each year; only 150,000 are in fact built. The greatest shortfall has been in multi-family housing.

Of the housing units built in California, many are unaffordable. In 2002, of the 30 least affordable metropolitan areas in the nation, 20 were in California. Understandably, numerous coastal cities were on the list, but so were inland communities such as Salinas, Stockton, Merced, and Modesto. As a consequence, only 27 percent of California households can afford a median-priced home.

Why is California housing so expensive? First, there is a shortage of appropriately zoned land where people want to live, especially along California's coast. This has forced many who work in coastal cities to move inland, driving home prices up in those areas. Second, many slow or no-growth groups resist the construction of new housing in their communities. Third, many city officials believe housing of any density does not generate enough property taxes to pay for the services they require. City officials prefer sales tax–laden auto malls and shopping centers that require minimal public services. As noted earlier, this has been called the "fiscalization of land use."

TRANSPORTATION POLICY

Getting around California and even one's own community presents another policy challenge. Californians spend more than 300,000 hours per day in traffic jams. Freeway speeds are slowing, and, on many urban freeways, the "rush hour" itself has disappeared into a cloud of heavy traffic—all day, every day. Bus and rail transit riders are not exempt from traffic delays. In fact, simple door-to-door commute times are shorter for automobile drivers than for public transit users.

Although traffic congestion is easy to see and experience, it is a very complex policy problem. Three factors help explain why. *First,* Californians, as other Americans, love their automobiles; they symbolize American individualism and personal choice. As a 1926 *Los Angeles Times* editorial put it, "How can one pursue happiness with any swifter and surer means than the automobile?" The consequence of what seems like a personal choice is cumulative for the state. Today, there are more vehicles than licensed drivers in California, and people can feel the impact. Once-picturesque residential streets are lined bumper to bumper with cars, and lengthy daily commutes are routine. *Second,* urban development patterns have encouraged congestion in California. As cities dispersed outward to accommodate growth, massive highway projects linked city centers with suburbs and beyond to exurbia. New highways are filled to capacity as soon as they become available, and many surface streets are as crowded as the freeways. *Third,* vehicular traffic causes a variety of environmental problems. While the state's smog problems are infamous, lesser know environmental effects include various automobile contaminants (oil, grease, antifreeze, and small tire particles) that wash into streams and waterways. Traffic noise, fumes, and road dust are also major problems, and the health effects can be severe. According to the Environmental Working Group, more than 9,300 Californians die each year by exposure to airborne particulate matter—more than by car accidents, homicides, and AIDS combined. Furthermore, this type of pollution affects the poor and non-Anglos more so than affluent or white communities.[10]

How have policymakers coped with these transportation-related problems? In short, *California's transportation policy has been to accommodate the automobile.* Local governments typically approve traffic-generating developments and provide the local streets required. They may require developers to pay mitigation fees to cover some of these costs. Large-scale state and national highways and the interstate system were shared responsibilities, but the primary policymaker has been the State of California. Historically, the gas tax is set aside for highway, not mass transit, funding. While public policy has favored the automobile, spending has not kept pace with that commitment. For example, highway capacity increased by only 4 percent in the 1980s and 1990s, while California's population grew by 50 percent. The result? Compared to other states in 2000, California ranked dead last in per capita highway spending.

Recent developments suggest some change in transportation policy. First, California voters have approved some, if not all, transportation bond and gas tax measures. At the local level, voters in more than 20 counties have approved sales tax add-ons for city and county road improvements. Second, a 1989 law permitted Caltrans to build toll roads—quite a departure for a state traditionally wedded to *free*ways. Amid controversy and criticism, several have been built in Southern California.[11] Third, efforts have begun to improve rail transit within major metropolitan areas. Planners also envision a high-speed rail system connecting San Diego, Los Angeles, the Bay Area, and Sacramento. Such a rail corridor would reduce air travel and airport-related automobile traffic. At present, the Los Angeles/Bay Area air corridor is the most highly traveled in the nation.[12]

ENERGY AND ENVIRONMENTAL POLICY

California's population growth has had a severe impact on the state's quality of life in two additional areas: energy and the environment. Energy policies address the oil, natural gas, and electricity demands of a complex, energy-hungry economy and the lifestyles of 35 million residents. Environmental policies address the impacts of economic and population growth on the quality of the state's water, air, land, and natural resources.

The electricity crisis of the early 2000s highlighted a host of energy-related concerns. Californians suffered both spiraling electricity prices and infuriating gaps in service—brownouts and blackouts. As the British journal, *The Economist,* put it, "One of the wealthiest regions in the world is on the brink of an energy crisis of third-world proportions. How did California come to this?"[13] The answer to that question lies in a confluence of public policies and events—electricity's version of the perfect storm. The key decision was the passage of Assembly Bill 1890, a 100-page law that sought to replace a patchwork of regulatory practices with an open-market approach.[14] Electricity generation did become more competitive, but other developments worsened the situation:

• Wholesale energy prices floated freely while policymakers froze retail prices.

• No new power plants were built to replace old plants and meet increased demand.

• Stable long-term energy contracts were disallowed.

• Energy generators and traders (like the infamous Enron Corporation) "gamed" the system by withholding capacity to spike short-term prices.

• Encouragement of energy conservation was neglected.

• The two largest public utilities became insolvent, requiring state aid to avoid bankruptcy.

In short, California's approach to deregulation failed. To many, the outcome was as much a debacle as a crisis—a bitter lesson in how *not* to deregulate. In response, Governor Gray Davis and the legislature offered still more reforms, including these: (1) using public funds to bail out financially strapped public utilities, (2) selling energy bonds to repay state costs, (3) renegotiating costly energy contracts, (4) streaming the construction of new power plants, (5) encouraging consumer conservation, and (6) researching alternative energy resources (such as solar and wind).

Continued efforts are also under way to address environmental pollution in the Golden State. In one respect, California's population growth adds nearly 2,000 new "polluters" daily. But population is only one part of the equation. The development of new technologies (silicon chips, synthetic materials, and industrial processes) also adds new toxins to the environment. The long-range impact of environmental pollution may well be global warming—the "greenhouse effect." This is caused by a buildup of gases that allow the heat of the sun to penetrate the atmosphere but prevent it from escaping. If this problem is as serious as some scientists claim, a permanent warming trend would raise ocean levels (inundating California's coastline), threaten the ozone layer (worsening the state's already high skin cancer

rates), alter plant growth patterns (endangering the agricultural base of the state), and diminish the Sierra winter snowpack (reducing California's water supply).[15]

The short-term impact of environmental pollution is more immediate and visible. Chemical spills, toxic waste dump-induced illnesses, and polluted beaches seemingly occur with greater frequency. The California Air Resources Board indicates that more than 90 percent of Californians breathe unhealthy levels of at least one air pollutant during some part of the year. The most vulnerable residents—children, the elderly, and those with respiratory problems—may be advised to stay indoors on "smog alert" days.

California policymakers have responded to these persistent problems using four approaches. One traditional approach has been to issue regulations, set standards, and order offenders to comply. Sometimes called "command and control," this approach has been implemented by numerous agencies. For example, the Air Resources Board mandated that vehicles sold in California be emission free; in 2003, it modified that regulation to allow manufacturers to meet its requirements through a mix of ultra-clean hybrid vehicles. In 2002, the ARB announced plans to reduce the smog-producing agricultural emissions that plague the San Joaquin Valley. The Integrated Waste Management Act required that 50 percent of the state's solid waste be diverted from landfills by the year 2000. In response, local governments required trash haulers to provide recycling opportunities.

Another "solution" to pollution in California has been to send it somewhere else. Indeed, by the late 1980s, more than 30 other states were receiving toxic waste from California. Due to resistance by neighboring states and receiving communities within California, such exports have slowed. With nowhere to go, many toxins are simply stored in garages, warehouses, and factory yards.

A third approach is market-based. By determining a price or market value for nitrogen oxide, government can create incentives for companies to offset existing sources of smog when plants expand. Pricing incentives assume a partnership between the private and public sectors, a relationship many environmentalists mistrust.

A fourth approach has been to replace fossil fuels and hydroelectric power with renewable sources of energy such as solar, wind, geothermal, biomass, and small-scale hydropower. Technological advances such as fuel cells, lower operating costs, and reaction to the electricity crisis are making these energy alternatives both competitive and attractive in environmentally conscious California.[16]

LARGER GROWTH STRATEGIES

If you now have the impression that growth-generated policy problems defy piecemeal policy solutions, you are not alone. Some policy reformers believe that future policy approaches need to be broader in scope than has heretofore been the case. They argue that there needs to be a comprehensive growth strategy. Such a strategy would both control growth itself and accommodate growth that cannot be controlled. Controlling California's population growth itself is a much more difficult challenge. It seems to be treated as a given that policymakers can do little about. After all, in a diverse, representative democracy, how does government tell families to have fewer children? How does a subnational government barricade an international border? How do local officials deny housing on land zoned for that use? No wonder policymakers are at best ambivalent about population growth control.

Reformers also believe that continued reliance on home rule ignores the impact decisions in one community may have on its neighbors. Interjurisdictional turf battles may result, but managing regional growth does not. Proposed solutions to the home rule "problem" include giving greater land use authority to existing councils of governments (COGs), establishing still larger superagencies to manage regional growth, and reducing the power of single-purpose, single-minded agencies that focus exclusively on water, air quality, or transportation.[17] Progress on this front is slow. Related to this, numerous reform groups now seek "smart growth" strategies that manage, steer, and coordinate land use decisions while decoupling them from their revenue impacts. Local communities should not feel compelled to choose between shopping centers and affordable housing.

Lastly, some groups favor controls on population growth itself, no matter the source—high fertility rates or over-immigration. Some of these ideas are controversial because they challenge behavior deeply rooted in the state's diverse ethnic and cultural groups. They may also seem heavy-handed, elitist, and reactionary. Yet any growth management efforts that ignore population growth itself will likely miss the mark in California.

Policies Stemming from Diversity

To conclude Chapter 11, we consider the cultural diversity of California and its impact on six policy areas: abortion and gay rights, education, higher education, social programs, and immigration. Policy conflicts in these areas are struggles among competing groups—cultural hyperpluralism and ensuing political conflict seem best to describe this state of affairs.

SOCIAL ISSUES: ABORTION AND GAY RIGHTS

Some public policy issues do not involve large expenditures of public funds. They cannot be viewed as government programs, run by permanent state agencies. Unlike the annual state budget, they do not consume vast amounts of policymaker time. Yet they stir human emotions, produce conflict, and divide Californians unlike most other public policies. We call these policies *social issues.* Here we focus on the two most familiar ones—abortion and gay rights.

California's policy on abortion is generally pro-choice. It is buttressed by the state constitution's explicit right of privacy (Article I, Section 1). While the legislature has periodically denied Medi-Cal funding for abortion for poor women, the courts have regularly overturned such restrictions. Furthermore, in 1997, the California Supreme Court on a 4 to 3 vote struck down a never-enforced law requiring teenage girls to obtain parental or judicial approval for an abortion (*American Academy of Pediatrics v. Lungren*). Interest groups have been active on this issue and have not limited themselves to the courts and the legislative process. Occasional protests have taken place at birth control and abortion clinics. In recent years, several court cases have limited the ability of pro-life groups to block access to those clinics. Abortion protests and counterprotests have become less frequent as anti-abortion activists focus more on counseling and abstinence education.

Californians' support for abortion rights is qualified and more nuanced than zealots on either side would admit. According to a 2002 *Field Poll,* nearly two-thirds of California voters support a woman's right to an abortion, but that support declines dramatically the longer the woman is pregnant. A majority favors parental consent for teenage abortions but also supports late-term abortions if the mother's life is in danger.[18]

Gay rights policy has produced mixed results in California. On the one hand, long-sought recognition of gay marriage has not been allowed. With Proposition 22 in 2000, 60 percent of voters included this language in the Family Code: "Only marriage between a man and a woman is valid or recognized in California." In the process, California joined 35 other states and the federal government by refusing to recognize formal civil unions between gays. On the other hand, gays have been more successful in the legislative process. For example, in 2001, Governor Gray Davis signed landmark legislation that granted "domestic partner" benefits to same-sex couples and heterosexual senior partners who register as such with the state. Gay rights have also advanced at the local level. By the early 2000s, eight counties and 29 cities had passed ordinances barring discrimination against gays. These rights vary from place to place, but they include public and private employment, public accommodations, education, housing, and lending practices.

EDUCATION POLICY

Unlike abortion or gay rights, education is a public service deeply rooted in California's political history. Yet the state's educational system faces unprecedented challenges. In 2001–2002, the state's 8,915 public schools in 1,065 school districts served more than 6 million students from kindergarten through high school. Another 631,000 students attended private schools, and nearly 16,000 were home schooled. In fiscal year 2003–2004, the state provided about 53 percent of K–12 funding, local taxes 26 percent, and federal funds 12 percent. Once the envy of the nation, one challenge after another now faces California's educational system, including enrollment growth, ethnic diversity, and social change.

Pressures, many beyond the control of policymakers, buffet California educators and students alike. Here we consider enrollment growth, ethnic hyperpluralism, social conflict, and funding challenges. The sheer growth of California's school-aged population is by far the most profound challenge. In the decade from 2000 to 2010, a projected 50,000 students will be added to California K–12 schools *each year.* To provide for these students alone would take 1,700 new classrooms. This growth, coupled with efforts to reduce class size in the lower grades, has created a massive and urgent need for added classrooms, new schools, and more teachers.

Sheer growth creates its own budget pressures. As stated earlier, education is the biggest slice of the state budget pie, but those numbers are relative. In absolute numbers, California spends far more on education than any other state, about $53 billion in 2003–2004—roughly $8,900 per pupil. Yet in terms of per-pupil, state-only spending, California's numbers are less impressive. In 2001–2002 (the most recent fiscal year available), Hawaii spent $8,995 per pupil while California spent only $5,163. Those numbers ranked California seventeenth in spending.[19] Compared to other states, California has seen both better and worse days. In 1964–1965, it ranked fifth in per pupil spending; in 1992–1993, it ranked forty-second.

The ethnic composition in California's public schools has been shifting for some years and will continue to do so well into the twenty-first century. Ethnic and cultural hyperpluralism are increasingly the norm. Today, no single ethnic group constitutes a public school majority. Latinos will continue to be the most rapidly growing group. Statewide, about 25 percent of K–12 students (1.4 million) are English learners (EL). That is, they are not proficient enough in English to succeed academically in mainstream English programs. That figure jumps to 41 percent for the mammoth Los Angeles Unified School District. While Spanish is the stereotypical first language for many students, it is by no means the only one. The state Department of Education "Language Census" records 56 major languages present in California schools—more than in all of Europe.

For many years, educators dealt with this language diversity by offering bilingual education. EL students were taught in both their first language and in English, with the goal of making them proficient in English. Growing frustration with the results of bilingual education resulted in the passage of Proposition 227 in 1998. It required all instruction to be in English unless parents objected. It also allowed EL students to participate in sheltered English immersion programs for a maximum of one year.

In addition to ethnic diversity, broader social changes affecting all segments of society have introduced new levels of conflict in California schools. Two-income parents, single parents, child abuse, parental neglect, and poverty have changed the very mission of public schools. Teachers have become disciplinarians, surrogate parents, counselors, social workers, detectives, and nurses. Problems stemming from gangs, gang attire, graffiti, guns on campus, and drug use are increasingly routine. California's schools are becoming more hyperpluralistic as students emphasize their own differences and identities based on race, ethnicity, income, gender, sexual orientation, and religious faith.

What have policymakers done to confront these challenges? First, they have addressed educational performance, a process that began several decades ago. The 1983 Hart Hughes Educational Reform Act increased high school graduation requirements and provided for longer school days and school years. The 1992 Charter Schools Act authorized the creation of 100 schools that would operate apart from and free of most state and local regulations. In 1996, after experiencing some of the highest student–teacher ratios in the nation, California launched a dramatic class size reduction program. In kindergarten through third grade, class sizes would be limited to 20 students. The results were immediate and mixed. While teacher morale and classroom manageability increased, so did local costs and shortages of classroom space and credentialed teachers.[20]

In 1999, Governor Gray Davis pushed for and the legislature passed four additional reforms: (1) A statewide system of individual school accountability was established. Based on new tests, all schools would be publicly ranked on performance and held accountable accordingly. Schools with high scores would receive cash bonuses; schools with low scores would receive grants in order to improve. (2) All students graduating from high school after 2003 must take an exit exam in language arts and mathematics. (3) A California Peer Assistance and Review Program pairs "exemplary" teachers with veteran teachers who need to improve subject matter expertise and teaching competence. (4) Six new reading programs were created and funded to increase student reading achievement.

Second, policymakers have focused on educational accountability through a succession of statewide tests. In 1993, the California Learning Assessment System (CLAS) replaced traditional multiple-choice achievement tests. As criticism over the test mounted, the Department of Education chose the Stanford-9 test to initiate its new Standardized Testing and Reporting (STAR) Program for grades 2 through 11.

Third, policymakers have struggled over how best to give California families greater educational choice. To many, choice is synonymous with the notion of school vouchers. Yet Californians rejected voucher proposals twice, in 1993 and 2000. The latter measure, Proposition 38, would have provided state-funded, tax-free grants of about $3,000 to children in private and parochial schools, including nontraditional programs. Voucher proponents contend that public schools are wasteful and overly bureaucratic; accordingly, parents deserve a choice of schools. Opponents fear that vouchers would drain public education budgets and deny real choice for poor families or "problem" students—the physically impaired, English learners, or low academic achievers.

While vouchers have failed in California, less radical "managed choice" options are available. Charter schools have provided educational alternatives, but for only a handful of families. In addition, state law now allows intra- and interdistrict transfers. In other words, students may attend public schools elsewhere in their district or in other districts; for example, where their parents work. Magnet schools attract students districtwide by offering specialized courses or approaches.

HIGHER EDUCATION POLICY

Historically, Californians have taken pride in their institutions of higher education. But population growth, increased cultural diversity, and chronic underfunding have raised some profound issues for the state's colleges and universities. Students and faculty know the symptoms of the problem only too well. Fees are raised, courses are cancelled, graduation plans are delayed, and needs outpace revenues. For many public university students, a four-year baccalaureate degree is largely a myth. How have these pressures come about?

Higher education policy in California is governed by the Donahoe Higher Education Act of 1960—commonly called the *Master Plan*. According to a legislative report, what began as a modest agreement between educational institutions evolved into a "world-renowned social compact" articulating a bold vision for the future.[21] The plan prescribed enrollment parameters for each level, assigned different missions to each level, and created governance structures to operate and coordinate relations with each sector.

The entire system grew beyond all projections in the decades that followed. Today, the overall system encompasses a huge complex of campuses throughout California. UC consists of 8 general campuses and one health science campus enrolling more than 202,000 full-time equivalent (FTE) students. A new UC Merced should open in a few years, funding permitting. CSU consists of 23 campuses and six off-campus centers enrolling 339,000 students. The state's 109 community college campuses and other sites enroll 1.1 million students. California's 125 independent colleges, universities, and professional schools enroll another 293,000 students.

Due to recent recessions, funding shortfalls, and enrollment growth, some Californians are questioning the adequacy of the Master Plan.

They are concerned about four interlocking issues: access, growth, pricing, and governance. First, access is an especially sensitive matter for California's college-bound minorities. To increase applicants from certain high schools, a new admissions rule extends UC eligibility to the top 4 percent of students *at each high school,* whether or not they were in the top 12.5 percent of all California high school seniors, the regular UC standard. To resolve larger access issues would require more campuses, classrooms, courses, and funding to match.

Second, to accommodate current and anticipated enrollment growth, each system needs several new campuses; but planning has been marred by competition for scarce budget dollars. More modest reforms include year-round instruction, greater on-campus efficiencies, increased private college aid, and more online (Internet) coursework.

Third, some reformers urge reconsideration of low higher education fees, especially for middle class and wealthy Californians who could afford higher fees. Opponents of higher student fees point to the continued need for access, growing numbers of price-sensitive minority students, and the relatively high total costs of attending college in California, including living expenses. In recent state budgets, the higher education sector was required both to raise fees and cut costs. Still, students' fees remain significantly below those at comparable public universities in other states.

If those issues were not enough, consider the challenge of achieving authentic diversity on California's campuses. Given the ethnic and cultural hyperpluralism in California, it is only natural that this hyperpluralism would be felt on campus—and so it is. Efforts to diversify California student bodies have been a partial success. The community colleges are the most ethnically diverse; UC and the private institutions are the least diverse. At one time, California's public colleges and universities used affirmative action to increase minority enrollments. This practice encouraged efforts to recruit, admit, and enroll students from underrepresented backgrounds (such as race and ethnicity). Although the U.S. Supreme Court, in *Regents of the University of California v. Bakke* (1978) rejected hard and fast numerical quotas for admitting minorities, they did laud the general goal of diversity. In 1995, the UC Board of Regents ended affirmative action in UC admissions. In 1996, voters approved and the federal courts affirmed Proposition 209, which banned racial and other similar preferences in all state programs, including higher education. Despite these setbacks, student bodies are more diverse now than they were decades ago. Diversifying California's professorate has been more challenging. The California Post Secondary Education Commission reports that, despite recent progress, higher education faculties are much less diverse than the students they teach.[22]

SOCIAL PROGRAMS

The Golden State has a long history of social programs that cushion the impact of life's slings and arrows. A patchwork of social programs reflects the different times in which they were enacted, mixed priorities and approaches, plus some measure of ambivalence toward those in need. In fact, the history of social policy typifies *ambivalent benevolence*—on one hand, a caring concern for California's "truly needy" and, on the other, reluctance to reward those who seemingly prefer "handouts" to honest work.

Taken together, California's social programs consumed more than 28 percent of the state's general fund for 2002–2003. When combined with federal funds, nearly $30 billion is devoted to the broad areas of health and welfare. In recent decades, this share of the budget has grown due to high birth rates among the poor, high levels of immigration, high divorce rates, and federal mandates.

Who are California's poor? Almost 13 percent of all Californians are poor; that number jumps to nearly 25 percent of all California children. Census data tell us that the highest levels of poverty occur among Latinos and African Americans (18 and 17 percent); the lowest rates among whites and Asians (8 and 9 percent). Contrary to popular impressions, most poor families are employed. Where do they live? The highest rates of poverty occur in the San Joaquin Valley (22 percent of residents there are poor); the lowest rates are in the San Francisco Bay Area (7 percent).

The largest welfare programs in California target needy families, children, those who are elderly or disabled, and other adults. California's major program to aid needy families is *CalWORKs* (California Work Opportunity and Responsibility to Kids). This program implements the federal Temporary Assistance to Needy Families (TANF) program that, under welfare reform, replaced the old Aid to Families with Dependant Children (AFDC). It provides time-limited assistance (food and shelter) to eligible families in times of crisis. The state's 58 counties administer the program. In 2003, a monthly cash grant for a family of three ranged from $607 to $637. For those families that tend to fall in and out of poverty, there is a cumulative five-year limit on aid. In 2003, about 1.4 million Californians per month received CalWORKs support.

Is the program working? Well, yes and no. Caseloads have declined and, according to one study, many families have moved off the welfare rolls and into jobs. But many find their paychecks provide little more than what they received from welfare. While many have been able to stay off welfare, they continue to need "transitional benefits" such as food stamps and Medi-Cal.[23] In addition to CalWORKs, the federal food stamp program provides nutritional assistance to eligible low-income families. Recipients receive coupons that can be used like cash at participating grocery stores. In 2002, more than 1.9 million Californians received food stamps worth roughly $70 per recipient per month.

Children receive further attention. Obviously, children benefit if a parent qualifies under CalWORKs. In addition, the Child Protective Services program intervenes when there is evidence or suspicion of in-home child abuse or neglect. The state's Out-of-Home Care System places more than 70,000 such children with relatives, foster families, or group homes. The Cal-Learn program assists pregnant and parenting teenagers to obtain high school diplomas or the equivalent. The Child Support Enforcement Program locates and requires noncustodial parents to pay court-ordered child support. In 2002–2003, child support collections in California exceeded $2.4 billion.

A variety of programs also assist the elderly and disabled. For example, the federal Supplemental Security Income (SSI) program is part of Social Security. It provides monthly cash aid to aged, blind, and disabled persons who fall below the program's income and resource requirements. California augments the SSI payment with an SSP (State Supplemental Payment) grant. In 2002, grants amounted to $750 for individuals and $1,332 for couples. Blind people received somewhat more.

What about those adults who are not covered by the programs just described? Several programs exist for them. The Adult Protective Services program assists elderly and dependant adults who are functionally impaired, unable to meet their own needs, or are victims of neglect or abuse. Lastly, the state's Refugee Settlement Program helps refugees from other countries who locate in California become self-sufficient.

HEALTH POLICY

California's approach to aiding the sick is multifaceted and increasingly expensive and includes three broad approaches: private insurance, Medi-Cal, and deinstitutionalization.

Private Insurance

In the United States, our health care system depends heavily on private insurance. In 2000, about 65 percent of California's nonelderly possessed either job-based or privately purchased health insurance. What about the rest? More than 6 million Californians have no health insurance of any kind. Only 2 million of those are eligible for Medi-Cal or Healthy Families, two major state programs. The balance are workers and their dependants. Their employers provide no health insurance whatsoever (a common practice in agriculture, construction, retail, and small businesses), yet they earn too much money to qualify for publicly funded care. Lack of health insurance disproportionately affects Latinos. Nearly 40 percent of Latinos under the age of 65 lack health insurance, and most non-citizen Latinos work in low-wage jobs that offer no coverage. In 1997, California partly filled this insurance gap with "Healthy Families." Under this program, otherwise uninsured families can purchase for their children low-cost government subsidized health insurance for as little as $6 per month. The plan covers usual health, dental, and vision needs. In 2003–2004, this program stood to benefit about 768,000 children.

Medi-Cal

California's version of the federal Medicaid program for low-income individuals is called *Medi-Cal.* The federal government requires and funds basic services such as doctor visits, laboratory tests, and hospital care. It also provides matching funds for any of 34 optional benefits such as hospice, adult dentistry, and physical therapy. More than 17 percent of Californians qualify for Medi-Cal, including CalWORKs and SSI/SSP recipients, pregnant women, and other groups. In 2003, Gray Davis proposed that many optional services and provider reimbursement rates be cut to balance the state budget.

Deinstitutionalization

A much less discussed health care approach in California has been the deinstitutionalization of the mentally ill. Historically, psychiatric patients were placed in institutions, apart from society and family. Prior to the 1960s, California had a reasonably progressive and balanced approach, including prevention and early intervention in mental cases. But in 1968 a new law, the Lanterman-Petris-Short Act, required that patients be "mainstreamed" in communities rather than confined in institutions. The ideal of community-based treatment fell far short of expectations. Anticipated community-based mental health centers never materialized. Many former mental patients did not return to families or live in group homes—they became homeless. Indeed, thousands of California's homeless population have disabilities, mental illness, or other health problems. Many call jail home because without close supervision or daily medication they lose control and commit crimes. Shelters, low-cost hotels, and other "transitional housing" accommodate only a fraction of California's homeless.

CALIFORNIA'S IMMIGRATION "POLICY"

In recent decades, pressures mounted for California policymakers to "do something" about illegal immigration, even though it is a federal responsibility (hence the quotes around policy). California's approach to immigration has been both reactive and proactive. Reactive policies are in response or opposition to some condition or trend. Ballot initiatives can be reactive in tone, purpose, and content. For example, in 1994 Proposition 187 attempted to deny publicly funded services (education, health, and welfare) to illegal immigrants. A federal judge declared 187 to be an unconstitutional infringement on federal immigration responsibilities.

Other approaches to immigration have been more proactive and less initiative driven. That is, policymakers have sought to accommodate high levels of immigration and/or cooperate with the federal government in controlling those levels and the costs associated with them. These efforts have included:

• Improving the reading performance of all California school children, not just that of English language learners

• Allowing some undocumented students to attend the University of California by paying low in-state tuition rather than nonresident tuition

• Seeking higher federal reimbursements for the costs of incarcerating undocumented felons

• Encouraging Border Patrol efforts to staunch the flow of illegal immigrants across the California/Mexico border

California's efforts to control immigration and its impacts reflect a fundamental political debate over the future of the state—what it is and is becoming. What we do know is that California never was a melting pot but rather a stew pot. Today, there are simply more ingredients than ever before. Immigration policy arguments now seem to center around the ingredients themselves. Will new and different ingredients enrich the whole stew, stand distinctively alone, or be left out of the recipe altogether?

Conclusion

As is evident in these pages, California's size, wealth, growth, and diversity create some interesting and, at times, sobering challenges and opportunities. These are expressed in policies encompassing state and local budgets and policies addressing growth and diversity. At the state level, California's annual budget is a reflection of its economy to be sure, but more important, it reflects what its policymakers regard as truly important. Surprisingly few policies consume surprisingly large chunks of the state budget. At the local level, budgets reflect local economies and local priorities, but they are also tempered by state and federal spending decisions. At both the state and local level, budgets represent group conflict in an increasingly diverse state.

Other policies have attempted to accommodate and manage the state's constant population growth. Some policies, such as the provision of water and transportation infrastructure, actually helped make California an attractive place to migrate to. Other policies have been in response to that growth, in particular, housing and a variety of environmental policies. Recent decades have been characterized by growing political conflict over what to do about population growth and its impacts. No matter what California policymakers choose to do, it seems they will be reacting to continued population growth rather than controlling it.

The diversity of Californians themselves leads to still other policies. Education policy in California is fueled by population growth, ethnic diversity, social change, and competition for scarce public resources. These pressures have been felt in the state's colleges and universities as well. California's social programs, including welfare and health programs, represent a hodgepodge of particular policies and a loose partnership between the federal government and the state. Lastly, immigration policy, although a federal responsibility, has had an impact on California in some profound ways. Although immigrants flock to California from all over the world, the focus in California has been on the impact of those from Mexico.

KEY TERMS

cruise control spending, entitlements (p. 140)
May Revision (p. 140)
trailer bills (p. 140)
general obligation and
   revenue bonds (p. 143)

fiscalization of land use (p. 144)
filter down housing policy (p. 149)
Master Plan for Higher Education (p. 155)
ambivalent benevolence (p. 156)
CalWORKs (p. 157)
Medi-Cal (p. 158)

REVIEW QUESTIONS

1. In what ways does California's economy affect state budgeting?
2. How do state and local budget processes work?
3. If you were to raise taxes and cut spending to balance the state budget, what decisions would you make and why?
4. Describe how policymakers use public policy to both accommodate and manage population growth.
5. How do policymakers address the needs of California's poor, sick, mentally ill, and the state's immigrants?

WEB SITE ACTIVITIES

California State Department of Finance
(www.dof.ca.gov/)
This agency advises the governor on the annual budget and makes available numerous documents on past and current state budgets and the state's economy. Each year, the Governor's Budget Summary provides the latest data on a host of state policies.

Business, Transportation, and Housing Agency
(www.bth.ca.gov/)

California Environmental Protection Agency
(www.calepa.ca.gov/)

California Department of Education
(www.cde.ca.gov/)

California Department of Social Services
(www.dss.cahwnet.gov/)
These are among the numerous state agencies that provide a wealth of data on the policies described in this chapter.

Bureau of Citizenship and Immigration Services
(www.immigration.gov)
Now a part of the U.S. Department of Homeland Security, this agency Web site features immigration statistics relative to California and elsewhere.

INFOTRAC COLLEGE EDITION ARTICLES

For additional reading, go to InfoTrac College Edition, your online research library, at http://infotrac-college.com/wadsworth

Seasons of Spending

Tax Loopholes Throw California State Budget for a Loop

The Real Cause of the California Housing Crisis

Road Pricing in California: Tolled You So

California's Welfare Rolls Fell More Slowly Than the Nation's

Gays Advance in California

NOTES

1. Deborah Reed, *California's Rising Income Inequality: Causes and Concerns* (San Francisco: Public Policy Institute of California, 1999), viii; see also *California Budget Project, Boom, Bust and Beyond: The State of Working Californians* (Sacramento: California Budget Project, 2003) (Available online at www.cbp.org/).
2. For more on the state lottery, see Joan Wilson, *The California State Lottery's Role in Funding Public Education* (Sacramento: California Lottery, 2001) (Available online at www.calottery.com/).
3. Michael A. Shires, John Ellwood, and Mary Sprague, *Has Proposition 13 Delivered? The Changing Tax Burden in California* (San Francisco: Public Policy Institute of California, 1998).
4. State Controller, *Cities Annual Report, Fiscal Year 1999–2000* (Sacramento: California State Controller, 2003).
5. State Controller, *Counties Annual Report, Fiscal Year 1999–2000* (Sacramento: California State Controller, 2003).
6. See *Dollars and Democracy: An Advocates Guide to the California State Budget Process* (Sacramento: California Budget Project, 1999).
7. Noel Brinkerhoff, "Water Marketing: Let's Make a Deal," *California Journal* 30 (August 1999): 12–17.
8. Steve Scott, "Restoring the Delta," *California Journal* 28 (May 1997): 36–43.

9. Ann Martinez, "Minorities Make Gains in Owning Homes," *San Jose Mercury News,* August 8, 2001.

10. Available online at www.ewg.org/.

11. Jenifer B. McKim, "For Whom the Road Tolls," *California Journal* 32 (June 2001): 46–50.

12. For more on recent transportation issues, see Sigrid Bathen, "Gridlock . . . and Beyond," *California Journal* 29 (November 1998): 36–39.

13. "California's Power Crisis," *The Economist* (January 20, 2001): 57.

14. For an overview of this deregulatory effort, see Steve Scott, "California's New Electric Bill," *California Journal* 27 (November 1996): 9–13.

15. On this last impact, see Edie Lau, "Sierra Will Be Hit Hard by Warming, Study Says," *Sacramento Bee,* June 4, 2002.

16. Peter Asmus, "California's Energy Legacy: A Desperate Innovator," *California Journal* 32 (January 2001): 16–21.

17. Elisa Barbour, *Metropolitan Growth Planning in California, 1900–2000* (San Francisco: Public Policy Institute of California, 2002).

18. Mark DiCamillo and Mervin Field, *The Field Poll.* Release #2043 (May 8, 2002).

19. Kendra A. Hovey and Harold A. Hovey, *CQ's State Fact Finder 2003* (Washington, DC: CQ Press, 2003), 211.

20. For more on teacher shortages, see Emelyn Rodriguez, "The Search for Qualified Teachers," *California Journal* 32 (August 2001): 10–17.

21. *Master Plan for Higher Education in Focus: Draft Report* (Sacramento: Assembly Committee on Higher Education, April, 1993), 2.

22. Available online at www.cpec.ca.gov/second-pages/stat0204.asp/.

23. Meredith May, "Welfare Reforms Not Ending Poverty: Study of Single Moms Says Paychecks Don't Provide Much Lift," *San Francisco Chronicle*, April 16, 2002.

Index

A

ABAG. *See* Association of Bay Area Governments
ABC syndrome-Anybody or Anywhere
   But California, 33–34
Abortion, 152–153
Abundance, politics of, 22–23
ADR-Alternative dispute resolution, 116
Adult Protective Services, 157
Adversarial justice, 114
Affirmative action, 44
African Americans
     judges, 112
     migration, 6
     poverty among, 157
     in prison, 118
     voting patterns, 57–58
Air Resources Board, 151
Allen, Doris, 45
American Academy of Pediatrics v. Lungren, 153
American era, 5–6
Appellate courts, 110–113
Appropriation process, 81
ARB. *See* Air Resources Board
Arbitration, 116
Articles of Confederation, 27
Asian Americans
     immigration, 6
     poverty among, 157
     voting patterns, 57–58
Assembly speaker, 84–85
Association of Bay Area Governments, 135
Associations, 71
At-large elections, 39

Attorney General, 102
Authorization process, 81

B

Baldassare, Mark, 3–4
Bear Flag Revolt, 16
Benchmark polls, 68
Big Four, 8, 17–18
Bird, Rose, 100, 113, 117
Birdsall, Wasco, and Associates, 72
Blanket primary, 65
Boards of supervisors, 128
Boxer, Barbara, 69
Brown, Janice Rogers, 6
Brown, Jerry, 23
     Curb incident, 101
     judicial appointments, 100
     personality, 96
     Proposition 13, 39
     as secretary of state, 102
Brown, Pat, 23, 96, 102
     judicial appointments, 117
     personality, 100
     progressive politics, 21–22
Brown, Willie, 6, 41, 78, 84
"Brown bag" advocates, 72
Bryce, Lord, 24
Budgets
     diversity and, 138
     economy's role, 139
     local
     expenditures, 146
     process, 141

Budgets (*continued*)
 revenue, 143–144
 social programs, 156
 state (*See also* Economy)
 debt, 141–143
 expenditures, 145–146
 external process, 98
 governor's role, 98, 140
 process, 139–141
Building industry, 72
Bureaucracy
 functions, 104–105
 powers, 105–106
 size, 104
 union, 106
Burton, John, 85
Bush, George W., 57
Bustamante, Cruz, 5, 85, 101

C
Cabrillo, Juan Rodriguez, 15
CALFED, 147
California
 national ranking, 10
 New York *vs.*, 13
 uniqueness, 2
 Washington *vs.*, 32–33
California Democratic Council, 66
California Journal, 61
California Learning Assessment System, 155
California Medical Association, 73
California Peer Assistance and
 Review Program, 155
Cal-Learn program, 157
CalWorks, 129, 140, 157
Campaigns. *See also* Elections
 contributions, 90
 professionals, 67–68
Capital punishment, 109, 119
CDC. *See* California Democratic Council
Centralized federalism, 31–32
Charter Schools Act of 1992, 154
Chinese-Americans, 6, 17
Cities
 councils, 131
 creation process, 130–131
 development, 139
 managers, 132
 mayors, 131–132

professional management of, 39
 without government, 131
Civil service. *See* Bureaucracy
CLAS. *See* California Learning Assessment System
Cleland, Robert Glass, 21
Clientele linkage, 61
Climate, 4
Clinton, Bill, 40, 55
Coastal protection, 44
COGs. *See* Councils of governments
Committees of Vigilance, 17
Community government
 budget, 141–142
 cities, 130–132
 counties, 127–130
 diversity of, 136
 limits of, 125
 regional, 135–136
 role of, 125
 San Fernando Valley succession, 123–124
 school districts, 134–135
 special districts, 132–134
Conference committees, 88
Connell, Kathleen, 103
Constituents. *See* Voters
Constitution, State of California
 1849, 27, 30
 amendments, definition, 79
 basic framework, 27–28
 boundaries, 27
 changing, 29
 convention, 29
 distinctiveness of, 29–31
 features, 28–29
 federalism and, 31–32
 impeachment, judicial, 113
 preamble, 7–8
 reapportionment, 83
 structural conflicts, 10
 women and, 28
Constitution, United States. *See also* Federalism
 founding principals, 31
 history, 27
 Tenth Amendment, 31–32
Constitutionalism, definition, 26–27
Constitution Revision Commission, 45
Contract lobbyist, 71–72
Controller, 103
Cooperative federalism, 31

Corporate tax, 142
Corrections, 119–120, 144–145
Councils of governments, 135
Counties
    boards of supervisors, 128
    clerks, 129
    fiscal officers, 128–129
    judicial officers, 128
    laws and charters, 126–127
    shape of, 126
    troubles, 129–130
Courts
    capital punishment, 19
    civil process, 116
    criminal process, 114–116
    district attorneys, 128
    divisions, 109–111
    initiatives and, 44
    interest groups use of, 73
    judges (*See* Judges)
    lawyers, number, 108
    Ninth Circuit, 44, 109
    policy making by, 117–118
    sentencing, 118–119
    social trends, 118
    system, 109
Crew, Robert, 96
Criminal justice. *See* Courts
Crocker, Charles, 8
Cronin, Thomas, 41
Cross-filing, 65
Crowd lobbying, 91
Cruise-control spending, 140
Cultural diversity and, 10
Curb, Mike, 101

D
Dahl, Robert A., 9
Davis, Gray, 103, 117
    2002 campaign, 68
    campaign costs, 68
    education agenda, 100, 154
    electricity crisis, 151
    executive orders by, 98
    gay rights and, 153
    image, 94–95
    liberal issues, 22
    proposition 187, 101
    recall of, 45–46

Death penalty. *See* Capital punishment
Declaration of Rights, 30
Defense of Marriage Act, 40
Deinstitutionalization, 158
Delegates, definition, 80
Democracy. *See* Participatory democracy;
    Representative democracy
Democratic theory. *See* Representative democracy
Democrats
    central committee, 65–66
    ethnic voters and, 57–58
    Latino support for, 55
    media bias, views of, 63
    strength, geographical, 56–57
    turnout, 54
Depositions, 116
Deukmejian, George, 22, 100, 102, 117, 119
Development privatization, 125
Dillon, John F., 125
Dillon's Rule, 125–126
Direct primaries, 39
Discovery, 116
Diversity
    budget policy and, 138
    cultural, 10
    demographics, 4–6
    economic, 7
    interests, 9–10
    ironies of, 11`
    land, 3
    local government, 136
    public policy and
    education, 153–156
    health, 157–158
    housing, 147–149
    social issues, 152–153
    social programs, 156–157
    transportation, 149–150
    regional, 3–4
    resource, 4
Donahoe Higher Education Act of 1960, 155
Drake, Sir Francis, 15
Draper, Tim, 43
Dual federalism, 31
Dust Bowl, 6

E
Eastin, Delaine, 33
Easton, David, 2

Economy, 6–7. *See also* Budgets
Education
    English learners, 154
    higher, 155–156
    higher, master plan, 21
    public policy and, 153–156
    school districts, 134–135
    spending on, 11
    superintendent, local, 129
    superintendent, state, 102–103
    teacher's salaries, 29
Elazar, Daniel, 14
Elections. *See also* Campaigns
    at-large, 39
    campaign professionals, 67–68
    importance, 66–67
    interest groups influence, 72
    national politics and, 69–70
    number held, 66–67
    role of money, 68–69
Electricity crisis, 150–151
Elite theory, 8
EMILY's List, 69
Endorsements, 66
End Poverty in California, 20–21
English only. *See* Proposition 63
EPIC. *See* End Poverty in California
Era of limits, 22
Eu, March Fong, 102
Excise tax, 142–143
Executive branch. *See also* Governor
    attorney general, 102
    fiscal officers, 103–104
    insurance commissioner, 103
    lieutenant governor, 101–102
    pluralistic aspects, 101
    secretary of state, 102
    superintendent of public instruction, 102–103
Executive orders, 97–99

F
Fair Political Practices Commission, 69
Federal Housing Act of 1949, 148
Federalism, 31–32, 32
Federal plan, 77
Feinstein, Dianne, 68
Ferrelo, Bartolome, 15
Filipino-Americans, 6
Filter down policy, 149
Fiscal committees, 88

Focus groups, 68
FPPC. *See* Fair Political Practices Commission
Fremont, John C., 16
Functional representation, 79–80
Furman v. Georgia, 119

G
Gann, Paul, 22, 43
Garamendi, John, 103
Garcetti, Gill, 128
Gay rights, 40–41, 152–153
Gender gaps, 57–58
Geology, 13
George, Ronald M., 117–118
Gerber, Elizabeth R., 42
Gerrymandering, 83
Gold Rush, 5, 7, 17
Goldsborough, James O., 34
Gore, Al, 56–57
Government
    councils of, 135
    duties, 28
    effect of Initiatives, 44
    limited (*See* Constitutionalism)
    regional, 135
Governor
    budget process, 140–141
    chief of state role, 101
    executive powers, 97–99
    judicial powers, 100–101
    leadership, 95–98
    legislative powers, 98–100
    public order and, 101
    salary, 96
Grapes of Wrath, 6
Grassroots lobbying, 91
Great Depression, 20–21
Gregg v. Georgia, 119
Grodin, Joseph, 100, 113
Growth. *See under* Population

H
Hahn, James, 123
Hamilton, Alexander, 31
Hanks, Tom, 67
Harris, Robert Alton, 119
Harrison, Gray Otis, 61
Hart, Gary, 103
Hart Hughes Educational Reform Act, 154
Health and welfare, 144

Health care, 157–158
Healthy Families, 158
Hearst, William Randolph, 61
Hertzberg, Robert, 85
Homeowner associations, 131
Home rule, 125
Hopcraft, Steve, 68
Hopkins, Mark, 8
Horcher, Paul, 45
Housing issues, 147–149
Huffington, Michael, 68
Huntington, Collis, 8
Hyperpluralism
    in community politics, 124–125
    cultural diversity and, 10
    definition, 9
    individualism and, 9
    initiative process and, 42
    interest diversity and, 9–10
    majoritarianism and, 10

I
Illegal Immigration Reform and Immigrant
    Responsibility Act, 35
Immigration, 6, 34–35
Immigration and Naturalization Service, 34
Immigration Reform and Control Act of 1986, 35
Impeachment, judicial, 113
Incumbent gerrymandering, 83
Indian gaming, 44
Individualism, 9, 24
Individualistic political subculture, 14
In-house lobbyists, 71
Initiatives. *See also* Referendums; individual
    Propositions
    constitutional changes by, 29
    courts and, 44
    elected officials and, 29–30, 43–44
    entrepreneurial aspects, 43
    faulty assumptions, 41–42
    impact on government, 44
    money and, 42–43
    process, changes in, 43
    reforming, 45
    role of television, 43
INS. *See* Immigration and Naturalization Service
Insurance commissioner, 103
Integrated Waste Management Act, 151
Interest groups. *See also* Lobbyists
    benefits, constitutional, 28–29

influence, 70
organizations, 71–72
tactics, 72–73
types, 70–71
well-financed, 39
Interests, diversity of, 9–10
Internet, 64
Interrogatories, 116
IRCA. *See* Immigration Reform and
    Control Act of 1986

J
Japanese Americans, 6
Jarvis, Howard, 9, 22, 39, 43
Johnson, Hiram, 20, 77
Johnson, Lyndon, 31
Joint committees, 88
Jones, Bill, 102
Jordan, Frank C., 102
Jordan, Frank M., 102
Judges
    disciplining, 113–114
    experience, 112
    selection, 112–113
    training, 111–112
Judiciary. *See* Courts
Judiciary Act of 1789, 109
"Junk" crimes, 114
Jury nullification, 117

K
Kearney, Denis, 18
King, Rodney, 51, 115
Knight, Goodwin, 21
Knight, William "Pete," 40–41

L
LAFCO. *See* Local agency formation commission
Land, diversity, 3
Lanterman-Petris-Short Act, 158
La Opinion, 61
Lasswell, Harold, 8
Latinos
    health care, 158
    housing needs, 149
    judges, 112
    media portrayal, 63
    party affiliation, 55
    political interests, 79
    political role, 5

Latinos (*continued*)
> population, 5
> poverty among, 157
> in prison, 118–119
> in public schools, 154
> 2001 reapportionment and, 83–84
> voting patterns, 57–58

Lawson, Kay, 61

Lawyers, 108, 113

Legislative Analyst's Office, 140

Legislators
> careerism, 83
> policy making by, 78–79
> recruitment, 82
> redistricting and, 83
> representation, 79–80
> rewards of, 82
> salary, 76, 82
> types of, 79–80

Legislature
> bills, 79
> budget process, 140–141
> civic education by, 81
> committee system, 85, 88
> congressional, 32–33
> constitutional changes by, 29
> district maps, 86–87
> executive oversight by, 81
> function, 76
> future challenges, 91–92
> governor and, 98–100
> history, 77–78
> initiatives, use of, 29–30, 43–44
> lawmaking by, 84
> leadership, 84–85
> media control, attempts, 63
> process, 88–90
> reapportionment, 83–84
> staff functions, 88

Leslie, Tim, 101

Lieutenant governor, 101–102

Litigation, 73

Livability, 10

Lobbyists. *See also* Interest groups
> function, 72
> influence, methods, 90–91
> types, 71–72

Local agency formation commission, 130–131

Locke, John, 26–27

Lockyer, Bill, 85, 102

Los Angeles Times, 61–62

Lottery, 143

Lucas, Malcolm, 117

LULUs-locally undesirable land use, 128

M

MacDonald, Katherine, 91

Madison, James, 31

Majoritarianism, 10, 22

Marshall, James, 16

Mass media
> influence, 61
> Internet, 64
> markets, 67–68
> newspapers, 61–62
> television, 62–64

Master Plan. *See* Donahoe Higher Education Act of 1960

Mayor, 131–132

May Revision, 140

McClatchy, James, 61

McClintock, Tom, 103

McWilliams, Carey, 42

Medi-Cal, 158

Mental Health, 158

Merit system, 39

Merriam, Frank, 21

Metropolitan planning organizations, 135

Mexicans. *See also* Latinos
> era, 15–16
> immigration, 34–35
> trade, 35–36

Milbrath, Lester, 41

Mockler, John, 94

Modernization, politics of, 17–20

Money
> in initiative campaigns, 42–43
> initiative process and, 42–43
> for national campaigns, 69–70
> role in politics, 68–69
> soft, 69

Montalvo, Garci Ordonez de, 2

Moralistic political subculture, 14

Mosk, Stanley, 117

MPOs. *See* Metropolitan planning organizations

Municipalities. *See* Cities

N

NAFTA. *See* North American Free Trade Act

Newspapers, 61–62

New York, California *vs.*, 13
Ninth Circuit Court of Appeals, 44, 109
Nordlinger v. Hahn, 40
Norris, Frank, 18
North American Free Trade Act, 35–36

O
O'Connell, Jack, 103
O'Connor, Sandra Day, 111
Oil, discovery of, 20
Olberg, Keith, 102
Olson, Culbert L., 21
O'Neill, Thomas P. "Tip," 125
Operation Gatekeeper, 35

P
PAC. *See* Political action committees
Participatory democracy, 7
Participatory linkage, 61
Partisan gerrymandering, 83
Partisanship. *See also* Political parties
    affiliation, 55
    geography and, 55–57
    voting patterns, 54
Patronage, 104
Pendleton Act of 1883, 104
Perceptual representation, 80–81
Phillips, Kevin, 2
Plural executive, 101
Pluralism, 8–9
Political action committees, 18, 69
Political culture, geology of, 13
Political development
    abundance stage, 22–23
    idea of, 14–15
    modernization stage, 17–20
    unification stage, 15–17
    welfare stage, 20–22
Political environment, definition, 3
Political parties. *See also* Democrats; Republicans
    California style, 65
    candidate selection, 66
    elections, 66–67
    endorsements, 66
    influence, 64–65
    minority, 65
    organization, 65–66
    surrogate, 66
Political Reform Act of 1974, 69
Political subcultures, 14

Political system, definition, 3
Political theory, 7–8
Politicians, 28, 45–46
Politicos, definition, 80
Politics
    definition, 2–3
    of fences, 35–36
    single-issue, 9–10
Polls, 68
Popular justice, 116
Population
    biracial, 5
    diversity, growth in, 4
    foreign born, percentage, 35
    growth, 146, 152
    migration, changes, 1–2
    school age, 153–154
Portola, Gaspar de, 15
Postindustrialism, 6–7
Poverty, 156–157
Power
    democratic theory, 7–8
    elite theory, 8
    hyperpluralism, 9
    pluralist theory, 8–9
Preliminary hearing, 115
Price, Charles, 91
Primaries, 39, 65
Prisons. *See* Corrections
Progressive era
    effects on local government, 126
    impact of, 20, 38–39
    legacy, 47
    legislature and, 77
    paradox, 47
Propositions. *See also* Initiatives
    5 (1998, Indian gaming), 55
    9 (1974, lobbying reform), 69, 78
    10 (1998, tobacco tax), 44
    13 (1978, property tax cut), 11, 22
    approval, 30
    consequences, 39–40
    national impact, 69
    revenue strategies and, 143–144
    roots, 39
    20 (1972, costal protection), 44
    22 (2000, gay marriage), 40–41
    34 (2000, campaign finance), 69
    38 (2000, school vouchers), 42–43, 58
    63 (1986, English only), 30

Propositions. *See also* Initiatives (*continued*)
    115 (1990, jury selection), 115
    140 (1990, state term limits)
    approval, cause, 78
    court approval of, 44
    effects on leadership, 85
    effects on legislators, 83
    187 (1994, illegal immigrants), 44, 55, 158
    198 (1996, open primary), 65
    209 (1996, affirmative action), 44, 69
    227 (1998, bilingual education), 154
    (1998, school bond), 72,
    (2000, Indian gaming), 73
    (1966, legislative reform), 77
    interest groups influence, 72
Protest politics, 51
Public policy
    definition, 138
    economy (*See* Budgets)
    education, 153–156
    energy, 150–152
    entrepreneurs, 9
    environmental, 150–152
    growth, 146, 152
    health, 157–158
    housing, 147–149
    immigration, 158–160
    making, 78–79
    paralysis, 11
    progress, 11
    responsive linkage, 61
    social issues, 152–153
    social programs, 156–157
    transportation, 149–150
    water, 147
Public relations, 72

Q
Quakenbush, Chuck, 103

R
Racial gerrymandering, 83
Rancho system, 16
Reagan, Ronald, 21, 22, 32, 100
Reapportionment, 83–84
Recalls, 45–46
Referendums, 30, 45–46. *See also* Initiatives
Refugee Settlement Program, 157
Regents of the University of California v. Bakke, 156

Regional governments, 135–136
Regions, diversity, 3–4
Reiner, Rob, 9
Renault, Dennis, 23
Representative democracy
    definition, 7
    participation (*See also* Voters)
    conventional, 50
    electoral gaps, 57–58
    exit option, 50
    protest option, 50–51
    political ideals and, 8
    shared linkages, 61
Reprieve, 100
Republicans
    central committee, 65–66
    ethnic voters and, 58
    media bias, views of, 63
    2001 reapportionment and, 83–84
    turnout, 54
Resolutions, definition, 79
Reynolds, Mike, 9, 43
Reynoso, Cruz, 100, 113, 117
Richardson, Friend W., 101
Riordan, Richard, 66, 123
Roberti, David, 85
Rodriguez, Gregory, 57–58
Roe v. Wade, 30
Rosenberg, Howard, 63
Rosenfield, Howard, 43
Rules Committee, 85

S
Sacramento Bee, 61, 62
Sales tax, 142
Sanchez, Linda, 5
Sanchez, Loretta, 5
San Fernando Valley succession, 123–124
San Francisco Examiner, 61
SCAG. *See* Southern California Association
    of Governments
Scalia, Antonin, 65
SCAQMD. *See* South Coast Air Quality
    Management District
Schneider, William, 2
Schools. *See* Education
School vouchers, 42–43
Schrag, Peter, 10, 41, 62
Schwarzenegger, Arnold, 67

Scott, Steve, 63
Secretary of State, 102
Select committees, 88
Senate Pro Tempore, 85
Serra, Father Junipero, 15
Shelley, Kevin, 102
Sheriffs, 128
Simon, Bill, 66, 68, 94, 102
Simpson, O.J., 114, 116, 128
Sinclair, Upton, 20
Single-issue politics, 9–10
Slate mailers, 66
Social programs, 156–157
South Coast Air Quality Management District, 135
Southern California Association
   of Governments, 135
Southern Pacific Railroad, 18, 47, 77
Spanish era, 15
Special districts, 132–134
SPR. *See* Southern Pacific Railroad
SSI. *See* Supplemental Security Income
Standardized Testing and
   Reporting Program, 155
Stanford, Leland, 8
STAR program. *See* Standardized Testing and
   Reporting Program
State Personnel Board, 104
Steinbeck, John, 6
Stewart, Potter, 119
Strauss, Levi, 17
Streisand, Barbara, 67
Superintendent of public instruction, 102–103
Supplemental Security Income, 157
Supreme court, 111, 112–113

T
TANF. *See* Temporary Assistance
   to Needy Families Program
Taxes
   cigarette, 44
   corporate, 142
   excise, 142–143
   gas, 150
   limiting (*See* Proposition 13)
   personal income, 141–142
   policies, 29
   property, 39–40
   sales, 142
Television, 42–43, 62–64

Temporary Assistance to
   Needy Families Program, 157
Term limits. *See* Proposition 140
The Curse of California, 18, 19
The Federalist, #17, 31
The Federalist, #45, 31
The Octopus, 18
The Wright Act of 1887, 18
Three Strikes Law
   criticism of, 119
   description, 11
   effects on courts, 110
   effects on prisons, 145
   Ninth Circuit ruling on, 109
Tobacco Settlement Fund, 141
Tobriner, Mathew, 112
Tracking polls, 68
Trade, 35–36
Trade and Commerce Agency, 35–36
Traditionalistic political subculture, 14
Trail courts, 110, 112
Trailer bills, 140
Transcontinental Railroad, 5
Transportation, 149–150
Treasurer, 104
Treaty of Guadalupe Hidalgo, 16
Truman, Harry, 21
Trustees, definition, 80

U
Unification, politics of, 15–17
Uniform Sentencing Act, 119
Unruh, Jesse, 77, 84
Unz, Ron, 9, 43

V
Vetoes, 100
Vietnamese Americans, 6
Villaraigosa, Antonio, 5, 85
Vogel, Nancy, 22
Voters
   civic education of, 81
   disenfranchised, 51, 53
   knowledge, 49
   qualified, 51
   snapshot of, 52
   turnout factors, 53–54
   unaffiliated, 55
Voucher programs, 155

W

Warren, Earl, 21, 22, 23, 96, 100, 102
Warren, Roger, 114
Washington, California *vs.*, 32–33
Water
    constitutional mention, 30
    importance, 4
    public policy and, 147
Welfare, politics of, 20–22
Wesson, Herb, 6, 85

Westly, Steve, 103
White, Theodore, 14
Willis, Bruce, 67
Willis, Doug, 63
Wilson, Pete, 22, 96, 100, 117
Women, 28
Workingmen's Party, 18, 50
Works Progress Administration, 21
World War II, 20
WPA. *See* Works Progress Administration

Credits